DISCOVERY OF THE SELF

Claire Myers Owens

Introduction by Dr. Anthony Sutich, Editor
Journal of Humanistic Psychology

THE BOOK TREE
San Diego, California

ISBN 978-1-58509-141-6

Editor
Erik Dobko

Cover art
© gudron

Cover layout
Mike Sparrow

Published by
The Book Tree
P O Box 16476
San Diego, CA 92176
www.thebooktree.com
We provide fascinating and educational products to help awaken the public to new ideas and
information that would not be available otherwise.
Call 1 (800) 700-8733 for our FREE BOOK TREE CATALOG.

Dedicated
with admiration and gratitude

to

Edmund Sinnott

F.S.C. Northrop

Henry Margenau

Wilmon Sheldon

Abraham Maslow

William Sheldon

Carl Jung

C.A. Meier

Aldous Huxley

Albert Schweitzer

Raynor C. Johnson

Hadley Cantril

Gordon Allport

Akhilananda

Nikhilananda

and to all the other readers of *Awakening to the Good* who wrote me warm, wonderful letters about it and especially to my always helpful husband.

Contents

INTRODUCTION

This is the autobiography of Clairene Myers, coupled with a projected extension, as written by her Niece Claire Myers Owens. It is a remarkable work about a remarkable woman. One could say it is two autobiographies in one, in view of Mrs. Owens' device of writing the concluding section as if she herself had taken up her Aunt's life where it had left off.

Mrs. Owens gives an account of a search that is becoming increasingly common in our contemporary Western world, namely, the discovery of the self. The nature of the self, its functions and its relation to the world have also become a matter of scientific inquiry in recent years. One of the most important features of Mrs. Owens' book, therefore, is her attempt to relate her own, as well as her Aunt's, process of discovery to the work of prominent Western psychologists and other scientists. Jung, Maslow, Sheldon, and others are among those she incorporates in her presentation.

Mrs. Owens and her Aunt give evidence on page after page of an earnest and determined effort to arrive at the direct experiencing of the Self. The most significant fact about their efforts seems to be that they repeatedly demonstrate the difficulties and hardships that are inherent in the pursuit of such a goal. Time after time there is a lyrical account of attainment, only to have it develop into discouragement, depression or even despair. So realistic is the presentation of the "rough side" of the road to the Self, that her very personal report concludes with the final stage still to come. Thus one can say that her book is more a portrayal of the ecstasies and agonies progressively experienced, rather than a version of "how-to-do-it," and over and over again she stresses that there are many ways and many methods available to the person who engages in the process of discovering his personal self, and each must find his own.

There is no doubt that professional psychologists may find themselves in some disagreement here and there with Mrs. Owens' references to contemporary scientific findings (for instance her rather uncritical acceptance of Sheldon's work). Nevertheless, she and her Aunt are to be commended for their impressive attempt to relate their own experiences to the work of outstanding psychologists.

Although she makes no claims to being a scholar it is obvious that Mrs. Owens and her Aunt have read widely and intelligently. It is also clear that Mrs. Owens is very modest in her claim that she is an ordinary woman. She writes with unusual facility. At times there is a certain lyrical quality in her presentation. A number of passages remind me of personal accounts of the psychedelic experiences I have been privileged to read and hear in recent years.

Mrs. Owens' book is a rewarding experience for anyone concerned with the discovery of the Self.

Anthony Sutich

FOREWORD

"To discover the self is to discover the secret of happiness, the meaning of life, the ultimate goal of living – and the greatest joy possible to man," so said my late Aunt, Clairene Myers.

But how?

In today's tumultuous world modern man is bewildered and frightened. The hierarchy of values constructed for him by economics and politics, philosophy and religion have all come tumbling down about his head.

For in spite of their obvious benefits they have been unable to bring peace to the earth.

Why?

The very goals for which Western man has struggled most diligently – political freedom, material wealth, scientific discoveries, and psychoanalytical understanding – despite their advantages, have not been enough to bring inner peace to the individual.

Why?

The more advanced psychologists now believe and Clairene Myers demonstrates – it is because Western man has failed to use a vitally important part of his mind – the deeper unconscious. This apparently is the source of his altruism, love of mankind, compassion, creativity, intuition, wisdom, spiritual experience and many other virtues. Virtues inherent in all men but too often dormant. Dormant because our materialistic, extroverted culture is dominated by rationalism almost exclusively.

Our sick society, however, cannot be regenerated unless the individual is regenerated, says Dr. Carl Jung. And the goal and meaning of individual life is individual development.

In short, the discovery of the "undiscovered self" may be the answer to many of our problems – personal and global. The conscious mind has given us much external progress but it also has given us the nuclear bomb, radiation, and world wars. Must not the conscious mind now be united with the healthy unconscious if man is to be whole as nature intended him to be?

9

That is the theme of this book. My late Aunt, Clairene Myers, appointed me her literary executrix. From her almost illegible notebooks, I have attempted to recreate a typical account of how an individual may discover the self, "lose" it, and strive to recapture it.

Her story could be anyone's story – with variations. All unknowingly she was merely obeying certain universal laws. Laws that govern the human psyche in the actualization of its potentialities for the good, the true, and the beautiful.

After her very puzzling experiences, she confirmed their validity by certain systems of psychology, philosophy, and religion. Systems whose underlying principle is that all men possess innate good, love of mankind, ability to live in peace with others and in harmony with the universe – if – *if* they exert sufficient effort to uncover these treasures buried within themselves.

But is such self-evolution biologically possible, one may ask?

Edmund Sinnott, the biologist, says that the scientists agree today that man has arrived at the limit of his physical evolution. The human body has not changed essentially for 10,000 years. In the future, however, mankind may evolve mentally and spiritually. Man, Sinnott asserts, now possesses the brains adequate to direct his own evolution at last.

Why does he not do it, he asked?

Such a possibility would have sounded utterly fantastic to my Aunt prior to her own initial discovery of the self. That experience transformed her character so incredibly, it convinced her we all might benefit by a new kind of education.

Because, she pointed out, our education in the West has been primarily directed at the conscious mind, at filling it with highly useful facts to use in the external world of things.

In the East, she noted, the emphasis has been on the development of intuition and the unconscious. This has produced a serene inner life, many saints, holy men, and great art. The cultivation of the conscious mind, however, has been deliberately neglected. Has not this resulted in poverty, illiteracy, and disease among the suffering masses and conquest by enemy armies? Witness Tibet and India.

Does not the tragic state of the world today, she asked, – West and East – indicate that neither is sufficient by itself? The individual man needs the development of the conscious and unconscious mind and the union of both to make him a fully functioning human being. Society desperately needs self-actualizing individuals, as Abraham Maslow reminds us.

She foresaw that the regeneration of society and of the individual must be attempted simultaneously by the man of tomorrow.

It is not easy to write another person's autobiography but the material in her notebooks and letters indicated this form. When my Aunt's recent book, *Awakening*, was published, it elicited incredible letters of appreciation from scientists and philosophers, psychologists and artists as well as many laymen.

Her files are full of letters from and to well-known scholars. Frankly, I feel her admiration for scholarship was a little excessive. Perhaps it was because she did not consider herself an authority on anything except beautiful inner experiences of the discovered self. And the natural language of the self is poetic not scientific.

But, as a famous Yale philosopher assured her, her intuitive insights produced the same truths, as did the rational efforts of the more advanced philosophers and scientists today.

Evidently, she hoped her concrete example of self-realization might constitute a modest contribution to the movement she considered one of the most important in the world today – the effort to find modern scientific means and methods to discover and develop the latent good inherent in the self of all men. For, she asked, have not all other methods of the West failed?

Her lack of self-confidence sometimes annoyed me. Three years ago when she first began compiling notes for this book – which she never lived to write, alas she asked a question of a distinguished Yale scientist. Should she not submit her manuscript to the scholarly authorities before she sent it to a publisher?

He laughed. "Why should you? You know more about it than they do."

(Mrs.) Claire Myers Owens
New Haven, Connecticut, 1963

STAGE I

AWAKENING OF THE SELF

Chapter 1

RESPONSE

Forecast

To discover the self is to discover the secret of happiness, the meaning of life, the ultimate goal of living, I learned recently to my utter astonishment.

It is to find a joy greater than wealth, power, or fame – greater than youth, love, or passion. It is the greatest joy possible to mankind – the discovery development of the self.

If these beautiful truths can be experienced by an average person like me, Clairene Myers, they can be experienced by anyone. The laws governing the psychic growth of the normal, healthy unconscious toward the actualization of its potentialities, or individuation, the good life, or Enlightenment, are applicable to everyone.

This is a true report of how I discovered the self, "lost" it, and strove to uncover it again. Skeptics may doubt such possibilities. But, as Jung reminds us, the most beautiful truths in the world are of no use unless the individual experiences them within himself.

An autobiography has small justification except for its possible universality. How universal is the discovery of the self? Are the methods, means, and stages the same for everyone?

The Self

But first, what is the meaning of this term, "the self?" It seems too indefinite to me. Yet it is the accepted term in those disciplines concerned with the inner man.

In the Analytical psychology of Dr. Carl Jung, the self means the total psyche. It embraces the conscious mind and the unconscious – both personal and collective. When it is functioning properly it seems to bring the individual into harmony with the laws of the universe.

In the Humanistic psychology of Abraham Maslow and his colleagues, the self is our intrinsic nature with a natural urge toward Being. He has conducted research on hundreds of subjects and discovered that everyone has peak experiences and a rare few actualize their potentialities.

In the philosophy of Plato, Socrates exhorts his pupils to "know thyself" because from the self-virtue flows forth. Plato, however, denigrated intuition and exalted reason. Yet, paradoxically enough Socratic dialectic can activate the deeper unconscious, I discovered, though it may be heresy to say so in the presence of classical scholars.

The modern philosophy of F.S.C. Northrop equates direct aesthetic apprehension with the theoretic, rational and scientific as a valid method of ascertaining truth. He advocates their union in East and West as the best way to international peace.

In Hinduism the self is called the Atman, which is the individual microcosmic self and at the same time the macrocosmic Self.

Buddhism claims the contents of the self are wisdom and love, and intuition alone can release them.

The teachings of Jesus exhort man to arouse his better inner nature. The intellect is not mentioned.

Thus we see that some authorities regard the self as the deeper unconscious, others as its union with the conscious mind, while still others postulate the identity or union of the personal self with the universal Self.

Literature abounds with records of the discovery of the self and, by any other name, it is just as sweet. Whitman's *Leaves of Grass* offers the glowing results of self-realization but not the process preceding it. *Walden, Faust, The Divine Comedy*, and *Pilgrim's Progress* relate peak experiences. Certain poems of Tennyson, Wordsworth, and Millay, the best essays of Emerson, certain writings of Jefferson and Lincoln, of Gandhi and Schweitzer contain an implicit awakening to the self. In Huxley's novel, *Island*, it is explicit.

The discovery of the self is universal and old; only the scientific, psychological explanation of it is new.

Location

Where is this mysterious self located? If it is considered to be the unconscious, it is said to be in the oldest part of the brain – the thalamus. Reason of course resides in the newest part of the brain – the cortex. The greater cosmic Self is sometimes felt to be in the collective unconscious and at other times "out there." Does anyone really know?

Methods and Types

How can this buried treasure in man's deeper, better nature be uncovered? There seem to be two methods. It can either be induced by systematic training or it can occur spontaneously. The method apparently is determined by the individuals' type of physique and temperament.

It has not been proven but it looks as if three constitutional types usually engage first in an effort to actualize their potentialities and achieve it last. As a rule they enlist the aid of self-actualized guides. The fourth type, the 4-4-4, often is given a glimpse of the self (and perhaps the Self), loses it, then must strive to recapture it. That is what happened to me.

In the search for individuation a long struggle is usually necessary for all types either before the awakening to the good in the self, in others, and in the world – or after.

Means

What means are employed in arousing the individual's intrinsic nature? Each discipline offers its own means. The aspirant may make his choice, in theory at least.

Analytical psychology offers Jungian therapy, which releases the collective unconscious. Humanistic psychology, so far, is concerned primarily with ends not means; but Maslow suggests self-therapy or a new psychoanalysis and education.

Plato offers Socratic dialogue to achieve "recollection of eternal ideas" and the good life. The Socratic method, I believe, arouses the conscious and the unconscious mind simultaneously. Reason is the means oddly enough.

Hinduism provides four main systems of yoga for the four main types of temperament. Enlightenment is induced under the direction of a guru. Buddhism is the same. Zen has its own masters and devices. Christianity makes faith and acceptance of an intermediary the prime requisites rather than inner experience.

All these systems of arousing the inherent good in man have proved more or less efficacious for some types. But what of the 4-4-4 type like me?

Stages

Poets, Western mystics, Christian saints, and some laymen are awakened involuntarily to the good, the true, and the beautiful. Does this mean they are all 4-4-4s? No one knows for sure. In the East it is the custom to induce reintegration.

Those who discover the self involuntarily, however, often regress. I certainly did. Some aspirants undoubtedly rest on their laurels, others strive to progress again by various means.

The means I employed might be used by all types, I believe. This has not been proved – yet. Methods and means and the sequence of events may vary. Goals and struggles are similar for all types.

Therefore, my story could more or less be anyone's story.

Those aspirants of a higher, happier life who have been visited by spontaneous psychological death and rebirth pass through definite stages of psychic growth. There are five according to the autobiographies of those who have achieved all the stages.

Stage number I is Awakening of the Self. II is Self-Discipline. III is Enlightenment. Stage V, which some consider the highest possible development of the human psyche, is usually inaccessible to an ordinary person like me, I fear. Besides, its goal heretofore has been either the exclusively religious life or that of a philosopher-king.

Modern psychologists like Maslow and Jung, however, postulate the Unitive life as a simultaneous functioning of reason and intuition, the senses and feeling, and muscles in harmony with the universal rhythm.

This phenomenon turns work into play, resolves dichotomies of the conscious and unconscious minds, spirit and flesh, good and evil.

The goal of the average, modern, independent aspirant of the West like me, is Stage III – the good life in the workaday world.

But enough of theories which, I hope, throw a little light on the universality of the search for self-actualization. Perhaps my personal story will in turn illustrate the theories.

How It All Began

One day (that lasted five years) I wrote a little book. I was certain no one would like it. I wrote it for myself, to clarify my own problems. It never occurred to me they might be other people's problems too. My theme ran counter to the current of the strongest tide in the world – public opinion. Today everyone was concerned with external things – or so in my ignorance I assumed. Yet my book dealt with the inner life. And what's more – with my inner life.

I was unaware then that a worldwide movement was quietly forming. It had different terminologies and methods but the goals were similar. Psychologists and philosophers, scientists and the religious were concerned with the realization of the individuals' undeveloped capacity for wholeness.

I was not a scholar. I was merely an ordinary woman who strove to run a large household, instruct her servants, keep her husband happy, entertain her friends, do community work, and follow the latest fashions in clothes, ideas, plays and books. I read omnivorously, studied and did a little writing.

One morning, I sat down in my writing room on the quiet third floor of our house in Connecticut. I attempted to read the final version of the manuscript of my new book, *Awakening*, coolly, critically, as if it had been written by someone else. I had revised, rewritten and cut it till it bled.

As I read, it seemed to possess some mysterious kind of authority. Yet I knew I was an authority on nothing – except beautiful inner experiences. But like millions of other Americans, I was lost in the confusion of the modern world, bewildered by global wars and nuclear bombs, sick to death of tension and fears and valueless values. So I poured out my problems and solutions onto paper.

It had all flowed up from the deepest part of my being in a manner I myself did not at the time understand. The urge to write it had been irrepressible. The urge to be honest at any cost had been inexplicable. As I read it, something inside me assured me it was profoundly true and therefore must possess some merit.

It was not in the fashion of the day and yet to think that it might languish in silence in my files forever was unbearable. So I sent it to a small publisher. But, because this firm was not equipped to promote it, I feared my book might be stillborn. Its probable sad fate almost broke my heart. Was it not incumbent on me to make some effort in behalf of my brainchild? But what?

Over and over again I murmured to myself, if only *one* famous and good man, interested in psychology and religion, philosophy and art, would read it, understand it, and like it – that is all I ask – just one!

Recently I had read a beautifully reassuring book by a Yale scientist. In it, he offered biological evidence that the protoplasm of every living organism contained goal-seeking properties and also displayed an inherent urge to wholeness. The instinctive, emotional part of mental life exhibited the highest level of goal-seeking. And the book also postulated the unity of matter, mind and man.

I wrote the author about his splendid book. I also informed him of my book, *Awakening*, soon to be published. I explained to him that it related my spontaneous discovery of the personal microcosmic Self and the universal macrocosmic Self. My rebirth had occurred at the very moment of my deepest despair concerning the tragic chaos of the world and the evil behavior of man who caused the chaos.

I went to the biologist's office at the university. After talking for half an hour, he kindly agreed to read the galley proofs of *Awakening*. He courageously gave me the names of twenty other scholars at Yale, Harvard, Brandeis, Princeton and other universities who should be notified.

After reading the galleys he promptly wrote a warm, wonderful letter about *Awakening* to be used on the dust jacket:

"This book is a moving account of how a keen and perceptive mind has met the ancient problem of the good and the evil in man through suffering, aesthetic insight, mystical experiences and especially the unifying concepts of psychology. She has reached a satisfying solution that will have significance for many in the troubled world of today." And there was much more. I was overwhelmed by sheer happiness and incredulity.

The forthcoming publication of my book also afforded me the long-awaited opportunity to write to a woman whose work I profoundly admired. She had edited a series of books by distinguished scholars on science, philosophy, and religion. She very generously offered to read the galleys of my book. Her letter left me incredulous with joy:

"You write with warmth and experience of the unity man and nature . . . it is this principle of unity for which science, philosophy, religion, indeed all men seek."

I suppose I should offer the customary apologia for being so immodest as to repeat the praises showered on my little book. It is not an apology, however, but a defense of what might otherwise be misinterpreted.

The whole point of such a discovery of the Self is that one realizes for the first time how low one's own station is compared to the heights possible to mankind. One realizes for the first time the infinite power and beauty of the life force.

The reactions of readers were not praise for my book so much as for the wondrous laws of the human psyche that made such glorious experiences realizable. I could take no credit for anything. I had merely served as an instrument through which some strange impersonal power had elected to flow – or so it felt. I had merely allowed nature her wonders to perform and then recorded the whole phenomenon as honestly as possible.

The last reason is, it is absolutely necessary to quote some of the warmest letters because they precipitated that prophetic incident – a vision of the man of tomorrow.

Other scientists and philosophers at Yale read *Awakening*.

"Your insights are deep and remarkable. Your book inspired me," wrote a physicist.

"Magnificent!" said one of the older philosophers.

"Your book is extraordinary," said a world-famous philosopher over the telephone. I had never met him. "Can you come to my office and talk about it?" I went and he said, "It is amazing that a woman can arrive by intuitive means at the same conclusions that the advanced philosophers and scientists are arriving at by rational means. Your book will take its proper place in the current of contemporary thought."

I left his office literally walking on air, I felt so highly honored. But I am sure I acted very stupid and inarticulate.

Later I received another sympathetic letter from a physicist in Australia.

Even the psychologists responded to it.

"I read it at one sitting. It is exciting and fascinating," wrote a professor at Brandeis University. He enclosed the names and addresses of one hundred scholars at various universities all over the world. This was absolutely incredible! By now my poor head was swimming.

A prominent psychologist at Harvard and another at Princeton sent pleasant notes. The founder of a new system of psychology at the College of Physicians and Surgeons in New York wrote in the flyleaf of one of his own books, "Your *Awakening* is a fine book."

The most famous psychologist in Switzerland assured me he had read it twice. A member of the Jung Institute in Zurich told me he had read it on the boat coming to America. Such a psychological rebirth, he informed me, was natural and normal and what was wrong with our Western culture that it did not happen to more people?

A Gesell Developmental psychologist, who was the author of several perennial best sellers and who cherished a totally different philosophy from mine, telephoned me. "My friends tease me and say some day I may be known simply as the friend of the founder of your new cult."

The reaction of the religious of various beliefs left me incredulous, bewildered, and dizzy with happiness.

A well-known student of Hinduism and Buddhism wrote from California, "It brings out the all-important fact that religion is concerned primarily with the immediacy of Being."

A physician – philosopher – musician – theologian in Africa sent me a kind note in French.

A Hindu monk in New York wrote, "I am much impressed by the book and the vast sweep of your mind. Many Hindus have had similar spontaneous experiences but they do not last:" It was impossible for me to believe such a tragedy at that time. Another Hindu monk in Boston wrote in a similar vein.

A well-known Vedantist commented over the lunch table, "You may become a sort of Western guru."

Already readers were bringing me their problems to solve, although I certainly was not competent to do so.

I listened carefully and sympathetically. The mere verbalization of their troubles, however, appeared to clarify them somewhat.

A Buddhist informed me over the telephone that she and another Buddhist student were studying *Awakening* together.

A Jew arose at breakfast in a hotel dining room and announced publicly, "I have been reading your book most of the night and I'd like to become your disciple."

A Negro schoolteacher from North Carolina wrote, "Everyone in the world should read it. It would solve all our problems."

A Catholic nurse said, "It will help everybody in this frightening world of today."

A Kentucky Protestant and housewife explained how she kept it by her bedside table to consult.

Another Protestant wrote, "I read it until four in the morning. It brought me such peace and happiness."

With each new response I was becoming more puzzled – and more delighted. But how could laymen of different backgrounds find nourishment in it?

"It is so beautifully written I can't lay it down," a businessman told my husband on the street.

"I can't leave it alone. I want to crawl right inside the covers." That was the reaction of a secretary in California.

"It is so beautiful I can hardly bear it, especially the poetic parts. Listen to this." And an elderly woman in tears read certain passages from *Awakening* to me over the telephone.

A psychiatric social worker in Illinois wrote a neighbor that she had read it three times and was now giving lectures on it.

"Your research lends conviction to your conclusions."

This was the verdict of a senator's wife in Washington.

"I nominate the author for President of the United States," wrote a member of the State Department – in jest of course.

One day I walked into Saks Fifth Avenue to purchase a hat. A clerk rushed up to me, took both my hands in hers and exclaimed, "Oh, I have just finished your book. It did me so much good I took it right over to a sick friend in the hospital. She is dying of T.B. and I thought it would do her more good than the Bible."

"It fills a deep human need," a New York musician explained.

But what need? I still failed to understand.

"I can tell you exactly why people like it so much," said a musician in Bishop's School for Girls much, much later. "Because it expresses what the rest of us have felt but have never been able to put into words."

At this particular time, however, I was still in a state of bewilderment and elation.

The warm, wonderful letters continued to arrive. Too excited to sit still, I walked about the house in a delicious daze. I could not read or think. I could not listen to conversation, music or news broadcasts. I could not write a word. I did not wish ever to talk again.

All I could do was to float voluptuously in the warm, sweet stream of success, of work rewarded, truth recognized, dreams fulfilled, of ideals expressed, exalted moments revealed and shared, of potentialities actualized, of the impersonal Self and the personal self discovered (terms I learned much later).

I knew the joy of communication with my fellow men on the profoundest level, not the frustrating superficial level of everyday human intercourse.

I felt deep gratitude that my book might have helped others for other men's books had so often helped me in a thousand ways through the years. Without books I really could not have lived. It was an enormous debt partially repaid.

"How does it feel to be famous?" asked my equally incredulous friends and family.

"But," I protested, "I did not write this book they are talking about. I am incapable of writing such a book. How could anyone book appeal equally to scholars and laymen, to scientists and the religious? I simply don't believe it!"

Chapter 2

FLIGHT

Such sudden, unexpected response stunned me with incredulity, left me dizzy with happiness and overwhelmed me with gratitude.

Day after day I walked excitedly from room to room, upstairs and down. I could not rest in peace until I could comprehend the reason people responded so personally and so passionately. In an attempt to fathom this mystery I decided to recapitulate the story for myself objectively as if I were telling it to some stranger.

After all, all the book had done was to relate how I felt despair at the tragic state of the world from the beginning of World War II in 1939 until 1950. How modern man's overt behavior – his world wars, hate and cruelty, his deliberate destruction of time-tested human values – destroyed my faith in mankind because it seemed to prove man was innately evil. I could not live in such a world.

So one morning as I lay on the old blue couch in my writing room unable to write a word I "died" psychologically. Then without my volition I was reborn in a glorious, mysterious manner. (At that time I never had heard of the "reconciliation of opposites" about which Jung and the Greek philosophers and Hegel and the Hindus speak. I knew Jesus had said one must "die" and be born again but I did not understand a word of it.)

In desperation I asked myself, could it be that only man's *conscious* actions were so evil? Could his *inherent* nature be good? I did not know.

Therefore, in order to save myself from repeated attacks of despair and psychological "death," I was obliged to institute a search for the innate good in man – if any. This search, however, soon devolved upon me. I was forced to look deep within myself for the innate good in myself – if any. Eventually all this led to a search for the good in the universe – if any.

In the process of being "reborn," without so much as a by your leave, a secret door within me seemed to open and memory flowed forth. I relived vividly the most beautiful incidents of my entire life as if to reveal the inborn nature of the self and its relation to others, to the arts and nature, and even to the cosmic mystery itself.

23

Thus, my book simply told a true story:

– how I conducted a kindergarten in a Southern mining camp and how the innate innocence of the miners' dirty little children mysteriously revealed to me the inborn purity of all men;

– how I read a beautiful but disturbing poem late one night in New York when I was twenty-five, how I pondered whether God existed or not, whether Jesus was divine or not, and suddenly the poem revealed to me that there existed a vast impersonal force in the universe, not a jealous, wrathful and avenging personal God who enjoyed punishing mankind as I had been taught as a child;

– how I quarreled with my husband, ran away, and was partially reconciled, then danced barefoot on sand of the seashore until the rhythmic movement of my own muscles united me with reality, cleansed away all pettiness, bitterness, desire for revenge, hurt pride, and renewed my love;

– how I wore a street dress to an English dinner party where all the other women were arrayed in formal evening gowns and half the crown jewels. Afterward I sat up all night pondering on the tyranny of all conventions in clothes, customs, and ideas, trying to throw off the power that clothes, politics and intellectual fashions exerted on me, on all women. Finally, sudden insight dramatically revealed to me that the supreme good was truth and that, henceforth, I was free of all men's opinions concerning fashion, politics, ideas, everything. I would do my own thinking. Truth had set me free – for a brief while;

– how one evening during World War II, I sat in our Connecticut garden and the odor of the earth at dusk so absorbed me back into the earth itself, so filled me with its elemental strength that I was able to face disaster, war, and death;

– how a great painting of an ugly old man in a New York museum purified me so astoundingly that I understood for the first time in my life why Aristotle asserted that the primary function of art is purification.

All that I recorded in *Awakening* were beautiful, personal incidents which I did not in the least understand when they occurred or even recurred. It told how one night in New York I had sat writing another book, a novel that had preceded *Awakening*. It was an allegory concerning three women in one or, rather, one woman divided into three characters – the feminine, the intellectual, and her *animus* and their unpredictable adventures. Suddenly a great shining river of words appeared to flow from "out there" like a river of light down into my own bursting brain.

Once I lectured on the profound meaning of the classic art I had recently seen in Europe. This discussion of beauty so aroused me, it suddenly flooded me with intense love for everyone present, for the whole human race, regardless of wealth or poverty, breeding or the lack of it, color or race, religion or the lack of it.

It flooded me with a desire to serve others, even to sacrifice myself if need be. All to my utter amazement, for love of mankind was an entirely new sentiment to me. It was like the feeling of falling in love with one man but multiplied a thousand fold.

My story related how once, in a moment of intense love and passion, I seemed to see the face of the Unseeable. It related how one summer my husband and I returned to the simple life in a small cottage by the sea. Living immersed in nature freed my deeper, better self and, to my utter astonishment, brought intimations of an immortality in which I heretofore had not believed.

One exceptionally fine opera at the Metropolitan in New York seemed so ennobling, it filled me with compassion and courage that were new to me.

My book told how I discovered that rhythmical, muscular motion if abandoned enough, nature and art if beautiful enough, thought when prolonged and profound, love and passion if deep enough, relaxation when complete could arouse both the personal self and the sense of a cosmic Self. It revealed how I learned that there seems to be a universal good – if man only knows how to live in rhythm with it.

There were many other glorious experiences but finally the accumulation of them seemed to allay all fears, fulfill all yearnings, and answer all questions. At last I knew all men contained inherent good because, to my surprise, my deepest, truest inborn self, for which I could take no credit whatsoever, seemed intrinsically good. And no one is unique.

Then there was trouble.

Awakening recounted how my own reason, kept so long in abeyance, now reasserted itself. It rejected all these fine irrationalities of the unconscious – unless I could verify them by science. I couldn't.

So I spent many months in hasty, hungry but superficial research. In psychology, philosophy, comparative religion and the poetry of the profounder poets.

These disciplines presented four new worlds to me and four new languages, which I found exceedingly difficult to learn. Later I found clarification and confirmation in all these disciplines but now I discovered *scientific* verification only in psychology.

I learned from Dr. Carl Jung's books that I was not peculiar but wonderfully fortunate. Discovery of the self usually is achieved only through the guidance of a trained expert – either in psychotherapy or religious practices. I understood nothing as yet of Plato and his different methods and means. The spontaneous variety of awakening is rare, Jung stated.

By the term "the self" Jung meant the collective unconscious and its union with the conscious mind and eventual harmony with cosmic principles.

I learned that the human brain is composed of two parts – the large cortex, the conscious mind with which we reason; and, attached to it, the smaller older part, the thalamus, the seat of the unconscious.

The upper layers of the unconscious are the area in which neurosis occurs, the only area with which Freud concerned himself.

But the deeper layers of the unconscious with which Jung was concerned primarily is the normal, healthy, though usually suppressed part common to all men. He termed it the collective unconscious. Our Western culture has rejected the deeper unconscious but, when it is released, out flow virtues we did not know we possessed – love of mankind, our ethical principles, esthetic sense, creativity, intuition, and even spirituality. Jung also spoke of evil but frankly I did not understand it. I had found only good in the deeper unconscious.

In psychological terminology, my ego had drowned in my collective unconscious – a state that feels like death, Jung says, and as I had discovered. Then the release of my collective unconscious was like a rebirth. All the dormant good was awakened. And there came a feeling of being in touch with, in tune with the mysterious but harmonious laws of the universe.

Reason is one of the glories of man, of course, and without it we should not have achieved such progress in science, wealth, law and materialism. But alone, I saw, it is dangerous and leads to the nuclear bomb and cruel annihilation of man.

I learned from William James that the mystical experience is a perfectly respectable, normal psychological process spurned by reason and science because they have not taken the trouble to understand it- until Jung came along.

I learned from William Sheldon's constitutional psychology that our type of physique determines our type of temperament. He did not say so but I deduced that it was usually to one type that the tremendous, dramatic, spontaneous discovery of the self is likely to happen. I was this 4-4-4 type his laboratory said.

From Richard Bucke, I learned that cosmic consciousness was a matter of evolution, not necessarily of religion, and depended on one's type of temperament. He named fifty famous people who had experienced a discovery of the self completely or partially. Whitman, Thoreau and Emerson; Tennyson, Wordsworth, and Blake; Dante; Pascal, Spinoza and Socrates; Ramakrishna, Moses, Paul, and Jesus; and Buddha, others.

From Abraham Maslow, leader of the Humanistic psychologists, I later learned that all that had happened to me was an actualization of those potentialities for the good possible to all people. He said the self-realized individual exhibits compassion, justice, happiness, kindness, optimism and many other virtues.

For the first time in my life I understood what Jesus meant: "Except a man be born again he cannot see the kingdom of God"; "he that loseth his life shall find it." "Unless you become as little children you cannot enter the kingdom of heaven." "The kingdom of heaven is within you."

For during my grand awakening I felt an unexpected, unprecedented sense of purity and innocence, the guilelessness and honesty of a child.

Nothing could surpass that heavenly state of mind resulting from the discovery of the self. And later I learned that this awakening of the deeper, better part of man's nature is the object of all the discipline and exercises of Hinduism and Buddhism, Taoism and Zen – to restore man's relation with his source.

Then, armed with the knowledge derived from various authorities, my conscious mind eventually accepted the contents of my collective unconscious because it understood these beautiful irrationalities. The two parts of my mind, however, still operated separately, they were not united.

So this was not the end.

I confessed in *Awakening* how I waited and waited for that union which Jung's books assert is necessary. Then one fine day, in a burst of glory while I was reading Northrop's *The Meeting of East and West*, my conscious mind united with my collective unconscious, my reason wed my intuition, and I was made whole – for an hour but not permanently as Jung says nature intends all men to be. But I noted his warning that completeness is not perfection.

And I knew, and said in the book, that what had happened to me could happen to anyone. No one is unique. Any man or woman could experience an awakening to the good in the self, in his fellow men, and in the universe. If not spontaneously as I happened to do, then it could be induced by psychology or any of the higher religions. I did not know then that it also could be brought about by reason and the Socratic form of dialogue.

Any man can achieve what Jung calls self-realization or individuation – a natural process of the normal human psyche and necessary to individual health and happiness and to universal peace between nations. So ended my story of *Awakening*.

I did not realize then that individuation was a lifelong process. I assumed that a glimpse of the high plateau of the good constituted permanent residence there. But there were many strange things about the discovery and development of the self a novice like me had yet to learn.

Also, I discovered that if your book achieves even a modicum of success, organizations invite you to lecture, strangers seek to meet you, people in restaurants ask for your autograph on menus though they undoubtedly have no intention of ever reading your book. Readers seek you out, rush up and clasp your hand in their warm hands that are positively electric, their eyes shining with a glow you have never seen before. You feel there is an indestructible bond forged between you forever. Strangers point you out from a distance. Skeptics stare at you with an expression unlike any other in the world. It is compounded of incredulity, anticipation, admiration and an intensity that almost frightens you, as if you were some strange monstrosity in a zoo.

In the first flush of my initial success, success itself seemed more intoxicating than champagne, more nourishing than food, more exhilarating than exercise, deeper than passion, profounder than thought, comparable only to the ecstasy of love – minus the concomitant anguish. Was it not the best gift life had to offer mortal man?

But no, I reminded myself, many men insist that man's ultimate ambition should be union with ultimate reality. Then why is fame so sweet? Why do all men long for it? Is it fame or success or the actualization of our best potentialities or the discovery of the self that lifts us to such intense exultation? I was willing to stop here. Or were there higher states?

I did not know. All I knew was that success seemed my defense against death. It offered me security and love and recognition more enduring – it seemed at the moment – than the love of parents, of friends or even marriage.

Parents, I told myself, however loving, surely die. Friends, however devoted, may prove fickle and fall away. Marriage, however loving, may terminate tragically. You may lose your home and health, your husband and money. Illness may cut the ground from under your feet. But if you have achieved success, however circumscribed, if you have been touched by fame, however modest, you become a citizen of the world.

You have gained the respect of your peers. You feel you never will be lonely again whatever happens. You have established lines of communication with kindred minds all over the world, a network of intellectual and affectionate companionship. You feel, momentarily, the sweet illusion that you can never die!

All the days of my life a quiet premonition had glowed within me like an unquenchable spark. Be patient, Clairene, your day will come, an inner voice bade me.

This inextinguishable faith in eventual recognition of the real me had sustained me in times of criticism – just and unjust. It had armored me against lack of understanding in my best friends, misunderstanding by acquaintances, and the indifference of strangers and personal failures. Now at last my day had come!

To realize potentialities you did not even know you possessed, I said to myself, how unutterably sweet it is! I am more deeply happy than ever in my entire life! But I am too happy! Something terrible is going to happen!

Chapter 3

VISION

Something did happen. But not what I had expected. It was unsought – unwanted – at first, until Jung's books later explained the meaning to me of this psychological phenomenon which is frequent in this stage of psychic growth.

This startling phenomenon descended on me one unforgettable day after more wonderful letters from readers had arrived. I lay down on my bed to rest, from habit, too exultant ever to sleep again. I sighed with sweet satiety, felt saturated with happiness, replete in every pore. Waves of pure undiluted joy surged through my body to the marrow of my bones, through my mind and heart and senses, until its sweetness was unbearable. I was afraid my skin would literally burst with happiness. I felt like one of those medieval wine skins filled to capacity with the new vintage. Surely one more drop of joy and my body would burst!

"Please, I beg of you, whatever you are, wherever you axe, spare me another word of praise. Please, no more, no more! I cannot endure another drop of happiness!"

As I lay there on the bed, I involuntarily threw out my left hand again and again in a passionate gesture. Why – I scarcely knew. Toward some unknown something, what – I scarcely knew. The need to offer thanks to something was insupportable. The pressure to render thanksgiving to someone was overpowering.

"Thank you! Thank you! Whatever you are – the life force, the creative principle, God, or whatever. Thank you! Thank you! Wherever you are – in outer space, in the human psyche, in the collective unconscious of the race or wherever. Please know, if nothing good ever happens to me again, so long as I live I shall be eternally grateful. Please know, no matter what disaster befalls me in the future, never shall I complain again about anything!

"But oh, please, never let me overestimate myself or my book. Let me remember that I – that any serious writer – seems but an empty vessel through which some universal energy elects to flow. Nevertheless I thank you for apparently speaking through me. I do not know where you are or who you are or if you are. But I *feel*, beyond reason and logic, the presence of some distant force, a thousand times more powerful than I. More omniscient than the wisdom of the human race accumulated merely in my own collective unconscious. I feel some mysterious, indescribable reality operating by universal laws I but dimly comprehend.

"I really wrote it all for *you*. Don't you understand? Not for myself – but for YOU! The inscrutable, ineffable It!

"Now for the first time in my entire life I understand why Johann Sebastian Bach said every note of music he ever wrote was 'for the greater glory of God.' Even against my will, against my reason, I feel my book, *Awakening*, was written for and by and about something better, higher, nobler than my small mere self. Whether this great life force is immanent or transcendent, existing in space and time or beyond both, or merely in the unconscious of the human psyche, my whole book is a tribute to the ineffable It!"

Then, as I lay there bursting with happiness, fulfillment and thanksgiving, the incredible happened! The impossible, the astounding! Suddenly, I saw a figure of a man about six feet away suspended in space, standing slightly above me and to the left. A clear distinct image of a beautiful young man with flowing white robes and flowing dark hair. He was smiling at me indulgently – even with amusement, smiling at me understandingly, even approvingly. It was a smile of ineffable sweetness, a face of inexpressible beauty, a gaze of indescribable intensity.

Who was it?

What was it?

Was it a vision?

My eyes saw it clearly while my mind realized the image was merely a psychological projection from itself. It seemed like a figure thrown on a motion picture screen. For some strange reason, I was not frightened in the least as I should have been.

It seemed quite a natural visitation, a confrontation in the nature of things. But who was it? It looked like a self-portrait of da Vinci, the greatest artist – some claim, the greatest man – who ever lived, a supreme artist and scientist. This image had flowing hair like Leonardo and no beard like Leonardo. But why the flowing white robes?

Or did this face resemble da Vinci's portrait of Mary, especially the one with St. Anne and the infant Jesus? It exhibited all the sweetness, the mysterious sadness and delicacy of a madonna. And yet, it was a man.

Well, then, could it be – ? No, no, I could not bring myself to think such a thing! It was too presumptuous. And yet, was it not more like Jesus the Christ? Like His traditional portraits except that the face had no beard? No, no, surely that could not be!

Or was this image supposed to be a composite of Christ and a woman and da Vinci, the spiritual-feminine-scientist-artist? In short, the universal man?

But why had this vision appeared at all? Was it accusing me of betraying Jesus? Because ever since college days, my reason had regarded Jesus not as divine but as a great spiritual leader like Buddha and Ramakrishna, or Moses or Mohammed. No, I did not feel there was any accusation in that face. There was affirmation and more – but what?

Was this figure smiling so indulgently, forgiving me for feeling too exultant at my small worldly success? No, it understood. I was confident that it accepted my exaltation. Then what was its significance? I stared for an indeterminate time at those smiling lips so full of wisdom.

Somehow, this presence filled me with warm reassurance, set the final seal of approval on my book, on my experience of the awakening self. My uncomprehending reason was unable to grasp its elusive, unspoken message. Yet there was a message – of that I was positive, and one of deep import.

I thought the vision would never vanish away. It lingered on, as clear as clear, never fading, never receding, as if determined that I should comprehend its silent annunciation, never saying a word, never taking its eyes from mine, never ceasing to smile that warm, wonderful, enigmatic smile . . .

Finally the figure began to recede slowly, reluctantly it seemed, as if disappointed that I had been too stupid to grasp its meaning. It grew smaller and smaller until it faded into the distance, until it disappeared into nothingness.

I lay motionless on the bed, strangely unafraid, scarcely surprised, accepting this phenomenon with unaccustomed serenity, viewing it with a new detachment, which in turn did not even amaze me. Everything seemed quite natural.

But what did it all mean?

Did this image signify that the greatest success of which man is capable is not the fulsome praise of many people, not worldly acclaim, however sweet, not creative achievement, nor even a spontaneous awakening to the self, but that the supreme success possible to man is to see a god?

But my reason regarded no man who ever walked the earth as a god. Besides, the greatest philosophies (so I had read) claim knowledge of reality is man's supreme experience. And all the greatest religions claim permanent union with ultimate reality is man's supreme experience – *Samadhi, Nirvana,* the Unitive life. And already I had very briefly experienced a fleeting moment of union with impersonal reality.

This was not a union at all, this vision of Christ was a confrontation and something more – but what?

I pondered and pondered, completely baffled, unable to fathom the meaning of this strange visual image without corporeal presence. Finally I rose, walked in a daze up the stairs to my writing room on the third floor.

I collected half a dozen books, stacked them on the desk, and sat there turning the leaves avidly, desperately. If anyone on this earth could explain the psychology of my vision, Jung could! But I failed to find what I sought.

In a sudden flash I remembered a little paperback book I had purchased recently and had not read yet, *Psyche and Symbol.* It was a collection of Jung's writings selected by one of his pupils, Violet de Laszlo. It saved my life.

In it Jung said that *a vision is merely a dream risen into the conscious mind, that Christ is a symbol of the self, that a vision of Christ in Christian culture is prophetic of a higher order of man in the future.*

Dumbfounded, I sat there trying to assimilate the wonder of such an interpretation! Motionless, I sat there, for hours it seemed, not reading, not thinking, merely trying to absorb these three stupendous ideas . . .

Eventually I emerged from my daze. If a vision was only a dream, why – everybody had dreams! So I was not peculiar after all. My everyday personality sighed with relief. For I felt uneasy at being unlike the people around me. None of my friends seemed to have visions. The only people I had heard of – at this point – who had visions were the prophets in the Bible.

Thank God for Jung, I thought, and pressed *Psyche and Symbol* fondly against my breast. Intellectual understanding was almost as exciting as the experience of the vision itself.

Why should such a dream rise into my consciousness at this particular time though?

Jung explained that today mankind is in danger of destroying the whole human race with radioactivity. Therefore some of us experience a strong resurgence of our instinct for survival. The activity of the deeper unconscious in many people nowadays is far in advance of the activity of our reason. And that is what the tragic world of today needs, he asserted.

But why a vision?

Jung had discovered after fifty years of studying thousands of people that when the unconscious is activated profoundly enough it always projects images externally. Well, certainly my deeper unconscious had been Violently activated by my recent experience of "dying," being "reborn," discovery of the self, writing a book about it, to say nothing of the profound agitation produced by the wonderful letters of readers. These letters touched the very core of my being, arousing something never aroused before.

Yet why should it be an image of Christ. Why not of someone else? Jung disclosed the fact that in our Western Christian culture, Christ was a psychological symbol of the self. Did this mean that if I had been born in a Hindu or Buddhist culture my vision would have been of Krishna or Buddha? Or if I had been Jewish might it have been a vision of their prophet Moses?

Jung's book stated that a person does not consciously intend to create a symbol. It springs from the deeper unconscious. It does not symbolize some known or even conceivable fact. It symbolizes something only vaguely conceivable.

But what did he mean by saying that a vision of Christ was prophetic of a higher order of man in the future?

I read further. The great psychologist suggested that the historical Jesus, existing in the outside world, might in time be transformed into the superior man within modern man himself. Western man would achieve a psychological state that corresponded to the experience of Enlightenment known to Eastern man. Such a process, he said, is a step in the development of man toward unknown goals of evolution. (This was so exciting it left me breathless!)

Jung's book warned me, however, that Christ is an archetype and also a psychological symbol of perfection to mankind. Therefore, temporary completeness does not constitute perfection. This meant the wholeness I had experienced when my deeper unconscious was released and united briefly with my conscious mind was not to be confused with perfection. Did this signify that individuation was a life-long process? That the effort at transformation of our character must continue indefinitely?

Did it mean that the man of tomorrow would be – perhaps not god-like or Christ-like but – at least a man who has released his deeper unconscious and united it with his conscious rational mind to create the whole man who can live in harmony with fellows and the universe?

But how to accomplish this?

This vision seemed to lay a tremendous obligation on me as to my future behavior. I was too happy, however, to feel its pressure for some time.

After the occurrence of these four unprecedented events – the vision, the wonderful letters from readers, the joy of writing the book about *awakening to the self,* and particularly the actual experience of the awakening – life was continuously blissful – for a period. My health was glowing.

I felt harmony with all people, with inanimate things, with my inner self, my body, and the universe. I felt capable of undreamed of feats – tomorrow! I was riding high on the crest of the wave, living on a plane higher than I had ever imagined possible me – for any ordinary woman or man. It surpassed every experience I ever had day dreamed of in my whole life. All my problems were surely solved for the rest of my life, I blithely assumed. It had revolutionized my marriage.

Then everything went wrong.

STAGE II

SELF-DISCIPLINE

Chapter 1

DESCENT

For eight incredibly glorious years I had been flying high above the earth. Like any self-actualizing person, I had been living in a state just this side of bliss.

Now suddenly, swiftly, without warning I was plunged to earth. The impact stunned me. An awful reaction of nervous exhaustion set in. Was it sheer excess of stimulation and happiness? Or was it permanent?

I feel numb, I said to myself. Nil. Void. Blank. Zero. As if I really am not here at all.

I who always reacted so intensely to everything – even things that did not deserve such reaction – now feel nothing. I who always cared so passionately about everything – even things not worth caring about – now do not care about anything.

I eat without relish, sleep without refreshment, talk pointlessly, walk aimlessly, perform my daily routine indifferently – waiting – waiting – for what? The next flight into the stratosphere?

What is wrong with me?

It has been my greatest joy to live in harmony with everyone. Now I am irritable and cross about trifles. I stumble and fumble, drop things – spill things worse than any awkward schoolgirl. My days are meaningless, my actions purposeless.

I am sick at heart that I am not sicker at heart at the loss of all those shining years of ecstasy. I am pervaded only by a dull, dry sorrow at the loss of something I doubt I ever possessed, assailed by a question that my deeper, better self ever was released at all – tempted to refute the existence of any better self in myself – or in any man or woman, doubtful that I ever achieved communication with the presence behind the phenomena, skeptical that such a source even exists.

I feel false to all my announced ideals, dishonest about all my published claims, a charlatan who cries spiritual wares she no longer carries. I am no longer living in accord with the ideas expressed in my own book.

What shall I do? Submit, succumb, degenerate into mediocrity again? Can I trust that same inscrutable principle which unbidden – heaped upon me – unworthy – all the glittering riches of self-actualization for a few shining years? Can I ever find the energy to trust anything again?

I vegetate. I regress. I grieve silently within. I appear stultified without. Has a vital spark within me been extinguished forever? Can so cold and dead a fire ever be rekindled?

I feel bereft, betrayed, deserted, forgotten.

Then gradually, there crept over me a grey fog of insomnia, irritability, indigestion, weakness, fatigue, nervousness – though never fear, only numb indifference. The memory of my past joys still cast a light over my whole life. Otherwise, I was struggling again with all the same physical problems that had tormented me immediately before my grand renascence which had banished them – forever, I had hoped.

Suddenly I no longer blamed It but myself. What had I done wrong? Wherein had I failed? Why had I lost all the glory and the wonder? Could I never again attain those "peak experiences" Maslow equates with Being – for all else is merely Becoming.

This was when it became all too evident that I had been like an astronaut permitted to soar to peaks of ecstasy, to view briefly the awesome heights to which man was capable of ascending psychologically or spiritually. Now it was as if by parachute I had descended to everydayness, to earthiness.

Nature apparently had not constituted the human nervous system so it was capable of sustaining great heights – even of harmony and happiness.

I must do something to correct this sad situation – at least the physical one. But how could I rehabilitate my poor, exhausted body? The condition had lasted a long time.

I tried doctors – rest – vitamin supplements – new diets. Nothing worked. Instinctively I sensed and said repeatedly to my husband that my body was suffering from some kind of deficiency, some terrible internal imbalance. What kind? No one knew. I least of all.

My family doctor finally suggested that I investigate Dr. Jarvis' controversial book, *Folk Medicine*. In desperation, I consumed astounding quantities of natural honey, unprocessed apple cider vinegar, and kelp tablets for their organic iodine.

Apparently, the minerals contained in them improved my health almost miraculously for a time. They generated so much energy – mental and muscular, nervous and creative – I nearly worked myself into another decline. Eventually, however, my nervous system rebelled against this over-stimulation and my alimentary tract against the vinegar.

I felt immeasurably better physically but now it was my state of mind that concerned me.

Like most Americans I was sick to death of continuous world crises, of cold wars, and hot wars, bewilderment and helplessness. Something vital was missing in the international scene. But what?

Something was wrong with our national life, too. I now realized to my utter dismay that all our precious political freedom, material wealth, scientific discoveries, and technological gadgets for *comfort* were not able to create a good society or world peace or good life within me, or in most individuals. Something vital was missing in our national life, too. But what?

Most of all I was dissatisfied with myself, with my personal life. It seemed extremely ungrateful of me for I had a nice husband, beautiful home, adequate income, modest success in my writing profession, pleasant social life, and good friends. We rushed to the latest plays, concerts, and art exhibits. I strove to read all the newest books, dashed all over New York senselessly for tomorrow's fashions, worked on a dozen committees without pay – civic, political, college, art, literary, charity. Yet some vital element was missing in my personal life.

It was obvious that what was lacking in me was a real, true inner life. For once anyone has attained the level where his feeling of harmony functions freely, where his deeper, better self predominates, he can never rest in peace until he attempts to recapture it. Recapture by conscious effort the glory he had once known without effort. But how to regain it?

Could I depend again on the spontaneous assistance from unknown sources such as I had enjoyed during the prolonged but spontaneous period of my rebirth? No, I was certain that was impossible.

If I longed to recapture that elevated plane of daily living I had once known briefly, I must climb mountain by my own conscious exertions – on foot, as it were.

Oh, but that was asking too much of anyone! It was too difficult, perhaps impossible. I did not even know how to begin, what path to follow, where to turn for guidance, what techniques of mental mountaineering to employ.

What of the state of the world? Was not that an additional incentive? It was worsening steadily. Every day World War III with its nuclear bomb annihilation of the whole human race, including me, drew nearer. I must find not an underground shelter but some elevated position from which I might attempt to withstand the onslaughts of man's political failures, scientific amoral horrors, ideological catastrophes, and senseless and savage behavior.

Was this what Jung had meant by survival? Survival by transforming our own characters? By realizing our potentialities for the good by conscious effort, as Maslow suggested?

But how?

Was this the man of tomorrow of which my vision had been prophetic? I did not know but must endeavor to find out.

So, after being spontaneously awakened to the self, writing a book about it, receiving wonderful letters from readers, seeing a vision, living briefly in harmony with all things and people, then in nervous exhaustion, and finally improving my physical health, I now felt an irresistible urge to set out alone in search of that higher, happier plane of life for my permanent residence – where the real true self could function freely.

Chapter 2

METHODS AND GOALS

I laughed at myself. Now I was right back with the beginners. For all my wonderful flight into the stratosphere I must struggle up the mountain from the starting point like all the other types of physique and temperament. Memory of that brief glimpse of the shining mountain top, however, might lend incentive to my efforts.

Was there no name for the high place I sought?

Self-realization? Individuation? Actualization of potentialities? Knowledge of the good, the true, and the beautiful? The good life? The discovered self?

I was not seeking the shining peak of Buddhist *Nirvana* or the Hindu *Samadhi*, or the Christian Unitive deified life.

I envisioned my goal as a halfway plateau on the highest mountain in the world, illuminated occasionally by the light of ultimate reality.

I was not seeking the exclusively religious life but rather the good life in the world, the complete life that made Greek culture the greatest ever produced by man, a life that embraced the intellectual, physical, sexual, intuitive, rational, spiritual, creative, political, loving and social life without undue emphasis on any one aspect. The full balanced life.

And what method should I employ? Should I *do* good first, thereby becoming good – presumably? Or try to *become* good first and thereafter do good – automatically? Our constitutional type seems to choose our method for us. Mine urged me toward the latter.

In short, I must first attempt to rediscover the self. I must learn how to release the collective unconscious.

But how? To discover the self one brief once was not enough. I must learn how to re-release it, cultivate it, develop it.

And what specifically were the goals of such a life as I sought?

I sat down one day and typed a list in an attempt to clarify and formulate the possible goals of the independent aspirant of self-realization in the West today – and especially my goals:

Can I deliberately awaken my inner resources to face our human predicament of nuclear bombs and the threat of annihilation, of men's senseless and savage behavior?

Can I learn to live in harmony with myself, with others, and the laws of the universe – permanently not periodically?

Can I revolutionize my relations with other people, sweeten my marriage – at will?

Can I attain a state of mind where prejudice against other religions, colors and races falls away – naturally?

Who will teach me to rise to a level where I love others as much as myself – almost; where I return good for evil – involuntarily?

Who will teach me not to control my anger but not to feel it?

How shall I achieve a psychological plane where solitude is enriching, creativity as natural as breathing, menial work an effortless rhythm – every day not once a year?

How shall I become so receptive to beauty in art, in nature, that it purifies me and actually alters my behavior – indefinitely?

Can I, can modern man in general, learn to cure that dichotomy between mind and body, reason intuition, matter and spirit that has blighted the West ever since the Greeks?

Can we feel the unity of all things at all times?

How shall I induce the joyousness unlike any other on earth?

How shall I merge myself at my own volition with the moral order of the universe – if the scientists have us any?

In short, how shall I liberate my deeper unconscious by my own efforts so that from it will flow forth harmony and happiness, peace and compassion, love and creativity and wisdom? How can I unite it with my conscious mind to make me whole permanently?

Chapter 3

OBSTRUCTIONS AND OBSTACLES

For days, weeks, months, I struggled to achieve my goals.

I was foolish perhaps, obstinate certainly. I imagined, however, that it was possible to make this desired journey unaided except by my own inner guide – my collective unconscious.

Promptly external obstructions loomed in my path like great rocks. Each morning when I first awakened I planned in earnest to achieve a transformation my character that very day. The news on my bedside radio announced that the world threatened to end not with a whimper but a bang, T.S. Eliot not withstanding. International crises, nuclear bombs, the cold war, the threat of global annihilation, and World War III. It left me helpless, bewildered and sick with anxiety, full of fear of death and of deformity from radioactivity.

How could I keep my mind on my personal goals? In the face of such global dangers how dared I, or anyone, think of inner personal problems?

At breakfast the newspaper headlines erected further obstructions in my path toward the discovery of my real self. They flung our national social ills in our faces. Juvenile delinquency, organized crime, the prevalence of mental illness, narcotic addiction, Johnny's inability to read, the denial of birth control clinics. They all demanded action on my part immediately – if not sooner. I would do what I could by sending small checks if nothing else.

After breakfast I consulted the cook, planned the menu, ordered the groceries. Then I lay back in my long reclining chair in the living room, closed my eyes, and attempted to relax, to cleanse my conscious mind of mundane affairs.

I bade my deeper unconscious come forth, please, and act as my guide on my journey into the self. She was too shy, too untrained. She had been repressed and suppressed for a lifetime – except for the glorious interlude of my initial awakening.

Besides, concentration was almost impossible. Distractions and noises were endless, from our otherwise convenient household conveniences – dishwashers swishing in the kitchen, vacuum cleaners grinding on the second floor where the chambermaid was cleaning the bedrooms, doorbells ringing, my husband making loud long distance telephone calls all over America in his office on the second floor. They all over-stimulated my nerves. These small metallic sounds struck me continually like minute bullets of an unseen enemy attacking an explorer in a jungle.

How could any expedition into the unconscious be conducted in sufficient peace and quiet in any household? How to find the solitude and silence essential for complete concentration. Jet planes blasted my nerves. Automobile traffic assaulted my ears. Life in an active, busy, noisy, mechanical, materialistic modern America was not designed for the development of one's inner personality. The role of wife and householder was not conducive to such projects.

After dinner every night my husband and I alternated music with books and magazines. I read about the recent discoveries of science and outer space, They stopped me cold, banished any thought of a personal goal.

Stunned, I gazed at the new universe all around us. We were faced by a universe of 500 million galaxies composed of swarms of billions of stars as large and luminous as our sun; confronted by satellites orbiting about the earth, rockets shooting the moon, space ships flying to other planets and soon – planets inhabited perhaps by a super or hostile race. We were surrounded by outer space so vast many scientists feared it might be infinite.

In the face of such a gigantic universe, of what importance am I, I wondered? Has the glory that is science and the grandeur that is space deprived me, perhaps all mankind, of our greatest strength – self esteem? Have not astrophysics and radio-astronomy struck the last fatal blow to man's feeling of centrality in the cosmos?

I for one was paralyzed by the enormity of it all, reduced to an ineffectual zero on an insignificant planet. Why should I, why should any person, strive to live a better life when atomic science undeterred by ethics had suspended the probability of life on earth? My fate was bound up inseparably with the fate of earth people everywhere. So I sat in my living room chair bewildered – witless – helpless.

Daily, hourly, society itself exerted invisible pressure on me, on any trainee for the higher happier life. It exerted it through our reading, through radio and television, magazines and books, conversations with friends, by the air of the culture we breathed.

Periodically I felt that so manifold were my duties and responsibilities – domestic and public – so many my activities and commitments, so continually was I being pushed and pulled and prodded, coerced in four directions at once by competition, convention and conformity, by government, society, fear and fashions, custom and tradition, above all by the ubiquitous advertising and the printed and broadcast word of our self-anointed spokesmen that I, for one, feared sometimes the centrifugal force that whirled me about in American life today would tear me into a thousand pieces. We had too much of everything – even good things.

And what was worse, in every mass medium, I found the writers urged me, urged all women, daily, hourly, unceasingly to be not only career women but ideal wives, models of fashion, psychologically trained mothers, expert French cooks, workers in national and local politics, in a dozen charities – Red Cross, mental illness, heart and polio fund collecting. Like all modern housewives I was hounded incessantly to be twenty women in one. Not to be exhausted when night came caused me to feel guilty. Our wonderful communications systems communicated too much, too often, from too many places.

No one, absolutely no one ever urged me to aspire toward a richer, fuller, inner life – to develop my potentialities for the good, to discover the treasures of the self – except the psychologists – Analytical and Humanistic, and later Psychosynthetic.

There were not only external obstructions to be overcome.

Inner obstacles prowled about my bed on sleepless nights like wild animals stalking some explorer's camp in the jungles of Africa. Fears –fears of war, radioactivity, disease, disgrace, poverty, old age, and death. Fear of losing social status, love or loved ones, of being left alone in the world.

How could I forget these fears that haunted me in the night? How could I eliminate my own weaknesses? Inertia, indifference, irritability, and my own innate cussedness? Anger, tension, fatigue, skepticism, and unmerited hostility, to say nothing of physical illnesses – cold, flu, and virus. They destroyed my confidence, distracted my attention, delayed my psychological advance.

The greatest internal obstacle of all to release of the unconscious was *reason* – my own reason on which I had prided myself for a life time. I was unaware as yet of the power of the conscious mind to release the true and the good within us through dialectic dialogue. Every time my timid unconscious emerged to guide my steps, reason spoke up loud and clear. It demanded to be my guide, but to another goal.

Should you not, my reason insisted, conform to the current intellectual fashion and help create the regenerated society for all first – trusting that the regenerated individual life will follow – eventually?

But, I protested, have politics and economics, determinism and positivism, materialism, science and technology brought world peace or inner happiness to the individual? Are they not all based on reason? Is it not high time for me, for modern man in general, to try some other means? Is it not time to seek the good life for the individual first – hoping the good society will result – automatically? Or must I, must contemporary man, attempt both simultaneously?

I continued my efforts to release my unconscious. All these efforts to transform my personality, however, required time, solitude, quiet, silence, relaxation, fewer distractions, less stimulation, and more concentration.

Consequently, I simplified my life, resigned – gladly to my amazement – from most of my committees and half my clubs in New York, stopped giving lectures all over the state, saw fewer people, entertained less, ceased rushing to every new play, concert and art exhibit, ceased dashing all over New York for tomorrow's fashions, traveled less, read fewer newspaper articles, listened to fewer broadcasts.

Physical inactivity was not enough.

Daily I struggled to overcome the distractions of all the external obstructions – the international situation, the national situation with all its social ills, the complexities and mechanization of our contemporary extraverted American civilization so splendid in many ways yet too full of tensions and pressures, stimulation and distraction.

I strove to overcome the internal obstacles of fear, doubt and inertia. Was it all not a task beyond my ability? My will power was not strong enough to control my body and mind.

I was on the point of stopping many times. But that meant I must return to convention and conformity, ceaseless activity and discontent forever – unless I received outside assistance.

I had hoped to make this expedition to the high place alone without direct outside aid of any kind.

Was indirect help permissible? Perhaps necessary?

Chapter 4

THE ARTS

What means should a modern independent aspirant of the West, like me, employ to discover and develop the self?

Should I abandon myself to the arts? Immerse myself in nature? Submit to Jungian or Humanistic psychotherapy? Or enroll for a course in philosophy at the nearby university? Should I seek a Hindu guru to train me daily in yoga? Look for a Buddhist master to teach me the way to a modified Enlightenment? Or withdraw to some Christian retreat for undisturbed silence and introspection for awhile? Where should I begin?

Well, in the past, which means had most quickly and easily released my collective unconscious? To my astonishment it was the arts!

So my husband and I intensified our trips to the museums in New York, in Europe. We poured over our collection of prints on Sunday afternoons. I studied paintings more carefully. They evoked mild pleasure. They failed to purify me as Titian's portrait of Pope Paul had done once.

I stood still and tried to abandon myself to the beautiful architecture in our town of which there were many examples. Its order and completeness brought internal order and completeness to me – momentarily. Its wholeness reassembled the scattered fragments of my personality – temporarily.

We exposed ourselves to exhibits of sculpture – modern and classical, pleased by the latter, deeply disturbed by the former.

We subscribed as usual to the drama season in our town. We saw legitimate Broadway plays before they opened in New York. Only one play, O'Neil's *Long Day's Journey Into Night*, aroused that purifying pity – though not the terror – which Aristotle said tragedy should arouse. Why was I unable to be transformed nowadays as I had been a few years ago in New York when Lawrence Olivier appeared in *Oedipus Rex*? Then my bones had melted with sheer delight. His wild animal howl of horror when he discovered he had married his mother curdled my blood. I came away from that great Greek tragedy feeling strangely ennobled.

Invariably I attended the theater as eagerly as a child. I expected to see noble characters struggling valiantly against adversity toward noble ends.

Today our most talented playwrights offered us a plethora of murderers, nymphomaniacs, homosexuals, alcoholics, drug addicts, derelicts, and neurotics, and above all golden-hearted prostitutes. Why had the prostitute become the favorite heroine of our best contemporary playwrights and novelists? The authors assured us they all deserved the "requiem of a nun."

Each time I would leave the theater saddened and bewildered, the foundations of my own life shaken, my values undermined, fearful for the future of mankind in our country. Was our civilization really disintegrating? Then how could I expect the drama to regenerate me?

We attended the ballet but I was still too apathetic from my recent descent from the heights. It titillated me only mildly. It was capable of doing much more. I was capable of reacting much more deeply. Not long ago I had experienced the same harmony the great ballerinas evinced – harmony of body and mind, harmony with the world and the universe beyond.

Ah, but poetry – surely it could come to my rescue. It would induce in me the revelation of these treasures I knew were buried in the deeper layers of my unconscious. I always blithely assumed poetry was my favorite literature. Today, in a moment of horrible honesty, I admitted that to one book of poetry I read a year, I read one hundred fiction and non-fiction.

It was a quiet Spring day – the cook's day off. I carried a stack of books of poetry into the garden. I returned to the old familiar words I had loved as a girl – Keats and Shelley, Wordsworth and Tennyson, Swinburne and Poe, Whitman and Millay. Beside my chair a bumblebee was rifling the honeysuckle of its sweetness. As I mouthed the wonderful words slowly, each luscious syllable dropped into my senses like a drop of nectar. It nearly made me drunk.

But contemporary poets – how could they be an instrument of readers' enlightenment? They offered little but a world that was a wasteland peopled with hollow men.

But the rhythm and rhyme of the lyric poets buoyed me up, assured me a second chance was possible, that I could make a success of my life yet, realize my potentialities.

My confidence was too temporary, too fleeting. By the time my husband returned home to take me out to dinner, the magic had flown. I felt weary, irritable, apathetic. Nevertheless, I continued to read and reread good poetry – periodically – hopefully.

What of music? It possessed less power than poetry, did it not? Poetry possessed meaning *and* music, involved reason and the senses. Music was meaningless, abstract, devoid of ideas.

On Saturday afternoons I listened to the opera "live" from the Metropolitan in New York. Each evening my husband played the radio with its frequency modulation records of the world's greatest music as we rested between the reading of our current magazines and books.

Each time, I concentrated as never before in my life. To my utter astonishment music proved to be the quickest and easiest avenue of all the arts to the good, the true, and the beautiful! My purification was only partial. It did not alter my behavior as music had had the power so to do – in the past.

I continued to listen night after night in anticipation of greater things.

The arts were a proven means to arousing the best in us but they presented serious difficulties. They required continuous repetition as a rule to be effective. I, for one, was unable to listen to music constantly. After a few hours my poor ears rebelled against those little hammer blows of sound. My husband, however, never tired of music.

Painting and sculpture were not easily available. They were few and far away in New York and Europe.

Architecture was accessible in one's own city yet if a woman alone stood on the street and stared at a beautiful building long enough to feel it transform her, men stared at her unpleasantly. If she sat in the car the top was cut off the top of the building. Of all the arts, books and music were the most easily available at home.

The arts involved other problems. Noises, distractions of television, radio, social life, cocktail parties, dining out, other stimulants like coffee and tea.

At night while listening to music when I was attempting to train myself in concentration, there were the voice of the cook entertaining a friend, telephone bells, jet planes blasting all other sounds out of existence, automobiles roaring by purposely making hellish rackets.

Finally, while the music was on, we disconnected the telephone, turned out the lights, refrained from all conversation, all movements. I discovered one secret was to relax the body completely but keep the mind alert. Not the conscious mind, that ruined everything. It was that "alert passivity" of which Aldous Huxley writes so understandingly. I placed my body in the most comfortable position possible that it might not distract my attention.

Now I appreciated for the first time the Hindu emphasis on posture, darkness, quiet, and solitude for the seeker after self-realization.

What about creative writing? I knew that on those rare occasions when the creative stream flowed effortlessly and joyously, it was able to arouse all the best in my nature, lift me to a moment's communion with the great mystery. In my present state of indifference and insensibility, I was unable to write a line.

Now I had repeatedly employed the seven arts – painting and sculpture, drama and dance, poetry, music and architecture as a means toward unfoldment. They had illuminated my life mildly and briefly but I was bitterly disappointed. Not in the arts. I knew they possessed the power, the magic power. I was disappointed in myself, in my inability to respond adequately.

If man-made beauty failed me at this time what of natural beauty?

Chapter 5

NATURE

Could nature open the doors of perception?

I immersed myself in nature. That was not difficult when one lived in Connecticut. Every glance out the windows plunged my eyes into a world of gigantic green trees. In the rear was a small garden – my husband's delight – full of flowers in the spring. Opposite us was a wild park with a river and mountain of red rock palisades that grew luminous in the level rays of the late afternoon sun. Yet we were only fifteen minutes by car from the Green in the heart of the city – thank goodness. We were both city people to the core yet felt an insatiable hunger for green growing things.

Repeatedly I sat in the garden in the sun or under the flowering dogwoods by the bird bath. I strove too hard perhaps – to let go, to relax utterly, to open all my senses, to release my deeper unconscious. Sometimes I succeeded in a feeble way.

At other times, the cook, the upstairs maid, the yard man, my husband would come by and speak to me. Or the tradesmen – the delivery boy with the groceries, the milkman, the garbage collector, the window washer, the man to read the water meter, or the man to read the electric meter, or the man to read the gas meter. Or it would be the man to cut the grass or trim the hedges, or the man to take the oak leaves out of the gutters, or a painter who wanted to paint something or a carpenter who wanted to nail something, or the man to spray the trees.

I always talked with them. I liked to talk with people. I liked to maintain friendly relations with all the people who served us and helped to keep the house in repair and the garden tidy.

But I soon found that to derive the full benefits from nature, solitude, silence and trained concentration were essential.

I waited and hoped for the permanent transformation of my personality I knew nature was capable of inducing. I trembled on the verge repeatedly. I was uplifted – for an hour only.

If a novice was unable to employ art or nature as a means to liberation, why not try psychology?

51

Chapter 6

PSYCHOLOGY

Jung

What of the various systems of psychology concerned with development of the normal, deeper unconscious? Did they offer the aspirant of self-realization techniques to extricate himself from that mire of mediocrity and misery in which I now floundered? Techniques suited for use to recapture *unaided* the lost psychological heights?

Had I failed to see that for which I was not looking at the time when I first studied Jung, for example?

Once again I searched through his profound but difficult books like a miner digging for gold nuggets. Primarily his system was designed to induce the initial discovery of the self. It alleviated a neurosis – if any – in the personal unconscious and released the collective unconscious. Afterward union of the patient's conscious mind with his deeper unconscious and harmony with the laws of the universe were supposed to follow. Greater mental health and happiness ensued.

But I already had experienced this release of my deeper unconscious. It was involuntary and solitary. I had passed through the first stage of psychic growth, awakening of the self. It contained several steps. My experiences had paralleled the steps Jung enumerates in the case of his patients – normal and otherwise. Despair; "death," when the ego drowns in the collective unconscious; rebirth, when the deeper layers of the unconscious are released; acceptance by the conscious mind of the contents of the unconscious; and finally union of the two.

The trouble now was that my awakening had not been permanent. It was Jung's books which had explained my strange, former, beautiful experiences to me and for that I would be forever in his debt. But now that the glory had receded, what to do?

He himself cautioned that individuation was a lifelong process. Did this not imply that it was necessary for his thousands of patients from all over the world either to consult him frequently through the years or to continue their own self-realization unaided?

Did he leave any instructions for them to use to further the development of their deeper, better nature? I failed to find any in his books.

Nor did he speak of regression or gloom such as this in which I found myself now bogged down. Did this mean the psychotherapy of Analytical psychology was so efficacious his patients encountered no difficulty afterward? Was the implication then that the method of self-actualization with the guidance of a trained analyst was superior to the natural spontaneous awakening of the self – such as mine? This was indeed disconcerting!

Was the slow, gradual arousal of the self more enduring than the sudden ecstatic visitation? Or was it the difference between the wild flower and a cultivated flower of the same species? Yet observe the great men whom no one had trained: Socrates (though he trained Plato and Plato trained Aristotle), Whitman and Emerson, Buddha and Ramakrishna, Paul and Jesus, Lincoln and Jefferson, Schweitzer and Gandhi. But then, of course, everyone of these was a genius. I was not.

Evidently Jung's psychotherapy opened the gate in the path that led up the mountain toward complete and permanent individuation. The remainder of the journey was the responsibility of the individual.

The Swiss psychologist did state, however, that age played an important role in this process. It was usually a project for the last half of life, for thirty-six or over. Well, I was well beyond that age.

Evidently Jung based his entire system of Analytical psychology on the scientific evidence that man was now able to direct and develop his own mental and spiritual evolution. He considered individuation a step in evolution toward a superior man of tomorrow. It might lead Western man to the enjoyment of the same kind of Enlightenment, he said, which men knew in the East when they became integrated with total reality. Would I ever achieve this goal? But how?

In all honesty I was disappointed in not finding in Jung the help I needed at the moment. I was unjust of course. His contribution to the welfare of the human race – and to mine – was immeasurable. His books had filled me with understanding and hope, courage and certitude. What more should one ask?

I chastised myself severely. I had fallen into error for the usual reason. I had *assumed* facts merely because I wished them to be there. Honest examination of his books revealed my mistake. Would I never learn not to make false assumptions?

But where would I find means of rescuing myself? What of other psychologists?

Sheldon

The primary purpose of the Constitutional psychology of William Sheldon was not the release of the deeper unconscious or the re-release. Knowledge of one's type of temperament, however, did indirectly serve such a purpose. He helped give us knowledge and courage to be ourselves. Were there any clues I might have overlooked in his books that might aid a self-actualizing person in a predicament like mine?

Briefly I reviewed Constitutional psychology. Sheldon had discovered that the individual's type of physique determined his temperament and ways of expressing himself. The person of round, soft, fat build, the endomorph, exhibits a viscerotonic temperament and expresses himself most naturally through *love* of food, comfort, and people.

The broad, strong-muscled, large-boned person he terms the mesomorph with a somatotonic temperament who expresses himself most naturally through *action* and overcoming obstacles.

The slender, small-boned, thin-skinned type of physique, the ectomorph, exhibits a cerebrotonic temperament in which the function of *thought* is predominant.

Then there is the 4-4-4 in which all three components are present in equal proportion. This fourth type expresses himself through love and action and thought. According to Sheldon's laboratory measurements on his seven point scale, I am a 4-4-4. Did this make my attempt at self-actualization more difficult or less?

Sheldon says that the endowment of the 4-4-4 may cause him a predicament but if he is able to harmonize his sometimes conflicting components, he may become an "elevated personality." An exposition of the way to harmonize them was not the province of his system of psychology.

In an earlier book, however, Sheldon described the Promethean Will as man's deepest wish to grow to his full stature. This was a different description of self-realization, was it not? Sheldon suggested new ways to educate the public over a long term by coordinating psychology, religion, and medicine but not methods for the individual to employ immediately and personally.

Nevertheless, I already had found knowledge of Constitutional psychology to be of immense value in understanding other people, as well as in my own pursuit of excellence. Such knowledge of their respective types would assist all types to fulfill their own potentialities, would it not?

He did not mention the descent of the mountain by the 4-4-4 or ways to ascend it again. No psychologist did. Evidently it was not considered their function. But there was a mystery here yet to be solved.

Nor did Sheldon indicate that the discovery of the self occurs spontaneously in the 4-4-4. Judging by my own experience and the rather unscientific research of the Canadian psychologist, Richard Bucke, it appeared as if it did.

Bucke

In *Cosmic Consciousness* Richard Bucke lists fifty famous persons who experienced the superior form of consciousness completely or partially. From Whitman, Emerson and Thoreau to Wordsworth, Tennyson and Blake to Pascal, Spinoza and Socrates, to Buddha, Jesus and Ramakrishna. Did they ever lose it or retrieve it? If so, how?

I reviewed his reasons for believing this higher type of consciousness was a result of evolution and that this in turn produced their particular type of temperament. The most successful examples possessed a temperament composed equally of the four humors of Aristotle: choleric, melancholic, sanguine, and phlegmatic. This was similar to Sheldon's classification but the latter was more scientific.

All these famous persons had discovered the self *involuntarily*. I searched diligently for Bucke's suggestion that they had lost it temporarily and striven to regain it. No clews.

Here again I foolishly and unfairly expected to find in a psychologist matter that was not in his sphere of interest. But I simply could not believe that nature would shower any person with such shining glory and then deprive him of it forever.

Whitman, I recalled, informed us of the glowing results of his cosmic consciousness but not of his struggle before or after. Millay's *Renascence* seemed a one-time grand awakening but exerted little influence on her poetry or future life. Wordsworth as we all know descended to pettiness after his intimations of immortality.

What of Blake and Dante, Pascal and Socrates, Buddha and Jesus and Paul – did they suffer reverses? I must investigate their lives from this point of view soon.

Bucke and Sheldon and Jung informed and encouraged me but did not offer the means for which I was at this moment seeking. What of the new "third force" in psychology?

Maslow

What of the Humanistic psychology of Abraham Maslow and his colleagues? Did it offer means to awaken or reawaken the self? I must reread the literature from this particular point of view.

I reread *New Knowledge in Human Values*, *The Self*, and the reprints of Maslow's papers in scholarly journals that he was kind enough to send me. I also read his book which was new to me, *The Psychology of Being*.

He has conducted research on living persons who have had "peak experiences" (a term he coined) which he equates with Being. He discovered that peak experiences come to different people through different channels – through natural childbirth, creativity in the arts, nature, art appreciation, love, intellectual insights, sports, religious writings and many more. The results however were similar:

Spontaneity, naturalness, simplicity, detachment, honesty, identification with mankind, better relationship with others, acceptance of self, of other people and nature, enjoyment of everything in life, gaiety, innocence, a sense of justice, tolerance, and playfulness. Also freedom from cultural pressures, loss of doubt – inhibitions – weakness – and fear of public opinion.

He emphasized even more markedly than Jung the good that is uncovered in the deeper unconscious. It was wonderfully heartening that Maslow found no instinct for evil in man. That was what had amazed me when I had my first awakening of the self. Did this mean that all evil behavior of man is due to an exclusive reliance on the conscious mind?

It was wonderfully reassuring to a discouraged seeker like me to learn from Maslow that many people in America today were actualizing their potentialities. This meant I was on the right road. But why were many other people afraid to pursue their own happiness and fulfillment?

Maslow believed that it was because they did not understand the nature of the core of their own being. They were afraid it might contain something horrible. They feared to open this – to them – Pandora's box. It might even be the way to insanity, they imagined. To me this ignorance was tragic and sad.

He noted, also, that there existed forces in our culture which discouraged modern man from seeking self-actualization. Political forces like Marxism, the psychological attitudes of the Freudians, and the mechanistic-scientific philosophy of our civilization.

Modern man should learn to look for his hierarchy of values in himself, within his own psyche, Maslow said. He no longer needed to seek his values outside himself – in a ruling class, or in sacred books, he believed.

Maslow foresaw that an increase of self-awareness might lead eventually to Eupsychia – a society based on psychological health, not a Utopia founded on material wealth.

Such research as his, he suggested, would make the Unitive life clearer and more available.

For years I had blithely and erroneously assumed that this new Humanistic psychology included means of achieving actualization of one's potentialities. Now I further assumed that it would instruct in methods of regaining this perpetually perishing power. Maslow stated unequivocally that the psychology of Being was concerned with *ends* not *means*. That stopped me cold!

When the Brandeis psychologist was interviewed on the radio, however, he was asked how in our culture we could work toward a psychologically healthy society. He suggested three means. Psychoanalysis (meaning for the non-neurotic as well as the neurotic, I imagine). This psychotherapy was available only to the few. Education for people in general. And self-therapy which he said was extremely difficult.

He had discovered that peak experiences occurred sometimes in moments of relaxation, at other times at moments of greatest excitement. They could not be forced at will. They just happened.

Certainly this was true but it gave me pause. Peak experiences I had learned from inquiry among my friends do happen spontaneously to all types of temperament. But I was now searching for means by which to persuade them to happen, or rather to prepare the interior soil of the psyche that they might burst into a second blooming. Was this impossible?

The purpose of this "third force," Humanistic psychology, was to promote theoretical and applied research. This, of course, I realized was invaluable to the welfare of the human race and to me.

The glorious results of self-actualization of thousands of subjects as discovered by Maslow was enormously encouraging to me. His work left me feeling I was not alone, not peculiar, but part of a great new movement working toward the happiness and health of mankind and toward eventual peace in the world.

Suddenly, I realized wherein I had been wrong. How could I have been so stupid, selfish, and childish as to expect every great discipline on earth to come rushing to aid one puny individual in her particular problem?

Unjustly I was asking of these psychological systems something they were not designed to offer.

Humanistic psychology was concerned with the incredible but desirable effects that evolve from actualization of man's unsuspected capacities. As science it may not have been its purpose but it did reveal to man realizable hopes for greater health, undreamed of happiness, and longed-for fulfillment of his real, true self.

Constitutional psychology primarily offered man useful knowledge of himself. Incidentally, it lent him courage to be himself, to know himself.

Analytical psychology was founded to effect the initial discovery of the self through Jungian psychotherapy. This led to wholeness and often to spiritual experience.

It was not until much later that I read Dr. Roberto Assagioli on Psychosynthesis and its scientific description of the different psychological stages of self-realization. It brought me immense relief and comfort.

In my great need I had been guilty of an old habit, reading into authors' books my own ideas merely because I wanted them to be there.

Actually Maslow, Sheldon and Jung made me feel I was swimming in the great current of modern thought toward some noble destination of mankind. And for this I was more than grateful.

Few of my friends or acquaintances displayed the slightest interest in this vitally important new movement. Many of my friends did not believe my character had been transformed even temporarily for the better during my original awakening to the good. Those who did believe it frequently resented it.

My whole life was changing. For, once anyone has experienced the wonders of self-realization-however briefly – he loses his taste for ordinary life dominated by the prevailing values of the conscious mind.

Already my erstwhile passionate interest in fashionable clothes, dinner parties, cocktail parties, the latest plays and even my formerly beloved novels was fading away. This rather left me stranded on a small, beautiful secret island of inner life in a sea of materialism and extraversion. It was lonely.

The reading habits of the candidate for liberation change drastically. Nowadays I devour a new kind of magazine. *Main Currents of Modern*

Thought, Spring (the journal of the Jungians), the *Journal of the Society for the Scientific Study of Religion*, and the *Journal For Humanistic Psychology*. Already I was a member of the Academy of Religion and Mental Health. Now I joined the Association for Humanistic Psychology.

It buoyed me up immeasurably to find psychologists, anthropologists, philosophers, sociologists, and scientists of all kinds in the universities all over America working on this same project – the actualization of man's potentialities for the good.

My initial discovery of the self (though momentarily under a cloud) and the whole "third force," psychology had opened up a new, wonderful world for me, for my future, for the future of mankind. It furnished shining goals to live for, work for, for myself and for others. I saw that the later years of life were destined by nature to be full of wisdom, health, a new kind of happiness and, above all, love of others. Already it had revolutionized my marriage, my entire hierarchy of values, my goals in life.

America laid too much emphasis on youth. But now I saw that even old age was not a time of striving for eternal youth, of dyed hair and diets to reduce. What did grey hair and wrinkles matter when a secret fire glowed within?

Recently I asked the latest visitor to Schweitzer, who was living the good life if anyone was, what his health was like at 88. "Vibrant," my informer replied.

That was the way nature intended old age to be. But how to regain the psychological heights that made one's health vibrant as mine had been during my renascence? Psychology did not tell me.

Was it my fault I had lost it all? Did it happen to others too? I must investigate other "case histories" – not of sick people who got well but of well and successful people who fulfilled themselves. Where were their autobiographies? They must exist. But where? At the moment it was more imperative to continue my search for means to me out of this Slough of Despond.

What of philosophy?

Chapter 7

PHILOSOPHY

If philosophy was the most respected of all disciplines, what techniques did it offer its students for achieving the good life?

In my girls' college there had been no course in philosophy. If there had been I was too hopelessly naive to understand so abstruse a subject. Only now in maturity was I ripe for it – I hoped!

Chronologically, I rushed hastily through the philosophic systems of the Greeks – through Plato and Aristotle; the Roman, Lucretius; the Egyptian, Plotinus; then through the Europeans: Thomas Aquinas in the 13th Century; Descartes and Hobbes, Spinoza, Leibnitz, Hegel and Schopenhauer in the 18th; then Comte and Mill, Marx, Nietzsche, and Spencer in the 19th Century. I examined the moderns briefly: Bergson, Croce, James, Dewey, Whitehead, Russell, and Northrop. I merely dipped into Sartre, and Heidegger, Weiss and other contemporaries.

A thorough study of all the philosophers, I realized, would require a lifetime and I was in a hurry.

To follow the philosophers as guides, however, was to scale many dizzy peaks in the mountain ranges. The view was so vast it took one's breath away. The air was so rarefied it was exhilarating. The temptation was to remain on one of these fascinating peaks of theory, to forget that plateau, that half-way house, where theory and practise were united, where the concrete problems of daily living were to be solved.

Which philosopher should I choose as my guide? Obviously, each philosophy contained many admirable ideas. But the philosophers disagreed among themselves. Each insisted his view of the world and reality was superior. At this I felt sorely puzzled and almost betrayed. I had placed my complete confidence in them to lead me to the good. Yet there were almost as many different theories of the good as there were different philosophers! This was incredible.

Then I recalled Sheldon's constitutional psychology. Even philosophers are influenced in their ideas and value systems by their type of physique and temperament to say nothing of environment, culture, neurosis or normality, masculinity or lack of it, and self-realization or lack of it.

All this would justify me, however, in formulating my own layman's philosophy – if possible.

In my first serious encounter with philosophy I was bitterly disappointed to find that few of the Western philosophers (with some grand exceptions) offered practical instructions or ways for the individual to achieve a more ethical, loving, harmonious, creative life. The majority of them appeared concerned with different aspects of the good society, the nature of ultimate reality, epistemology, ontology, cosmology, phenomenology, or metaphysics in general.

In all honesty I did not read Plato at this time. I made the terrible mistake of reading commentaries on him. I did not know then that one cannot understand him until one *experiences* his truths. I was afraid to approach him. All my life I had anticipated the great day when I should be mature enough to understand Plato.

In my random reading many scholars referred to Plato's unique greatness. Others pronounced him the greatest thinker the world has ever produced. I had a strong premonition that Plato might become one of the high points of my whole life – in what way I had not the faintest idea.

At this time, however, I still imagined he might be too abstruse for me to read, or worse, to understand. Not until much later this same year did I actually study Plato's own books. That was after I joined the Great Books Discussion Group. Thereafter, I read avidly several different translations of all his dialogues. He was so exciting and important.

When I finally did begin to understand Plato months later, I was stunned. Had I not for some time been striving to revive my deeper better self, revivify insights into universal truths through my collective unconscious? I had been struggling to *quiet* my conscious mind! And now here was Plato advocating the conscious mind, reason, and dialectic as the best means to achieve the good life. And I had been seeking solitude yet Plato's postulate was that dialogue, that is, public discussion was the ideal method!

This plunged me into an awful quandary!

Plato – or was it Socrates? I could never tell which – contended that dialectic, philosophical reasoning, training the mind to discuss abstract principles, would reveal the essence of things and eventually the nature of ultimate reality. Dialectic or skill in asking and answering questions – the

Socratic method of dialogue – could cause a man to recollect eternal ideas, universals, and to communicate with the supreme good, and himself become as pure and wise as he was before he was born.

Well, frankly, at first I simply did not believe Plato because I did not understand him since I had not yet experienced his glorious truths. Eventually I was to learn how correct Jung was when he said *the most beautiful truths in the world are of no use until the individual actually experiences them in himself.*

At this particular point in my journey, however, it was a relief to hear the great Plato identify the essence of the universe with the good. Many philosophers did not.

Socrates said "know thyself," for from such knowledge virtue flowed. This left me jubilant. It proved I was on the right road. I pounded the book, struck my forehead, laughed aloud for joy.

He said truth was dormant in all men. But I was amazed when the mighty Socrates exalted reason. For he himself had had mystical experiences and listened to his "inner oracle," and what was that but his collective unconscious?

Plato pronounced reason the only source of valid knowledge and intuition inferior, even evil. Yet what was his famous allegory of the cave except a description of the release of the deeper unconscious? But he did admit that beauty perceived by the senses constituted a window that revealed to us the good and the true.

I was obliged to laugh at Descartes and Pascal who also exalted reason above all human faculties. Descartes himself was launched on his career of reason by a great mystical experience. It lent him insight into the possibility that he might find a new method through logic to science and truth. He also had had three very impressive dreams on which he acted – even making a pilgrimage to Italy – yet he pronounced dreams unimportant. These intellectuals were blinded by their worship of reason even to the processes in their own bodies and minds. Why were they so ashamed of intuition – because Plato had branded it as the feminine principle of the universe and reason as the masculine?

It literally staggered me to hear so great a philosopher as Aristotle say happiness is the chief good, and the end of man. Not saving the world, not self-sacrifice, not creating the good society and neglecting the self. He said the good society should be formed in order for man to live the good life. But he also said "it is worth while to attain the end merely for one man, it is more god-like to attain it for a nation."

The way to achieve happiness, or the "good life" according to Plato was to engage in dialogue with a Socrates. It brought clarity out of my confusion when he distinguished between opinions and true knowledge of eternal ideas, between Becoming and Being – terms that had puzzled me heretofore.

It was astounding to find that three of the greatest thinkers who ever lived, Socrates, Plato, and Aristotle believed in God. (Today's scientists and intellectuals often laugh at God.) They believed in an immortal soul, too.

Before birth, Socrates said, the soul was not only pure but possessed knowledge of all things, lost it on birth, but "should be able to call to remembrance all that she ever knew about virtue, about everything," through the right kind of dialogue. For "all nature is akin." Wasn't that the kind of unity of all things I felt so strongly?

It stopped me cold, however, when Socrates in the *Meno* said "virtue comes to the virtuous by the gift of God." But I interpreted this to mean after a long struggle. Then the initial or final reward would appear as if from some impersonal outside force. Or was it simply the realization of one's own potentialities as Maslow said and Jung implied?

Evidently all three, Plato, Jung and Maslow were right. The aspirant of the good and the true could achieve them either though his *conscious mind or his unconscious!*

Not until the end of the year did I finally understand Plato's postulate that the "tendance of the soul (psyche) or the development of a rational ethical personality should be the chief occupation of all men." Then I went wild with joy!

How to reconcile Plato with Jung and Maslow? In dialectic did the conscious mind awaken the collective unconscious?

I wrote to several philosophers about this. They evaded the answer. Was it because they had not studied the new psychology of growth? Or because they personally had never experienced Plato's beautiful truths? Theoretical knowledge of Plato's system was not sufficient to understand its deeper significance.

Later I attempted to answer my question by examining my own experience during and after engaging in more or less Socratic dialogue with a Great Books Discussion Group and with acquaintances. Not until I had experienced the awakening to the good was I able to understand Plato's *Symposium* particularly.

To understand Plato or Jung or Maslow one must *experience* truths through different parts of the body – the conscious mind and the unconscious, the muscles, senses and emotions.

At this time I concluded that to practise Plato's method of attaining the good life would require a modern Socrates. I had no Socrates. And it was impossible to take a course in philosophy at the nearby university. Outsiders were not admitted.

At the moment I felt that art, nature, the mere knowledge of psychology and philosophy – though each had helped me enormously – had all failed to bring me permanent liberation of the unconscious. Or had I failed them? It seemed an unbreakable circle. I depended on these various means to produce in me the proper state of mind that in turn would allow me to benefit by their magic power.

I was becoming very discouraged.

What had other, greater, persons done in such a quandary?

After I had rushed like a breeze through 2300 years of Western philosophy, I was ready once again for Northrop's *The Meeting of East and West*. The first three times I read it I could not understand it. Now perhaps I was beginning to be ready for it.

As I read, my hands grew icy, my heart pounded, I laughed aloud with delight. I found many scholarly confirmations of some of my feeble layman's ideas. Northrop disagreed with Plato's dictum that reason was the only reliable and valid source of truth.

Northrop's exposition and analysis of Eastern art, philosophy and religion delighted me. It lent me added proof – beyond my own experience (which I did not trust intellectually, quite yet) that the aesthetic (that is, felt) factor in the nature of things is as important as the theoretic. He said it is a justified criterion of knowledge, and of the good, and of the divine. It is primary and ultimate and its truths as valid as those derived from reason.

Northrop demonstrated why the nations of the world required both and implied that the individual did likewise if he were to be a whole man living a complete life. He advocated that the philosophy and education of the future must unite the theoretic, scientific, and rational with the intuitive, aesthetic and emotional.

In short, the good life of the individual and the good society must harmoniously combine science, politics, economics, law and philosophy with art, religion and psychology.

He was the only philosopher I had read who believed in the equal value of the conscious mind and the deeper unconscious. It distressed me, however, that in this book he did not have a chapter on Jung. Later he did give a memorial address in praise of the great psychologist.

Philosophy was an ideal way to achieve the good life but at the moment it seemed too difficult, though I had Jung and Plato and Northrop on my side as well as Maslow.

But to what discipline could I now turn for assistance in releasing my collective unconscious?

Chapter 8

DISCIPLINE OF THE BODY

Could the body aid the seeker of a better life?

I omitted the miracle drugs that opened the doors of perception and induced the beatific visions about which Aldous Huxley wrote so glowingly. I wanted no artificial stimulant unless all other means failed.

Always I had labored under the delusion that it was noble to ignore the body. I constantly taxed my body beyond its endurance in order to write longer, read more, work harder.

Always I had been guilty of too much activity. Too much work. Too much fatigue. And worst of all, too much haste, over-stimulation and nervous tension. The wrong foods. Too little sleep. Too little exercise out of doors. Too little relaxation. Too little solitude. Too little idleness and reverie. This was the accepted American way of extraverted, over-active, materialistic life.

I was beginning to learn an invaluable truth. A sick body renders the good life almost impossible. A healthy body aids it – up to a point – beyond which the body becomes a hindrance.

I labored daily to transform my faulty habits of a lifetime – faulty habits of eating, sleeping, working, exercising and resting.

Eating is a major problem probably to every aspirant. I considered cooking (by others) a subtle art, myself something of a gourmet. Every good meal was like a symphony, every separate dish like a different instrument. As the sounds of sweet music played upon the ear and vibrated along my entire nervous system, so the flavors of delicious food played upon my palate. Eating was an exquisite pleasure three times every day – when one had a good cook.

But alas, I had an endomorph's love of food but an ectomorph's small nervous stomach. I was possessed by an absolute passion for rich French wine sauces, caviar, curries, chili and tamales. They usually made me deathly sick.

Always I had been tall and slender so weight was not my problem. Also I ate too fast. Now I strove to eat simpler foods, less, and more slowly. I concentrated on each mouthful. All this improved the flavor, my health, sleep, and disposition. Yet the wonderful, complicated, highly-flavored dishes were almost irresistible, a temptation in every restaurant and club. Fortunately at home I planned the simple balanced menus for my husband and I ate the same things.

It was almost impossible to buy pure foods any longer because our scientific genius has overstepped its bounds, but I struggled daily to purchase only fresh natural even organic foods with their purity, flavor, vitamins and minerals intact. I avoided frozen, processed, preserved, packaged, prepared foods too often too full of harmful additives, or poisonous insecticides.

For the first time in my life I had a powerful incentive to choose simple foods – because of my search for a higher, happier, healthier life through a reawakening of the unconscious, of the self.

Sleep seemed an insoluble problem. For years I had been a poor sleeper. Now I discovered that sleep at night depends on one's activities during the day. The kind and amount of food consumed, the exercise or rest taken or omitted, the work engaged in, the presence or absence of over-stimulation of all kinds – even talking too much.

I attempted to control my days but sometimes they appeared to possess a will of their own and ran away with me like wild horses.

Exercise was something I did not care for – except the rhythmic ones of dancing and swimming. It was impossible to engage in either most of the time. A minimum of exercise was essential to sleep, digestion, relaxation, and even brain work. I forced myself to walk half an hour or more every day slowly, calmly. The vigorous exercise recommended so vociferously by extreme mesomorphs was too stimulating to my nerves. Also I invented a simple set of exercises to be taken slowly, morning and night while lying Hat on my back in bed.

I scheduled an afternoon nap. This bored me. I much preferred to write or think or read or even work. But I battled to follow my routine. Thinking was the worse obstacle to sleep or relaxation. Ways to stop the wheels in the machinery of the mind was a major project. Paradoxically enough, the old motion pictures on television prevented my mind from whirling about and put me to sleep or the reading of a good second rate novel. The good novels made me think.

Relaxation and *posture* were vital. I no longer scoffed but understood why the Hindus insisted posture is extremely important. For my type of tall, loosely-joined bone structure a long reclining or contour chair was the only chair I ever had found in my life that really permitted me to relax. It claimed to be scientifically designed.

Relaxation was the most difficult habit to acquire. After a good hot meal or a short quiet walk I would lie back in the hideously, ungainly, comfortable, red reclining chair in our living room. It clashed grievously with all our 18th Century mahogany furniture and had to be whisked surreptitiously out of sight when guests arrived.

This mere bodily posture, however, often opened the barrier that damned up my collective unconscious. At times, there was a physical sensation as if a great inner flower were slowly unfolding its petals in my brain case, or at other times, beautiful truths or creative ideas or poetic prose would swim up to the surface of the unfathomable lake of the unconscious like silver-shining fish until my conscious mind could grasp them. There was something almost magical about this delicious process of apperception.

Consequently, instead of following the old American maxim drilled into me, into every American child, to always be a busy little bee and improve each shining hour, I set aside specific times each day to do nothing, to relax, to dream, to meditate, to indulge in reverie. It was not drowsiness, not indolence, it was the alert passivity that often is richly rewarding.

Tempo – I found I must change my whole tempo of living, slow down my mad American pace, learn to walk, talk, work, write, type (that was the hardest of all) slowly and calmly. It was amazing to observe how my quick, nervous, illegible handwriting about which my friends complained, grew large and legible and become a voluptuous pleasure to me to execute.

Haste was the enemy of everything good in life. So I endeavored never, never to hurry. But I had been hurrying for thirty years. The fast pace I had learned in New York had become a habit.

Slow tempo, calmness, relaxation caused the writing on my manuscripts to flow with greater ease and pleasure. I strove to perform all my activities calmly, quietly, and did so – for fifteen minutes. Then I attacked the task in hand fiercely with frenzied haste as if I were literally fighting fire. Tension had become my second nature – as it has with so many Americans.

Calmness not only allowed my unconscious to flow more freely, it permitted my conscious mind to function more accurately. It filled my muscles with a kind of sweetness, lent me a sense of well-being. So I continued to practise the difficult art of relaxation. Of course the secret was that once one had attained the desired plane, one automatically moved slowly, worked calmly, thought clearly.

The difficulty was that I must train my mind to train my body. I relinquished all stimulants – liquor, tea, and coffee, I missed my breakfast coffee painfully but relaxation was more rewarding.

Concentration. I discovered if I concentrated on anything I was doing, it became more interesting, consumed less energy and I did the work better. I would concentrate wonderfully – for a few minutes, then my mind would fly away. Our dynamic, active Western culture has taught us that to do twenty things at once is a virtue. My mind was not trained to concentrate. A woman's life in a household prevents concentration. Telephones, door bells, ringing. Urgent telephone calls that must be made immediately or there will not be any meat for dinner. Household noises constantly distracting from concentration on anything. Nevertheless, I exerted my every brain cell in an effort to concentrate because it was incredibly rewarding.

To transform all one's habits of a lifetime – habits of body and mind and nerves at a mature age was not easy.

The irony was that when I succeeded in a modest way, my body still interfered constantly. It demanded sleep or rest or food at a time when I wanted to write or study, demanded exercise when I preferred to work. Worst of all, my body continually caused me to be aware of itself – I itched, I ached, I had indigestion. It distracted me from my efforts to become oblivious to the body. In short, my body was always interfering with my struggle to rise to a plane of intuitive insight, unadulterated feeling, pure thought, or effortless creativity.

Finally I became discouraged. Discipline of the body could at times elevate a trainee to a higher plane remarkably. But could the bodily condition alone sustain it? Not in my case. It was all becoming too difficult. I was ready to surrender my search for the reactivated self.

One means, however, remained which I had not yet tried.

Chapter 9

RELIGION

Approach

Last of all I turned to religion for guidance to discovery and development of the self. I did not wish to devote myself exclusively to religion, merely to the good life in the world illuminated, permeated, by its basic principles.

Surely though I could borrow practical techniques from the religions without accepting all their dogmas, creeds, and rituals – or systems of instructions.

So next I studied the religious systems I heretofore had merely scanned – Hinduism, Buddhism, Zen, Taoism, Christianity and the teachings of Jesus.

I was shocked to find that the primary aim of all the higher religions was not at all what I had assumed it was. Without thinking, I had believed that their chief purpose was to help the individual achieve a better life in the world. That was not true.

The primary aim of all the higher religions is the same – to lead man toward union with ultimate reality or God. Not to improve one's worldly life, not to create an ideal political state.

In the process, however, surely man's real self must be aroused. For only through that was man able to communicate or unite with reality or the Self. It was this preliminary stage of the good I sought, not the final religious state of *Nirvana, Samadhi*, or the unitive, "deified" life of the Christian saints.

So I pursued true understanding of the various religious systems through thickets and brambles of my own erroneous preconceptions and misconceptions, dashed off on a dozen false trails, became lost in bewilderment, was misled by a score of self-appointed guides, tripped over my own hidden prejudices like unseen roots, struggled through intricate growths of ideas that were centuries old.

In Hinduism the self or Atman is the individualized self and also the principle of the cosmos. Buddhism believes the self contains love and wisdom. Taoism is a psychological state and at the same time the state of the universe. Jung defines the self as the psychic totality of the individual. Christ realized the idea of the self. Maslow finds the self to be an ethical creative unconscious.

Jung himself conceded that the Eastern system of thought had delved far deeper into human psychology, that is, of the deeper unconscious, than any psychologist in the West – himself included. But he was not very complimentary about their intellectual attainments or use of the conscious mind. In the East they claim they never suffer from neurosis – is this because they have cultivated the deeper unconscious from childhood?

Hinduism

At first Hinduism bewildered me because of its many gods and elaborate ceremonies. The Vedanta philosophers assured us the many are but manifestations of the one God. And the rituals and public ceremonies are chiefly for the populace. The elite – intellectual and spiritual – seek union with an impersonal force.

What was the goal of Hinduism? Enlightenment, liberation, self-realization, God-realization, *Samadhi*. And how was such a goal to be accomplished? Through one of the yogas, the several ways to discover the self and unite it with infinity.

As a last resort would it be necessary for me to practise yoga? If so, which yoga might be most suitable for me?

Would the four main yogas correspond to the four main types of physique and temperament as expounded by Sheldon's Constitutional psychology. If so, it would be easier for me to accept on a scientific basis. And should not my constitutional type guide me to the proper choice?

Bhakti yoga follows the path of love and devotion to a personal God. Was not this the way that might be chosen by the endomorph with the temperament that expresses itself most naturally through love – of people and of food and perhaps a personal God? This method of realization applied only partially to me. I did not seek a personal deity.

Karma yoga is the way of action, of good deeds. Would not this be most suitable for the mesomorph? One who temperamentally and naturally turns to action, power, and the overcoming of obstacles? This too applied to me but only partially.

Jnana yoga is the path of knowledge – meaning to the Hindus, spiritual knowledge of Braham. Would not Jnana appeal perhaps to the slender, small-boned, thin-skinned type dominated by his nervous system – the ectomorph who often displays a passion for knowledge? I exhibited some of the characteristics of this cerebrotonic temperament but not all certainly.

Raja yoga is known as the royal path. In it the aspirant seems to practise all the other methods to attain Enlightenment. It also includes the 84 postures which bring health and the innumerable exercises to control the breath as stipulated by *Hatha* yoga.

The conclusion might be that *Raja* would appeal to the temperament which fulfills itself through love *and* action *and* knowledge. At first glance it looked as if it might be the yoga suitable to my type of temperament – the 4-4-4 – until I studied it further.

To my dismay I learned that *Raja* and all other forms of yoga necessitate renunciation of the world, of family, marriage, love and sex. It prescribes celibacy, chastity, poverty, obedience, mortification, ascetic practises, repetition of the word OM thousands of times, concentration on a point of light or one's own navel indefinitely, prolonged meditation and many other exercises. It requires solitude and silence. Often the aspirant withdraws to a cave alone high in the Himalaya Mountains for three years of meditation without distractions.

And all yogas require daily instructions by a *guru*, a spiritual teacher – preferably in a monastery. These requirements stopped me in my tracks. I was married and liked it. I lived in the world and liked it. But I was literally stunned with disappointment and frustration. I had imagined yoga might furnish me with all the necessary techniques to achieve a complete transformation of my character at home alone by my own efforts without external guidance.

Nevertheless, I experimented with breathing exercises. My body felt as if it had disappeared completely, all awareness of myself vanished right away except awareness of my concentrating mind. It was the most delicious sensation I had ever known – absolutely indescribably but on arising there was a frightening pain in the back of my neck. I heeded the warning of the Hindu writers that to attempt these exercises without the proper guidance of a *guru* could be dangerous.

Also, I concentrated on a point of light – a highlight in a painting of which I was especially fond. I never moved my eyes, tried not to blink, tried to empty my mind of all thought, and found it worse than difficult. Finally I was rewarded with unprecedented physical relaxation, not with spirituality as I had expected but with a strong urge to create. So I wrote a little free verse poem then and there.

The extensive Hindu literature proved to me that yoga methods can and do produce enlightened men – even saints, who display extraordinary powers of all kinds. For instance, Ramakrishna, like Jesus, by his mere presence, or a word, or the laying on of hands could induce instantaneous Enlightenment or *Samadhi* in some of his disciples. Both exhibited transfiguration or self-illumination.

When the pupil arrives at a certain state of development, *Siddhis* or psychic powers automatically appear in him. Many holy men of the Orient claim they can heal the sick, walk on water, control the temperature of their bodies at will by mental power, sit naked in the snow, smell invisible flowers, hear inaudible music, display signs of levitation, and extrasensory perception, becoming clairvoyant, telepathic, and so forth.

When the devotee sees a light or a vision of a god, he has not reached the greatest heights yet. In this stage he is still in *savikalpa samadhi*. Not until he merges his individuality with the Universal Mind does he attain the final goal, *nirvikalpa samadhi*.

Some of the psychic powers are considered unimportant except as sign posts along the way toward liberation. Sometimes they are even considered a hindrance. I laughed at myself, for I, in my ignorance of all such manifestations, had considered my seeing a light and a vision of Jesus a tremendous leap forward!

The results of yoga training is that it transforms men, makes them good, selfless, and compassionate. It brings detachment, purity, ethical living, self-control, harmony, serenity, joy, love of mankind, and tolerance.

Were not these the very qualities for which I was striving? How frustrating that it was impossible for me to employ the methods of Hinduism by myself without continuous instructions.

I read the biographies of great Hindus and innumerable books about Hinduism. It was encouraging to know that it was not all theory. In at least one country today, India, there existed, thousands of persons who by their own efforts – with the aid of expert assistants – actually did live in harmony with all things and all people, who actually did return good for evil, really loved their neighbors as themselves regardless of color, race, or even religion.

They were happy laughing people. Many of them evinced that purity of the child without which Jesus said you cannot enter the kingdom of heaven which is within you.

Neither Hinduism or Buddhism claims it is the one and only true religion as do Christianity, Judaism and Islam. The Eastern religions admire Jesus, Moses, and Mohammed. They contend that the goal of all the great religions is the same – man's union with ultimate reality. Different religions merely follow different paths up the same mountain. I believed this too.

Western philosophy (with the exception of Plato) *informed*; Eastern philosophy *transformed*. In the Orient, unfortunately, their profound religions failed to produce the good society for all. Even most of the enlightened appeared oblivious to the poverty, illiteracy, and population explosion of the suffering masses.

They believed in reincarnation. They considered man's present suffering his punishment for misdeeds in a previous life on earth. In the West, reason, science and materialism worked for the public welfare though not always for the rich inner life of the individual, not for world peace or love of mankind as the religions of the East did.

Obviously the world and the individual needed both the outer material life and the good inner life. The whole world seemed to need a new philosophy, or a new psychology, or a new religion, in fact a synthesis of the various disciplines.

Even if I wished to practise yoga, where would I find a *guru* in our town of 200,000 people? It was impossible.

Nevertheless I borrowed gratefully some of the techniques of Hinduism. The simplification of life, reduction of ceaseless, useless activity, solitude, silence, concentration and meditation – though it would require many years to become proficient in meditation in the Hindu sense.

One difficulty was that the Hindu process was the reverse of mine. The aspirant strove for years and then achieved a great awakening. He seldom had a mystical experience first and so he evidently never did regress as I had. Yet many of the instructions for achieving the psychological heights were like those I now sought.

Although it was impossible for me to follow all its practises, Hinduism was wonderfully reassuring. It indicated that good is innate in man, that by his own efforts with assistance, he can realize it by releasing his deeper unconscious. It demonstrated that it is within my power, anyone's power, to live in harmony with the self and others, and with the rhythm of the universe.

Surely Buddhism might offer me a simpler method?

Buddhism

Buddhism considers itself a philosophy not a religion. It does not believe in God, the soul, or immortality. It relies on natural laws not on the supernatural or revelation. Buddha, like Socrates, was adept at dialectic.

He spent six years in the practise of austerities. Yet it was the moment of mystical insight, the release of his unconscious, as he sat under the famous Bo tree that caused him to attain his goal – Enlightenment. Intuition is the only means of achieving this says Christmas Humphreys.

Buddhism also believes it solves the problem of evil by reincarnation and the concept that there is unity in the universe. This unity includes what men call evil as well as good. The opposites are reconciled to form a new kind of good.

The object of Buddhism, I learned, is not union with God as in Hinduism but a psychological state of bliss, Nirvana.

Frankly, the description of these two states seemed strangely similar to my way of thinking. The means were different, the terminology was different, the intellectual interpretation *after* the experience was different. And I discovered that most scholars referred to Buddhism as a religion.

Buddha pronounced the world a place of suffering. The way to escape suffering is to eliminate desire. And the way to eliminate desire is to follow his Four Noble Truths and his Noble Eight-Fold path. This eventually leads to *Nirvana*.

The West describes Buddhism as a pessimistic philosophy. But by suffering could not Buddha have meant living the ordinary, materialistic, physical life dominated by the conscious mind? Anyone suffers in the conventional extraverted mode of life if he has ever heard of, or experienced even briefly, that other form of life of serenity, harmony, and wisdom, in individuation.

It was necessary to remind myself continually that the enlightened spoke from another plane, their words did not mean what we meant by them.

What techniques, I asked myself, does Buddhism offer by which this delectable mental and emotional state can be acquired? Renunciation of the world, withdrawal to a monastery and the practise of innumerable austerities under the constant supervision of a teacher as in Hinduism. It, too, is primarily concerned not with one's relation to one's fellow man or society but with realizing one's potentials for the good and the reaching of *Nirvana*. Is that not selfish?

All Buddhists were not able to reach the supreme bliss in the prescribed way and therefore other forms of Buddhism arose – notably Zen. Also, some Buddhists believe Buddha is their savior as some Hindus believe Krishna is their savior and as Christians believe Christ is their savior. Some Buddhists and Hindus resort to rituals and ceremonies and personal gods and some to none. In Hinduism and Buddhism the aspirant is given a choice.

Hinayana Buddhism explores the heights within and through the self. *Mahayana* Buddhism explores the fullness of spiritual knowledge through the world as well as through the heights within. (Frankly all this was Greek to me until later a strange experience with cooking, of all things – clarified it for me wonderfully.)

The results of Buddhism as of Hinduism are a transformation of character, a release of the inherent good within each man, tolerance, selflessness, joy, a return of good for evil, serenity, peace, and compassion, a discovery of the undiscovered self.

Again I said to myself, but are not these the very virtues for which I am striving daily? But must one renounce the world and the body, ignore the suffering of mankind, do nothing to correct social evils, and retreat to a monastery to accomplish these desired objectives?

Buddhism seemed a noble system of self-actualization but was it designed for women and wives and mothers? After all someone must bear the children if only that they might become holy monks! Was it designed for modern active Western life in the world? If everyone followed it to the letter the human race would become extinct. Could Zen Buddhism solve my dilemma?

Zen

Zen Buddhism appeared to obviate some of these difficulties. Its tenet is that Enlightenment is attainable through flashes of insight – not through the study of scriptures or prescribed exercises, rituals and meditations or life in a monastery. Though Zen has its monasteries to which householders often go for brief or intermittent periods.

A radical departure of Japanese Zen Buddhism is the idea that liberation can be achieved through ordinary activities – walking, working in a field, or any form of work. Anything is capable of liberating an aspirant from his ego. (That was exactly what I was attempting to do. It seemed to me the most natural method but perhaps the most difficult?)

By what techniques does one achieve Zen *Satori* – the first step on the road to *Nirvana?* A master is necessary for daily guidance. He employs a strange devise called *mondo*, a form of rapid question and answer, and the *koan*, which breaks the barrier of the illusory self and lets in the flood waters of the universe.

In short, the master drives the trainee to the point of utter frustration and even deals him a physical blow. Such means often induce a direct/sudden flash of that pure Enlightenment which made Buddha the Awakened One, awakened to the light within.

The object of Zen is to develop intuition, the faculty of direct knowledge of reality existing in every mind but too often dormant. This leads to knowledge of *Dharma* or Supreme Reality. Zen employs different means than psychotherapy but the channel through which Enlightenment or individuation flows is not reason, not the conscious mind but the deeper unconscious.

Zen, like other forms of Buddhism and Hinduism, ends all fear of death. In Zen one passes beyond the opposites.

All three of these Eastern religions are joyous in spite of their reputation in the West of being pessimistic. This misconception is due to lack of personal experience of Enlightenment and therefore misunderstanding. These religions of the discovered self suffer also from translation into English I sincerely believe. Most of the translations I read appeared to be by intellectuals who never had known the joy of awakening their deeper, better self. They attempted to explain it from outside not from the inside.

But where would I find a Zen master in the first place? And I still was obstinate enough to wish to achieve the transformation of my character and the plane of harmony and joy, love and selflessness by my own unaided efforts – if possible!

Thousands of saintly monks in India, China, Japan, and Southeast Asia have proved that the techniques of Buddhism and Hinduism do awaken the good and the God in man. They demonstrate the existence of a vast store of unused moral, ethical, intuitive, and spiritual virtues in the self. I heard little, however, concerning esthetic and creative traits. Nevertheless, Japanese and Chinese paintings, pottery and poetry and Hindu architecture and poetry attest to the creativity induced by their illumined state of mind.

If the independent Western aspirant like me was unable to accept all the practises and obediences and spiritual leaders and renunciation that the Eastern religions required, he certainly could adopt many of their methods and techniques and benefit by them immeasurably. Solitude, silence, the simple life, simple diet, meditation on the nature of things, re-examination of our goals, ideals, and values, reduction of unnecessary luxuries, complexities, noises, pressures and tensions that hamper the trainee in America.

In Eastern systems it requires from three to twelve years for the aspirant to achieve Enlightenment depending on his own capabilities. How long would it take me?

Oriental religions were concerned primarily with the development of one's own spirit or mind and its relation to ultimate reality. But I had no wish to ignore my responsibilities to society. Yet had not contemporary Christianity rushed to the other extreme? Did it not concentrate on the social gospel, man's service to his fellow men and rather neglect the individual's own spiritual unfoldment? Were not both highly desirable?

Could *Tao* help me?

Taoism

Would *Taoism* offer an easier method for me to adopt? It advocated immersing one's self in nature. It postulated that when the adept achieved harmony with nature) then he would be in harmony with other people, society, the self, and even the universe. Taoism had been highly successful at one time in China in a circumscribed area.

Already I had tried this method unsuccessfully though no doubt it would work wonders with some people with constant application and concentration.

I turned away from my prolonged and enormously helpful and encouraging study of the religions of the East. I felt deeply grateful, full of admiration, wiser, and more hopeful of my own success eventually. I was still, however, without a system proper for myself. The methods and means of Hinduism and Buddhism were different from those of psychology but certain results were similar. Yet none of them could I apply to my own mental growth without outside assistance.

Christianity

What techniques would Christianity or the teachings of Jesus offer me, or any contemporary aspirant seeking for the discovery and development of the self?

All my life I had postponed an attempt to really understand these mysteries. I feared there would be too many misconceptions, erroneous interpretations, and false assumptions I must rid myself of before I could see Christ objectively as he really was against the background of other religions and modern psychology. Certainly the outmoded teachings of my childhood in a small Southern town must be corrected.

Secretly I felt resentment against Christianity. It had attempted to cast a blight over my childhood. My chief memory of the Protestant ministers was that they harangued me and all church members every Sunday. They never offered techniques for discovering the innate good in ourselves. They declared that all forms of pleasure were Wicked, that I, that all men, were born sinners before we had even breathed our first breath.

Today I endeavored to apply Jung's explanations of religious symbols, allegories and myths. Bible stories that made no sense whatever when taken literally began to glow with beauty and psychological profundity.

Could it be, for instance, that the "Sin" of mans eating of the tree of knowledge was caused by nature's addition of the conscious mind to the old unconscious? Was not this the process of evolution? To live simply like healthy animals from the instincts alone might be a paradise on earth as Rousseau suggests. And certainly reason alone could bring "Sin" – like the nuclear bombs, for example, world wars and dictatorships.

Another stumbling block to modern, rational, scientific man – certainly to me: Christianity forbade you to become a Christian unless you accepted Jesus as a god who had come to earth in the form of a man. How did you believe this? By will power? By experience? No, by faith, they said.

Did Paul become a Christian through faith? Or was it by the great mystical experience on the road to Damascus? And St. Augustine and many other Christian saints? It was by the *experience* of God, either of Christ or of a personal God or an impersonal power.

Another difficulty arose at the very beginning. Christianity was based on the belief that Jesus was your savior and without him you could not release the good in the self. In Hinduism and Buddhism you were offered a choice. You were free to regard Krishna, Ramakrishna, and Buddha as your saviors or not. In Christianity the belief that Christ was your savior was mandatory.

In fact, did not the organized church exclude the person who had had a spontaneous awakening through nature, or art, or however? Conformity to the rules of the institution were necessary,

The teachings of Jesus must possess countless virtues of which I was ignorant otherwise Christianity could not have endured for two thousand years.

All my life I had heard and read that Jesus exhorted us to love our neighbors as ourselves. But how? Such feelings were diametrically opposed to the seemingly natural impulse of selfishness in most of us. How could we change it? Not by will power certainly as anyone knows who has tried it. Where were the necessary Protestant techniques?

Jesus exhorted us to return good for evil – but how? Can one deliberately practise such a virtue when the usual reaction to insult or injury is anger and a desire for revenge? I knew that once one rises to a plane of love and harmony one would feel a natural desire to return good for evil. I myself had not achieved this permanently but I hoped to someday. Where were the Protestant exercises to enable one to attain this high psychological plane?

Jesus said you must become as little children to enter the kingdom of heaven which is within you. Although at other times he referred to heaven as being outside, wholly other. I myself had felt first one way then the other – so this did not seem like a contradiction – immanence and transcendence. To become as a child must mean to release one's true real self dormant in one's collective unconscious. But how to release it by the instructions of Jesus, I failed utterly to see.

Christ also said we must die and be born again, on this earth was his implication, in order to see the kingdom of God within us. I interpreted this to mean the kind of psychological death of the ego I went through years ago when my ego drowned in my collective unconscious. But where was the Protestant technique to accomplish this in case it did not occur spontaneously – as it did not to most types of temperament?

Christ by the very radiance of his presence undoubtedly could transform his disciples. But who was there today who could induce Enlightenment in us by his presence, or by a touch as Ramakrishna did to his most advanced followers?

The methods Jesus advocated were similar to those of Hinduism and Buddhism. He advised aspirants to renounce the world and the flesh, forsake their family, wives and children to follow his way of life. He believed in poverty, celibacy, and obedience. He saw nothing strange in this for, according to Schweitzer, Jesus believed the end of the world was imminent.

And what means did the Protestant church today offer the person who sought to realize the potentialities of the good in his undiscovered self? The social gospel – Work – Action – Service to others! That is the way of the mesomorph. Is it suitable or natural for all types? Did this not bring about a neglect of the spiritual development of the individual?

Catholic Christianity of course formed monasteries and nunneries as did the East. I could not discover.. exactly what methods and means were offered to lay Catholics.

I went over to the university. I asked, what techniques did the Protestant church offer? A famous scientist who was himself very active in the church said: An inspiring minister, communication with the congregation. And I added, beautiful architecture and sometimes good music. It was seldom enough to reawaken the deeper self. He admitted it.

According to Jung, Baptism, Confirmation, and the Mass were symbolical of man's deep psychological needs and were supposed to arouse and satisfy him. Incense and ceremony and ritual also were designed to purify him and evoke the psychological state in which his unconscious could unfold. Protestantism threw all these adjuncts out the window – to their present sorrow.

Christianity asserts it is the only true religion. It did produce many saints, mystics, and good men. But the religions of the East produced far more. So how could anyone believe such arrogance? No wonder Arnold Toynbee, himself a Christian, castigated the three Judaic religions for their exclusiveness. For Islam, Christianity, and Judaism each claims it is the only true religion. How can three religions be the one and only true religion?

After experiencing an awakening, not only to the good within but to the impersonal life force in the universe, how can anyone believe such claims of exclusiveness? And Jung's therapy led to an experience of God in the patients' own breasts.

There was room in the world for all the higher religions and all methods.

Jesus preached love of our fellow men then how could any Christian condemn Hindus or Mohammedans or Jews – especially since Jesus himself was a Jew as were his apostles and disciples?

In the East, the long conscious struggle of the individual for Enlightenment occurs first and the final liberation happens afterward. Strangely enough, in the West the saints and mystics usually experience the mystical moment first and afterward find it necessary to work to sustain it – even in the case of Jesus. Is this due to a difference in types of physique or what?

If one knew the history of religions and mythology one knew that other countries and other religions have their virgin births and immaculate conceptions, resurrection, transfiguration (Ramakrishna was often transfigured in a way for all to behold) walking on water, healing of the sick and other "miracles."

Now it seemed to me that whether Jesus ever actually lived or not really did not matter. For was not the story of such a person with his painful death, resurrection and ascension to heaven an EXTERNALIZATION *of each individual man's psychological and spiritual progress?* Had not I, and millions of others, despaired, "died," and been "reborn" and experienced a sense of union with the infinite that was a sensation of ascension? Did not all successful aspirants of liberation at some time die to the ordinary self and ego and become reborn on a higher selfless plane?

At this startling insight I was able at long last to accept Jesus not as a divinity, as I was able to accept no man, but as a beautiful psychological symbol of everyone's inner life. Undoubtedly simple people of a simpler era 2,000 years ago required a dramatic symbol – even such a bloody one as crucifixion.

This solution of an old puzzle excited me so much my heart began to race. Relief and joy ran through my blood. A great surge of happy tears rose in me because the struggling human race could be so wise, so profound, so great as artists to create this great Biblical story, to dramatize and personify immortally man's own inner psychological and spiritual struggle and possible triumph.

It filled me with pity and love for the human race greater than I had ever experienced before in my entire life! I longed to embrace the whole world in my arms!

All religions, including Christianity, I now saw, meant that man in spite of his follies and cruelties and blindness, was forever striving for the good in all countries, in all ages, among all races. The great religions that had endured for centuries proved man yearned to be god-like, become reintegrated with the blissful source from which he originally issued. Hope for myself, for mankind, flooded through me like a shining wave.

The practical instructions I had hoped to find in the teachings of Jesus were not apparent to me, admirable as many of his precepts were. But at long last, after years of hostility rooted in my orthodox childhood, I had made peace with Jesus as a wonderful spiritual and psychological symbol. Only fugitives from the hound of heaven realize such relief.

Also I realized how eternally grateful I was for the ethical principles Christian culture had instilled in me – in most Americans – through the home, school, society, laws and church. With our mother's milk we imbibed the precepts not to lie, or steal or murder or commit adultery. It was too easy to take all our wonderful heritage for granted and to see only its faults.

Any of the great religions could teach me to discover the undiscovered self, if I submitted to their training. If not, they still encouraged and enriched me. And, I gratefully borrowed their techniques.

But what now?

Chapter 10

SYNTHESIS

Was I doomed to failure? I had reached the end of my resources. Would I never find a way to release the once discovered self again, to develop it until I achieved the good life?

Had I not employed all the natural means of which I was aware? The arts. Nature. Discipline of the body for ordinary health. Knowledge – though not the therapy – of psychology. Knowledge – though not the practise – of Socratic philosophy – as yet. And I had borrowed and put into practise some of the invaluable techniques of religion, though I had not submitted to its training system.

What had they accomplished, I asked myself? The arts not only afford the self-actualizing person intense pleasure, relaxation, and purification, they wash away the daily debris. Their effects, however, are too transitory – at least in my case at this point.

The beauty of nature soothes and calms, lends a mysterious kind of strength and reassurance but its benefits, also, are too fleeting – as far as I am concerned, right now.

Psychology furnishes the self-knowledge that aids self-development, to a limited extent. For full self-knowledge, the psychotherapists contend, is achieved only through psychotherapy that liberates the normal deeper unconscious. They offer no techniques the independent trainee is able to use alone at home to activate or reactivate the collective unconscious. Jung and Sheldon – in his earlier book – and Maslow assure mankind, however, that he possesses unused virtues that can be released.

Philosophy offers man infinite knowledge. It informs, it does not transform – except in the case of Plato. Plato's system if put into practise would lead the aspirant of the good life to use his reason, engage in dialectic, discuss abstract truths in a method of question and answer with a wise Socrates. He then might recollect eternal ideas, universals, communicate with the Supreme Good, become as wise, good, and pure as he was before birth and so live the good personal life. Such dialogues required a Socratic teacher. I had none unfortunately – or so I assumed at the moment. But paradoxically great stimulation of the conscious mind could arouse the deeper unconscious, it seemed, until both functioned simultaneously.

Religion teaches that man possesses innate good which can be released to the point where he is dominated by good and achieves a happy, harmonious, loving life. But if his regeneration is induced he must submit to spiritual exercises and constant daily instructions and practises under a trained teacher. Usually he must also accept certain dogmas and doctrines.

Sensible discipline of the body proves that clear thinking, good writing, the release of the deeper unconscious, love of others, are aided by calm nerves, good digestion, and the sound sleep of health. A healthy body alone is not sufficient.

Each of these six means had elevated me partially and periodically to a high psychological plane but no one alone was able to sustain me there long enough. Certain temperaments – like mine – required all of them apparently. Perhaps all types did. I certainly required a synthesis of the different disciplines if I was ever to achieve my goal.

Where is such a system to be found that synthesizes the basic disciplines, psychology and philosophy, religion and art? Today knowledge is highly specialized. It is fragmented. Man is not. In man, all disciplines meet.

So in my amateur way, I attempted to form a synthesis of natural means to awaken the dormant unconscious, at least to reawaken it in the type which discovers the self involuntarily and then loses it and wishes to rearouse it. Might not the same means initiate the discovery of the self in all types? This has not been tested yet.

Hereafter I filled my days with more art, more nature, more philosophical discussions, greater practise of religious techniques, further research in psychology, and more stringent discipline of my body.

I pored over the *Bhagavad-Gita* and *Upanishads*, the teachings of Buddha, the *Tao te Ching* of Lao Tzu, the Bible – surprised and delighted to see that the deeper unconscious always spoke in poetry or poetic prose. But for a modern they all required psychological interpretation.

I studied Suzuki and Watts on Zen; Christmas Humphreys on Buddhism. And of course I read Nikhilananda and Akhilananda on Hinduism and other commentators on various systems – amazed that the authorities so frequently disagreed. Specific instructions for the independent aspirant of today in the West were few and far between.

Every day for weeks, months, years I struggled. I experienced a few small triumphs and many failures. I seemed to progress then suddenly slipped back down the hill to everydayness, irritability, and helplessness. A dozen times I decided to relinquish all my beautiful plans and efforts to achieve a higher, happier way of life, to transform my obstinate, recalcitrant character so determined to go its own wrong way. My own conscious resistance was incredible though I could see the shining mountaintop ahead.

What had happened to other aspirants? Had they, too, fallen from their original glory? Surely not. But I should inquire.

Chapter 11

STAGES IN PSYCHIC GROWTH

Other people had experienced the discovery of the self unaided. Could their lives throw any light on my problems? Surely they had never fallen from grace. But if so, what did they do to rehabilitate themselves?

As a last resort I now read the lives of those whom I always had avoided – the great mystics and saints of the West. All my life I had laughed at the Christian saints about whom I knew nothing. In my ignorance I assumed they were abnormal, surely neurotic, perhaps pathological, sometimes insane.

I did not believe in the unnatural practises of austerity, fasting, celibacy, chastity, mortification, poverty, unquestioning obedience to authorities. It all seemed unhealthy, almost an insult to the creative principle of the universe – which after all created the body and sex and the senses and our power of enjoyment.

If people truly believed, I argued with my unseen opponents, that the life force was omnipotent, omniscient, and all-loving how dared any human being tell it what to do through prayer? Their continual praying bothered me. In their autobiographical passages, their constant calling on God and Christ obscured their other meanings. Why not release the good in themselves?

I chanced to come upon a most illuminating book by Evelyn Underhill. She described the lives of Eckhart, Boehme, Teresa, and the two Catherines, the Quaker Fox, St. John of the Cross, Paul, Jesus and others.

Always I had assumed that nearly all saints renounced the world, withdrew into selfish isolation in a monastic life and let the world and its miseries go hang.

Many in the East did. In the West, however, most of them, I learned, were actives as well as contemplatives. They worked in hospitals, schools, even politics, busily writing, teaching, and preaching.

I literally held my breath as I now read about the different stages of psychological growth common to many aspirants of the good. So eager, so excited did I become I attempted to comprehend an entire page at one swallow and was obliged to return and reread it.

Underhill said aspirants in the West who had attained them found that there were five stages in psychic growth traversed by those to whom the discovery of the self came first *spontaneously.*

Were they all the 4-4-4 type of temperament and physique, I wondered? No one will ever know.

Stage Number I was Awakening; II, Self-Discipline; III, Enlightenment attained often by artists, poets and mystics who might or might not be religious. Stages IV and V were seldom attained by any except the greatest saints. I could never achieve the final heights and did not wish to do so. I was not seeking the exclusively religious life like a nun but the good life in the world. Stage IV was the Dark Night of the Soul, a period of gloom and doubt and helplessness far exceeding that in which I now floundered. Stage V was the Unitive or Deified life, where one remained in continuous communication with the infinite.

Each stage exhibited its own characteristics. My heart pounded deafeningly as I read Underhill's list of characteristics:

Stage I, Awakening of the Self: Sudden awareness of the Supreme Good, realization of ultimate reality, the leaving behind of one's everyday conscious personality, exalted joy, seeing a radiant light such as Walt Whitman described as "light rare untellable, lighting the very light," brief union with the infinite; in short – the awakening to the great cosmic Self, and discovery of one's own small personal self – a reflection of the greater infinite power, or so it felt.

Had not I had many of these experiences during my initial awakening when I first discovered the Self and the self involuntarily?

Stage II, Self-Discipline of the Self: Getting rid of unwanted traits, habits, and external obstructions not in harmony with reality. The fall from the heights, the remaking of one's character, acquiring greater self-knowledge, the acquiring of goodness, simplification of one's life, attempts to eliminate one's lower nature, getting out of Plato's cave, the coming of humility, death of pride, passionate longing to escape from the old ego, discomfort, conflict, pain, getting rid of complications of ordinary life, consciousness of one's unworthiness, oscillating from the initial ecstasy to sharp pain. Dante describes it in his journey up the Mount of Purgation. One may lose friends, become ill, know failure.

So that was it! I covered the book with my hands and quietly wept with relief and joy. So my regression was not all my own fault. It had happened to others far greater than I. It was a natural step in the process of self-realization apparently. For even the religious experience was a psychological process.

I scarcely dared read further. I could scarcely wait. I removed my hand. What came next in psychic growth?

Stage III, Enlightenment: One feels internal purification, the sensation of living in harmony with the rhythm of the universe, intuitive insight into the secret plan of the cosmos. One adjusts to new standards of conduct, sees ultimate reality in all people, all things, feels the "saving madness" of which Plato spoke, acquires tremendous new vitality – physical and psychic, keener response to beauty. There is an integration of personality, union with the Self though still retaining one's separate consciousness. One sees the world as Being and Becoming, becomes aware of the transcendent and immanent reality. One often achieves worldly success at this time, peace, serenity, security, certitude, perceiving splendours that were always there. There appears desire to write poetry, clairvoyance, enhanced intellectual powers, increased power over external things. The barrier between the human and the nonhuman disappears. One listens to the inner voice, enjoys reverie, concentration, is able to heal the sick, sometimes exhibits self-illumination or transfiguration.

I stopped reading. I stopped breathing. It was all too wonderful to be true, too beautiful to even hope for. A quiet tide of painful happiness surged through me. Would I ever attain Enlightenment?

So I was not peculiar, not remiss to descend to earth again after my initial flight. To discover that I was merely obeying the universal laws of the human mind in its psychic growth – it was an almost unbearable relief. I sat motionless, overcome with awe for the wonders of nature, overwhelmed with incredulity that such marvelous things should have happened to me, to any human being and filled to bursting with gratitude for this new knowledge.

How comforting to know that I was not alone, not peculiar. I was remarkably fortunate. I was part, a lesser humble part, of a vast human process – for what? Evolution perhaps? Religion and science could and would support each other. Someday the psychologists of tomorrow would conduct scientific research into these psychic stages beyond the initial discovery of the self, into its complete development.

But how was I ever to attain Enlightenment? I reread the characteristics of Stage III and read it again. It filled me with new hope and energy and confidence.

To attain Enlightenment, undoubtedly those whose goal was the exclusively religious life withdrawn from the world would pray and fast and mortify the flesh, practise chastity and other austerities. But a layman like me could only plunge deeper into use of the only natural means I could find.

But would I ever ascend to this high plane unaided through art, nature, the mere knowledge of philosophy and psychology, a few borrowed techniques of religion – relaxation and concentration, solitude and silence and the improvement of my physical health?

The rewards promised to be so glorious I determined to continue struggling to climb toward them with all my power, passion and energy – now in so low a state.

Of course those who aimed at the unitive life probably would progress a hundred times further and faster than I through their meditation and contemplation. If I could achieve the first few steps on the plane of Enlightenment, I should be content. Never mind Stages IV and V.

Underhill was fine for the emotional and religious explanations but my reason, my conscious mind, insisted on finding scientific psychological explanation of the different stages in self-realization. It was resistant beyond belief!

Then as if by magic I came upon the writings of Dr. Roberto Assagioli of the Institute of Psychosynthesis of Florence. It had affiliates in Paris, Athens, and Delaware, U.S.A.

Psychosynthesis was the psychotherapy that attempted to synthesize the various elements of man's nature. It was especially interested in releasing the higher psychological functions – intuition, artistic and mental creativity.

Assagioli stated that the ebb and flow of different stages in self-realization was natural. All nature moved in rhythms – night and day, summer and winter – and so did the growth of the human mind.

An individual, he explained, should expect a physical reaction of the nervous system after the first joy of awakening, should expect a period of insomnia, nervousness, exhaustion, inertia, loss of will power, and aversion to action. He considered these temporary disabilities, however, never too high a price to pay for the glory of discovering the self. And it would be undoubtedly followed by a flooding of the tide. That is, the channel between the conscious and the superconscious levels would open up.

Jung had divided the mind into the conscious, the personal unconscious and the collective unconscious. Assagioli divided it into seven parts. In self-realization one became aware of the contents of the superconscious – ethics, esthetics, altruism, and so forth. Then one experienced joy and serenity, power, understanding and radiant love.

The highest aspect of the awakening of the self, however, Assagioli said, is realization of essential Being, of identification of the individual self with the Universal Self. This highest aspect he termed "religious" but the others he termed "spiritual" in which state one might or might not rise to the religious experience.

His conception of the spiritual did not quite correspond to that of Underhill's state of Enlightenment – hers was more religious. And in the East, Enlightenment meant more – it meant *Nirvana* or *Samadhi*, if I understood those terms.

But did not laymen need a stage of Enlightenment, too? Artists and scientists and intellectuals might attain a high degree of self-actualization of their potentialities without having an experience of the Self.

Assagioli interpreted the coming out of the cave in Plato's allegory as coming out of the darkness into the light of an inner awakening to the self.

He did not state whether there were periods of regression in those whose awakening was induced by outside help or only in those to whom it came involuntarily.

I smiled, understandably enough, when I read that he believed awakening of the self when spontaneous was better than when induced – even by psychosynthetic therapists. He said it also could be achieved through self-training, and education.

In a footnote he admitted that there are various techniques which may hasten the process of bio-psychosynthesis. They should be applied by educators and therapists but many of them could be self-applied. They were not listed unfortunately but would appear in later publications. Irony of ironies!

That meant I should still be forced to rely on my own home-grown techniques.

But to know that scientists in Europe were also investigating this process through every stage of fulfilling the best in the human mind and personality was terrifically exciting and reassuring. And at this low ebb I required great reassurance from the scientists.

Then my abysmal ignorance was further dissipated by further reading. Eric Neumann, a Jungian psychologist – and the Hindus for centuries before him – divided man's life into four great natural periods. I read with amazement what should have been obvious to any really thoughtful person.

Until 18 we are dominated by the desire for pleasure, until 36 by the desire for success in the world, until 54 we feel an urge to contribute to society, to do our duty. From 54 on we feel the natural desire for integration with ultimate reality, for self-realization, for becoming what we really are.

I clasped my hands in utter disbelief! My initial discovery of the self occurred *when I was exactly 54!* I could take credit for nothing. I was subject to the laws that govern the human mind. I felt I was fulfilling nature's purpose. This knowledge was unbearably strange and frightening and exciting!

Jung had discovered that self-realization usually begins after the age of 36, it is a project for the last half of life.

To some geniuses, the tremendous spontaneous awakening to their deeper, better nature occurs not at 54 but about 35 or 36. For example Walt Whitman, Buddha, Jesus.

Books, books – how could we live without them? They contained all the wisdom of the world all going utterly to waste unless we were able to *experience* their great truths. Reason is never enough. We must educate our unconscious as wen as our conscious mind.

With a tremendous new impetus I began my search again. For weeks, months, I read and reread, studied and restudied, pondered and puzzled, wondered and waited, experimented on myself, disciplined my recalcitrant body, endeavored to train my conscious mind, to release my collective unconscious at will. I longed and hoped, I grieved and gave up and began again.

I sorely needed a road map to Enlightenment so I might not stray off in the wrong direction.

Chapter 12

RULES

I searched for rules applicable to the modern independent seeker after self-actualization like me. I was obliged to establish a set of rules for my own daily guidance. Might they not be applicable to all types in all stages?

I typed three copies. One I stood up on the desk in my writing room on the third floor, another I concealed in my bedside table on the second floor. The third carbon I secreted on the table by my reading chair on the first floor. The original I carried in my purse at all times.

I studied it on the long motor trips through the country I took with my husband. He liked me best when I talked least. He was the most taciturn man in seven states. He saw no point in eternal discussions. Results – that was all that mattered.

I read it on the train on my increasingly more infrequent trips to New York. When I first moved from the city to Connecticut I went down every other week. This mad desire was fading away. Often I had observed priests and nuns on the train studying a little black book – breviary, was it? I had thought it affected. Now I understood as I studied my little list of homemade crude rules. I realized that this effort to transform one's character internally was a full time occupation.

Hopefully I studied my list of rules:

> Simplify your life.
> Eliminate unnecessary activities.
> Reduce unneeded stimulations.
> Decrease unwanted distractions.
> Cease to whirl about.
> See fewer people.
> Do less work.
> Do nothing more often.
> Avoid haste.
> Avoid fatigue, illness, and tension.

Abandon yourself to the arts – more completely.
Immerse yourself in nature – more deeply.
Know yourself through the psychologies.
Relax and let your unconscious flow forth.
Open yourself to cosmic forces you do not understand.
Discuss abstract ideas with intellectuals dialectically.
Absorb the great books of all countries.
Borrow techniques from religions.
Listen to your body's faint voice of wisdom.
Eat simpler food and less more slowly.
Exercise in moderation.
Plan your day to bring deeper sleep at night.
Work slowly with complete concentration.
Seek solitude and silence.
Learn to control your conscious mind.
Learn to control your deeper unconscious.
Learn from your failures.
Learn from your successes.
Ask yourself daily, am I this minute engaged in an activity that will be an avenue to the good, or the true, or the beautiful?

Day after day, week after week I struggled and strove to follow these 29 simple rules. For months I tried and failed and tried again with occasional small triumphs. I despaired and gave up, then began once more.

Finally the accumulation of my years of effort began to bear fruit. Did I really produce the fruit? Or had I merely cultivated the soil? In any case, the winds of chance blew stray seeds upon it and the results astonished no one so much as they did me.

Incidents began to occur that seemed to illustrate profound principles of psychology and philosophy, esthetics and religion and thus to prove my personal experiences were universal – with variations of course.

My efforts over the gloomy helpless years of Self-Discipline now created a different state of mind. *Ordinary episodes produced extraordinary effects.*

My system of rediscovering and developing the self, one's deeper, better, unused nature, might be amateur but was not any system of behavior known by its fruits?

I could not believe I might be approaching a layman's stage of Enlightenment.

It all began very gradually.

STAGE III

ENLIGHTENMENT

Chapter 1

LECTURE

One night my husband and I went to the nearby university to a lecture expecting nothing extraordinary.

It was not academic. It was not dry. It was not juiceless. It was alive, dynamic, vibrant. His words struck you in the face like bullets. Ideas rained down on your unprotected head like a machine gun attack.

It was sensational on four counts. Its delivery was passionate. Its content original. Its wording delightful. Its mannerisms hypnotizing. I not only felt, I saw the passion of his delivery. I sat the third row, directly in front of his wildly gesticulating forefinger. He threw himself into it with the force of a minor hurricane. Every nerve, every muscle, was employed in this strenuous exercise. He was in love with his own words, his own ideas; in love with the words and ideas of the writers he was raising from the dead.

His eyes – how extraordinary they were! I was sitting near enough to observe the fevered shine of exultation in them. Intensity of emotion had dilated his pupils abnormally. The entire irises were like black diamonds glinting with every reflected light.

Periodically, the verbal storm subsided. He stood silent, motionless, his eyes piercing the audience like sharp, shining stilettos stabbing into your very vitals. He pinned you down in your seat. You couldn't escape. You were compelled to attention. He all but hypnotized us.

The motionless audience watched his keen thought plunge mercilessly into the very heart and bowels of his writers, probe Thoreau's secret places as relentless as a surgeon probes for a bullet.

Everyone present seemed to follow him breathlessly as he traced a character trend through England across the ocean to New England like a supernatural hound pursuing a fox unerringly. We heard him mouth aloud each separate word of a Dickenson poem like a gourmet tasting some rare vintage wine. And his joy became our joy. His vitality became our vitality. My God, what a performance! Will our home town ever again achieve such distinction even by the skin of its teeth?

What was the source of this impassioned dramatic force? After all, the speaker was a playwright. Perhaps his sense of drama had been sharpened ten-fold by his recent experiences. The long early morning hours he spent, he told me later, with producers, authors and casts after every tryout at the local theater. Our town is the workshop where new plays are mauled and beaten into shape before they are shown to New York's hypercritical eyes.

But what of content? Style without content is sound and fury satisfying no one. This lecture had content. Its points of original research flared out like little tongues of flame – licking at your mind – lighting it up. You could hear the profundity of thought every time it struck bottom like a stone dropped in a deep well.

He traced the origin of the early New England spirit down to its very lair. The fierce independence. The inarticulateness. The dissenting with the dissenters. The almost pathological love of individual freedom and privacy in some cases, notably that of Thoreau. The utter indifference to what any man in particular or society in general thought of him. What an illumination of the New England enigma this lecture was to me.

This man had decided to say his say without caring a damn what anyone thought of him or his ideas. Proudly, defiantly, he wrapped about him the cloak of originality of his New England dissenters.

Words – how he played with them. Caressed them, as if they were pet kittens. Tossed them into the air like a skilled juggler. Threw polished phrases out into the audience like cool shining marbles for us to feel between our own fingers. I particularly liked his description of Emily Dickenson – "the articulate inarticulate." He said she often followed tradition in her poems until the last line, then "the bottom dropped out."

Ripples of laughter, then tense silence attested to the alertness of all his listeners. He seized phrases, held them up for our delectation, done to a turn, as if on the prongs of a toasting fork. Greedily, I snatched and consumed them as fast as he passed them out. Ever since my removal from New York's nourishing literary life it seemed a thousand years since I had met anyone who loved literature with consuming passion. And who was not afraid to show it, thank God!

And his mannerisms! No one should speak of that history-making lecture without commenting on those incredible gestures. Some people might condemn them as too extravagant. And so they might have appeared if they had not seemed an outward extension of an inner excitement. He strode across the stage like a milder Khrushchev. He pounded the lectern with his fist. He thrust a forceful forefinger at the audience to drive home a pointed remark.

That was not all. He delicately twirled his left hand from the wrist with the amazing skill of a Shankar whose classic Hindu dances I had seen in New York recently. Sometimes both hands rippled incredibly through the air performing little dual dances independent of his immobile body. A difficult accomplishment – impossible I had imagined to anyone except Hindu and Siamese dancers trained for a lifetime. I've never seen anything like it. Neither have you. It was hypnotic! Never, never had quiet, inhibited New England witnessed such a dramatic spectacle as Thornton Wilder treated us to this January night. It was a work of art.

And the subject of this unprecedented talk? It sounded academic, dry, juiceless. "Some Reflections on American Classical Literature." The classics were Thoreau, Melville, Dickenson, Whitman and Poe.

That night, when the lecture ended, the whole audience was so stunned by this dramatic performance it was struck motionless. Finally it rose *en masse* and burst into a prolonged ovation.

Van Wyck Brooks and his wife sat next to me. I asked him what he thought of it.

"Brilliant! Brilliant!" he said generously for it was about the flowering of his own New England territory.

"That's the best lecture I've heard in all my fifteen years in this town!" declared a famous Pulitzer prize-winning professor.

"It's the best lecture *ever* given at this university!" exclaimed another veteran of the war of words in this university town – where of the giving of lectures there is no end.

I had come to this lecture without great expectations. I had heard this man speak before. It was nothing unusual. I had seen his plays, read his books. Some I liked, others I did not. Also I had heard most of the contemporary world's literary greats speak – T.S. Eliot, Somerset Maugam, Thomas Mann, E.E. Cummings, Rebecca West and others. Writers are seldom good speakers.

Tepid and timid speakers usually even when interesting and talented. Men brilliant in their fields, profound in their specialized knowledge but often deadly as chalk dust on the lecture platform.

But, as Wilder's tornado of words whirled across the stage my very body had begun to respond. Gradually my heart swelled with excitement. Then my brain felt a sharp cold wind sweeping the cobwebs out of it. Fresh blood leaped through my veins. All life, at least all my life, commenced to flow in one direction – strong, irresistible, confident with a definite visible goal. No more wavering, wandering or wondering. My own destiny became clear once again. Even in a world that worshipped little but materialism, science and politics, it was imperative that I, that others, struggle to write not only of timely things but of timeless things. Things that have puzzled, delighted and sustained mankind for centuries – the inner life, self-development, the good life.

I was liberated! Restored to my true self. Not by yoga or standing on my head, or renunciation of the world or fasting or meditation, not by Jungian psychological therapy – excellent as they all were – but by art. This was not a lecture! It was art! And the primary function of all art is purification, as Aristotle assures us.

It liberated me from the pressures of public opinion of my day, lifted the burden of "what others think."

For, I felt, every book, every article was evaluated not by its literary merits, not by its intrinsic contents but by its political and economic slant. Every person was judged not by his accomplishments or intellect, not by his character or spirituality but by his political interests. Politics permeated everything in modern life. A book without politics was dismissed.

But thanks to this man on the platform, the art of human speech had liberated me from dominance by my conscious mind that bade me conform to the mores of the times.

I felt it lift me to another level – it was almost a physical sensation – lift me to another plane where my deeper unconscious opened like a flower under the sun, where my better, truer nature could function, on a new plateau of harmony and naturalness, creativity and joy.

I felt intensely grateful to Thornton Wilder – and to art.

I was liberated – mildly – temporarily at least. Now I was ready to perform wonders – I hoped.

Chapter 2

LOVE AND THE INFANT

There are no miracles, the Tibetan Buddhists maintain. There is only man's knowledge of the nature of things and the nature of human beings. Or is there something other?

One day an acquaintance telephoned me. "Would you like to drive out and see my daughter's baby? You said to let you know when she came to visit me."

"Oh, yes, I'd love to see her. When would it be most convenient?"

"Now. Only I should warn you the baby is crying."

"Oh? Then I'll come some other time."

"No. She cries all the time – been crying for months."

"How terrible! What do the doctors say about it?"

"They've all examined her. They can't find a single thing wrong. My daughter is flying back to California when her husband comes for her tonight. So if you want to see the baby—"

"I'll be right out as soon as I can drive there."

I drove quickly through the lovely woodlands leading to Mrs. K---'s house. Her beautiful spring garden was in full bloom. Her house was the newest style – a long, low ranch house of stone. I knew her furniture would be ultra modern too. She prided herself on following the latest fashions – in some things. I rang the bell and was ushered in by her pretty young daughter.

Mrs. K--- was sitting with a beautiful little baby girl on her knees – not on her lap, mind you, not in her arms, but at the very extreme edge of her knees. It was in danger of falling off onto the floor at any minute. The infant was dressed in an exquisite lacy dress. Previously, Mrs. K--- had told me of the many luxurious clothes, jewelry, bassinets, and the like she had sent to this, her first grandchild.

"What an unusually pretty baby!" I said.

It was crying persistently, piteously. The mother ignored it, as she smoked steadily.

The grandmother jiggled her knees impatiently. "My daughter is getting tired of changing diapers and heating bottles in the middle of the night. She wants to go back to that advertising agency in Los Angeles where she made such a success before she was married, remember?"

The daughter laughed. "Guess I'm just a career girl at heart. I didn't get a college education to be nothing but a nursemaid to a crying infant twenty-four hours of the day and night. I don't mind admitting I'm pretty fed up."

"Well," the grandmother said, *"I'm* getting fed up with this constant crying." She shook the baby. "Stop it! Oh, why won't you stop crying! You've been at it for months now. You're driving us out of our minds."

"But," I said to Mrs. K---, "you've had four children of your own, I should think you'd be an expert on handling them by now."

"Oh but – well – oh, that was so long ago. I've forgotten."

What a strange atmosphere in that room – like cold draughts of air! It was most peculiar. I watched the grandmother trying vainly to quiet the crying infant. Suddenly I thought in horror, what she'd really like to do is throw that baby on the floor! Her hostility is so strong it emanates from her like an electric current. Even I can feel it. Poor, poor little thing!

Finally in exasperation the grandmother thrust the child toward the mother. "Here, you take her. She's your child. You make her stop crying. It really is a disgrace."

The young mother took the child, threw it up in the air, blew in its face and shook it. "Now you stop that crying! We just fed you and burped you and changed you, so you have nothing on earth to cry about. Haven't you any company manners at all!"

The baby cried more loudly than ever. Above the slow, persistent noise we continued to discuss careers versus marriage.

I watched the baby. Its cry seemed to rise from some deep-seated misery. My heart bled for the poor, helpless little creature. No one loves you, I said to myself, no one anywhere loves you one iota, you poor, poor little thing.

Even the mother's rejection of her child chilled the air so much I could feel it across the room like an icy wind. She talked on and on about how troublesome children were. I commented that I thought she was fortunate to have a child at all. The baby never ceased crying for one instant.

Finally I stood up. I knew nothing about babies. I had never had one of my own. There were no younger children in our family for me to practise on.

But now I took this pitiful, crying infant in my arms and pressed her close against me. As I felt her warm, soft little body against my breasts, I caught my breath. Was there anything on earth so sweet to a woman as holding a baby? My heart swelled with joy. My whole being melted at her touch. I did not even look at her, but such a warm flood of love poured from me, it felt like a great rush of mother's milk.

I did not utter a word – aloud. But inside myself I was shouting passionately, silently, I love you! I love you! Maybe no one else loves you, you poor, miserable, unwanted little creature but I love you with all my heart! I'd love any baby on earth who needed love as badly and obviously as you do, you poor, poor darling!

Instantly the child ceased to cry. Immediately she began to utter those delicious gurgling sounds of a happy baby. It was so poignant, so touching it would have melted the heart of an iceberg.

"Good heaven!" the young mother exclaimed. "You've charmed her. You laid a spell on her. It is magic!"

"She's healed her," the grandmother said. "It's a laying-on of hands! It's a miracle!"

Chapter 3

LOVE AND DEATH

Is suffering sometimes nature's method of purifying us?

"Your husband must undergo a major operation at once. It is very urgent!"

It is our doctor. Our trusted doctor of long standing making this shocking announcement over the telephone.

My heart begins to pound. Sickness strikes in the pit of my stomach. I sit there at the desk frozen, listening to the details, to his warning of its extreme seriousness, its possible fatality.

Slowly, I lay the phone down. I remain motionless at the desk, stunned by the suddenness of the shock, by the enormity of it, the unexpectedness.

No, no, I protest to myself. I won't believe it! I can't! He has scarcely been sick in twenty years. But oh, the poor, poor darling. What has he ever done to deserve such a fate!?

Gradually my body feels as if it is filled with a hot seething mass of warring elements. It will fly into a thousand pieces any minute unless I do something immediately. I cannot sit still another second.

I rise and begin to pace the floor back and forth, scarcely aware of what I am doing. Through this room and that, round and round in a circle – resisting, protesting, fighting against such unmerited cruelty.

I am alone in the house. I am between cooks. It is not the day for the upstairs maid.

I rail at life, at fate, at the unknown, at the horrible injustice of it, at the unnecessary tragedy of it all. I attempt by sheer force of protest, of non-acceptance, to thrust it all out of existence.

Abruptly I stop and clasp my hands together fiercely. "Oh, don't let him suffer too much, oh, please! He does not know how serious it is, thank heaven! He must not know. I must try to lend him strength. But how can I? I am helpless now when he needs help the most. Only the surgeon can save him now."

The sickness in the pit of my stomach begins to spread through my entire body. I walk on and on, around and around like a wild animal caught in a cage, being tormented by some inescapable prodding force from outside.

Unheeded, great hot rivers of tears begin to stream down my cheeks. I continue to walk around and around through room after room. I have not wept like this since I was a child. In fact, never have I wept like this before in my entire life – from depths deeper than I knew existed. I feel as if the roots of my life are being torn up. The last line of defenses are being attacked – defenses I had considered impregnable. The last inviolate citadel of selfhood is being invaded as I had thought nothing ever in this world could invade it. My last protection against despair and destruction are crumbling. The integrity and strength of my deepest being, the hard central core that sustains my living, without which I would be but a helpless jelly – it is shaken, threatened. I am in danger of being destroyed here and now, instantly by the impact of this sudden, unsupportable blow . . .

Now fear rises in my body like a cold tidal wave. Fear that I may succumb, that I may be unable to meet this most terrible challenge of my entire life, that I may fail my husband in this crisis, fail my own self-esteem, and simply disintegrate and . . . and . . .

The prospect is too terrible to contemplate! I call on the last remaining ounce of my strength, resistance, pride and love.

Finally after hours it seems, the tears run dry. They have alleviated the dangerous tension somewhat. I grind my teeth together, clamp my eyes shut, clasp my hands together painfully. I *must* meet this challenge, I *will!*

Stop thinking of yourself, I chide myself. Think only of him. He is the one facing suffering and the danger of death. You must bear up for his sake. If you went all to pieces would that not double his burden? How can you even think for a minute of your grief, your loss? He is the one who is going to the hospital, not you!

Compassion for him melts my heart to a warm, useless liquid. But I must gird myself to do all in my power to help him, never mind about selfish little me. I am frightened for him but for myself also. What if I should be left alone? He is all I have in the world! The idea is unthinkable. I thrust it away.

I pause and gaze at his photograph on my chiffonier. "He has always been the strong one. You have leaned on him and he liked it – so did you. He has spoiled you and waited on you. You're nothing but a clinging Southern vine. He always drove the car for you when it was stormy and snowy or the traffic was heavy. He advised you what stocks to buy and sell – everything. And now – now – "

The next day I drive him to the hospital in complete silence.

I return home and for days I walk about the world in a state of shock. I bathe and dress automatically from sheer habit. I am scarcely aware whether I have slept or eaten or what I am wearing. I am waiting for the awful day of the operation. The doctor forbids all visitors.

Our acquaintances and neighbors rush to comfort me. Friends buoy me up by their kindness, call me every day, every hour, carry me off to meals I cannot eat, to familiar restaurants I cannot recognize. They surround me with solitude. Their support prevents me from collapsing. Surely trouble and tragedy awaken the best in everybody proving that good lies dormant in everyone only waiting for circumstances to call it forth. Their warm selfless generosity carries me through the days of waiting. I knew I should never forget their kindness so long as I lived. No matter what happened there would always be a special corner in my heart for them.

But then there are the nights – the unspeakable nights. I lie awake and think of him lying alone in that cold, impersonal hospital room waiting at the door of death perhaps and my heart quietly breaks. Is he facing the prospect calmly? Is the poor darling suffering too horribly? Is he afraid? He never mentions it. But then he is the world's most taciturn of men. He does not imagine and foresee and fret and regret as I do. He accepts accomplished facts without ado and takes up his life from there. Or was that a brave front? But I noticed he put all his financial affairs into final shape.

The nights of wakefulness are long in a cold lonely bed. But in the mornings I am awakened by that awful word – alone. One morning when the upstairs maid had offered to bring up my breakfast, I sat there unable to eat, staring at my once beloved home. It was cherished heretofore as if it were my child and his. It was a comfort to me, a solace, its beauty bringing pleasure, its rich colors bringing warmth.

Today it is suddenly meaningless. I no longer love it. I cannot love it. It is nothing but sticks and stones and useless colored stuff.

If anything happens to him, I would never want to lay eyes on this house again – a constant reminder probing the wound. I try to eat my breakfast. Suddenly a strange, tasteless taste comes into my mouth. It is like ashes. Life has the taste of ashes. So that is what that old expression means! I have never tasted ashes, no one has. Yet that is exactly what it tastes like. Without companionship living would be a waste of effort. Why try?

As I sit there playing with my food, I feel anguish for him but no matter how ignoble it is, I feel sorry for myself. I feel sorry for any wife or husband left alone after years of a happy marriage.

Slowly, the full meaning of loneliness invades me like a cold tide. No one to be close to, to be first with. No one to care what happens to you. No one to do things for, to lend your endeavors incentive. No one for you to care about daily, deeply, rewardingly. Alone – that terrible word echoes like the sound of some bell sounding my doom through all the long corridors of my mind and heart. Terrified by unknown horrors and fears, I feel exiled on a small deserted island in a dark and story sea, helpless, all the urge to fight drained out of me. Can I face such a fate, drowning in a sea of loneliness? Foolishly, frantically, I attempt to bargain with It – some unknown powerful It.

"If you let him get well, I'll be an angel to him the rest of his life. If you only let him come back to me – even as an invalid – I will do anything you ask – anything!"

I seek out other women whose husbands have been struck down by the same illness. I make elaborate plans to take care of him. I read all the literature on the subject.

Finally the day of the operation arrives. Our doctor forbids me to put my foot in the hospital that day. "He would not recognize you. There is nothing on earth you can do for him. You would suffer unnecessarily. You may come the following day. But even then I want you to stay only fifteen minutes. I will telephone you the minute I come from the operating room and report to you."

So I sit by the phone at home waiting – waiting from eight in the morning when the operation begins, until nine, until ten, until eleven, until twelve. Four interminable hours of suspense. Every hour I telephone the hospital and inquire. Some kind woman's gentle voice says, "No, your husband is still in the operating room."

To be patient, hopeful, noble, courageous – it is a desperate struggle. Slowly I fear I am beginning to die inside.

Finally something begins to break. I believed I had prepared myself to lose him forever. Yet somehow I am unable to bear this suspense another minute. I throw myself onto the generous warm bosom of my sympathetic maid and burst into tears.

At last the message comes. After five hours on the operating table he has come through it still alive. I feel relieved and happy for him. But isn't the message too late? I have already died a little death.

The next day and the days that follow I visit him in the hospital – a white, unfamiliar, thin face. He lies there so patiently, never complaining, trying to smile – a smile that sends me from the room in tears. The doctor pronounces him the perfect patient. Of course the danger is not past.

I endeavor to wait on him, to sympathize. He wants no fuss made, no discussion. Illness he regards as a blot on his masculine escutcheon, sympathy as belittling to his manhood. How strange men are. So proud, so brave, so self-contained. My pent-up feelings are not allowed to flow out in sympathy to him. For many women, for me certainly, the best medicine on earth is sympathy – and lots of it. It soothes you, sustains you, diminishes your pain like an anodyne.

All is not sadness, however. His personal friends and business friends deluge him with flowers. They telephone me long distance to inquire about his condition. These practical, hard-headed business men grow emotional, their voices warm, their words singing my husband's praises with a depth of sincerity that moves me deeply. I am pleased to know they held him in such high esteem.

And at the hospital my husband's best qualities emerge. He plays a humorous verbal game with his nurse. Her ability to handle a sick man is a gift to be admired. He also achieves a rapport with the surgeon, whom he trusts implicitly. I have known the doctor socially but in the sick room he is a different person. He is marvelously calm, quiet, confident. His voice is low, his manner unhurried, his touch of amazing gentleness. I can see there is a healing power in those sensitive hands as they examine my husband. A deep bond is forged between these two men that promises to endure for the rest of their lives. Ironically enough without the operation and illness this splendid relationship might never have been created. Out of evil a little good comes sometimes.

I have never been in a house alone at night. The first two weeks I hear burglars in every room in the house. By the third week I have trained myself to be oblivious to noises – almost. During the long sleepless nights, I strive to *think* my way into an acceptance of this dilemma. Of what earthly value is our reason if it cannot help us when we need it most?

Why, I cry out to an indifferent universe, why must suffering exist? Is it necessary? Is evil necessary? Is illness due to man's ignorance? Is evil due to man's ignorance? But who – what, made us ignorant? Would good be impossible without evil? Is the world really balanced between the poles of the opposites. The Orientals and the great psychologist, Carl Jung, maintain this to be true.

Is evolution the resolving of contradictory elements into unity? Is evil a step toward the good? I cannot see it. Yet when I myself experienced a psychological and spiritual awakening a few years ago, I "died" psychologically first, then was born again. At that time I experienced a "reversal of the opposites" to create a new good. But now – no, I do not feel it, I do not understand what is happening.

Is Western philosophy wrong to postulate a duality, a conflict between good and evil as a law of the all-controlling principle of the universe? Or is the old Taoist, Lao Tzu, much wiser? He saw *yang* and *yin* as two counterbalancing opposites – male and female, darkness and light, good and evil that invade each other's territory and eventually create unity.

Do good and evil derive from the same primordial force? But if this universal force is omnipotent and omniscient, then it obviously cannot be all-loving. Or if it is benevolent it obviously cannot be omnipotent. It is the age-old question that man has been asking and unable to answer ever since he began to think, since he ate the symbolical tree of knowledge of good and evil, that is, since evolution added reason to his instincts.

Why should such a small insect as man arrogantly assume that he should be able to comprehend the incomprehensibility of anything so vast, so magnificent, so complex as the cosmic scheme? That, however, is small consolation, because my reason demands an understanding. Look, for example, at the apparent decay and evil of moulds. Yet they produce healing penicillin. Well, you could accept evil if good always issued from it. But does it? If my husband died, that would be pure evil.

So reason failed me completely in my hour of tragedy.

Even after the operation, my husband was still in dire danger. Every minute of everyday for three weeks I had resisted suffering, rejected it, refused it. Yet resistance and tension only increased the pain.

Suddenly, one day in utter exhaustion, I let the stormy waters of grief, fear and pain flood into every corner of my being like a spring flood. I accepted suffering. I no longer rebelled against the inevitable, the irrevocable. Perhaps life was wiser than I.

And then a strange thing happened. This torrent of suffering that had threatened to destroy me began to recede. I found it had washed away old accumulations of pettiness, selfishness and dead egotism. Now it offered love and selflessness and tenderness a new opportunity to grow and flourish like little green plants.

So suffering could be purifying, I realized with utter amazement!

Finally I am allowed to bring him home from the hospital. He sits idly in his chair so pale, so weak, so miserably thin, it makes tears rush to my eyes. I must slip out of the room to prevent his noticing them.

After a long while he seems stronger again, goes out and attends to business. But I watch him like a hawk in continuous fear.

He never refers to his operation, discourages others from discussing it. Nothing is said between us. Nothing is different and yet everything is different. He too has been purged by his illness – more than I undoubtedly. We both move on a new plane, live in a different climate. A new tenderness envelopes us both like a warm light whose source is concealed. It pervades our home, brightens our lives.

I realize anew the welfare of another is more important to me than my own, and frankly I am surprised anew to find this a sweet and satisfying sensation. Our little, annoying personal habits no longer annoy each other, most of them disappear magically. His presence is more desirable than ever, his virtues more apparent, his life and health the things I guard more than my own.

When I was alone I had felt I was nothing – useless – footless – rootless. Food was tasteless – effort useless – life meaningless. But a husband completes a woman's life, I realize more than ever. I see that to care about someone – to love someone is a rare privilege. To be cared for – to be loved by someone is a necessity. To be first with someone is the prime law of life. To share with another, small things and large, satisfies some deep, strange need beyond explanation. Since my husband came home from the hospital our only friction is to vie with the other in doing things for each other. It is like the early days of the honeymoon and promises to remain that way.

As I go about my daily chores, I say to myself, this thing called marriage is beyond comprehension. It is not so ecstatic as falling in love, not so romantic as being in love. But married love is deeper and richer, more enduring. It is nourishing, like soil to a hungry tree that is bare at times but blooms again perennially. It is like a still, deep pool. Little waves of irritation may ruffle it occasionally but they are only on the surface. Nothing disturbs its serene depths. Surely marriage sustains and supports our inner being as does no other human relationship possible to the race.

To my astonishment I discover that I, too, have undergone an operation. Suffering is like an operation. Pain plunges its cold, cruel blade deep into your very vitals, cutting out the malignant growths of pettiness, of selfishness and cruelty (of which you had scarcely been aware). It leaves you more gentle, more loving, more selfless.

Perhaps suffering is designed to be one of nature's curative powers. So when will I learn to stop resisting the current of inexorable events, to stop attempting to manipulate life? When will I learn to swim with the rhythmic tides of existence that may someday lead me to my goal of understanding and harmony?

Chapter 4

FRIENDSHIP

Professor

For many years I had dropped in occasionally at the office of a professor of comparative religion at one of the divinity schools in which our city abounds.

He was an elderly man and consequently, some of his sources and authorities were outdated in the light of modern psychology of religion. His basic ideas, however, were beautiful and I believed he really lived by spiritual precepts. He was tolerant of all religions and races, generous and helpful to scores of people, and had many followers among both students and faculty.

Often I hastened to him when I was struck by an unanswerable question or some exciting new idea. For years, I sat gratefully and admiringly at his feet. I was indebted to him because he had lent me a helping hand on this strange new road to a new kind of psychological and spiritual life after my years of agnosticism.

When my new book was published, he pronounced it a beautiful book. He purchased many copies and distributed them far and wide. As wonderful letters from both scholars and laymen began to arrive my professor friend glowed with pride at the accomplishment of his pupil. He telephoned me frequently to inquire if new letters had arrived from readers.

One morning he laughed and said, "Probably in the future I shall no longer be the leader of my group but known merely as a friend of the originator of your new cult of self-realization."

His position was more than secure, especially in the hearts of his many followers, I assured him. One afternoon, however, I took him a long, especially complimentary letter I had received from one of the most respected scholars at the nearby university. I expected my divinity teacher to wax as ecstatic over it as I had.

He read it and turned on me, his face contorted with rage, his eyes like black ice so deadly cold with hate they frightened me. Was he going to strike me?

"All right, young lady, you may have had mystical experiences and I haven't. But that does not make you any sort of authority on the psychology of religion or anything else. I was teaching all the living religions and a lot of dead ones before you were ever born. If you really were as intelligent as you think, you would agree with me that the only way to save the world from tragic destruction is for America to surrender now to Russia and Communism and so prevent World War III."

Too stunned to speak I stared at him in consternation. Instead of the expected anger, a wave of compassion surged through me. Slowly I rose, walked to the door, then turned back toward him.

"You shock me to the very marrow of my bones. All I can say is that I am not a scholar as you are. But if I have any contribution to make to the welfare of others it lies in sharing my beautiful psychological experiences, for which I can take no credit because they were all spontaneous. You understand the history of religions better than I ever shall. You have been a wonderful teacher for me. It was you who gave me encouragement when I was stumbling blindly along this new road years ago. I shall be indebted to you forever. And I have treasured our friendship probably far more than I ever expressed to you. And I thought we were discussing psychology and religion not politics."

Then I turned and walked out of his office.

Later our friendship was renewed on a firmer foundation.

Novelist

One weekend my husband and I invited one of our closest friends from New York to stay with us at our cottage at the sea shore. Eagerly I anticipated long leisurely hours of lying together on the beach discussing endlessly all our deepest interests – especially the problems raised by my new book recently published. There never was time for long, intimate, profound talk in our too busy lives.

Before my new book was published I had imagined the warm reaction of my friends to it. Surely it would arouse all the good inherent in them. At last they would become acquainted with the deepest, most real me after our years of pleasant but unsatisfying, superficial social chatter. My book surely would strengthen all my friendships with indestructible bonds.

Friday night our guest arrived.

She was a successful novelist, younger than I, pretty, charming and much sought after though she never had married. In her letter accepting my invitation she commented three times that she had *not* read my new book.

At breakfast Saturday morning, three more glowing letters from readers of my book arrived. I showed them first to my husband who exclaimed, "Wonderful!" Then I passed them to my friend expecting her to be happy for me at my small success.

She did not read them but tossed them to the table, rose and walked away even though her host and hostess were still eating.

"I'm going to the beach – *alone*," she announced angrily. "Way off by myself."

She was very late in returning for lunch though I had told her we had reservations at a restaurant famous for its baked stuffed lobster – her favorite. As I drove the car along the shore road I talked gaily of impersonal matters as if nothing had happened.

In the restaurant she spied some friends at a nearby table, went over, and talked with them a long time. I sat alone at our table – wondering. She returned for dessert, then placed her purse on the table and said, "Take care of this for me. I have to make a long distance phone call."

I sat alone at the table until everyone had left the restaurant. Why was my friend suffering so mysteriously and striking out at me? Intuition warned me to say nothing. Yet as we drove home I did say, "I want to be a good hostess. If there is anything I can do to make you happy, please tell me."

She threw me an agonized look and tears rose in her eyes. My heart went out to her. This would clear the atmosphere and return things to normal between us, I felt sure.

At dinner that night she made a point of talking exclusively to my husband. I might have been a plate on the table. She laughed and flirted in that delightful way of which she was past master. My husband blossomed under her charming attentions. I thought it was good for him.

I sat there thinking that she always had been a spoiled child, demanding that she should be the center of attention at all times in all groups. But why? Was it because she had not been a spoiled child at home, that her parents had not loved her enough as an infant? Now as an adult constant attention was not sufficient to compensate for her early rejection. She felt the need of more and more adulation in order to maintain her self-esteem and self-confidence. Even success in her profession did not heal her childhood hurt.

Did my modest little success and glowing letters from readers make her feel painfully insecure and unsure of herself? Had I hurt her unwittingly and so she was striking back? Then what could I do to restore her good opinion of herself?

She had just had her blond hair tinted a more golden color. It was unusually attractive. I asked my husband if he did not think she looked younger and prettier than ever. He did. I praised her new dinner dress, and her latest novel. They all deserved genuine praise. She remained angry, cold, and sarcastic.

After that fateful visit we continued to see each other when I went to New York. I was careful never to disagree with her even about the weather. I deferred to her opinion on many affairs in New York about which she really knew more than I. Gradually she began to bloom again in my presence in that old charming way. My book was never once mentioned.

Painter

We gave a dinner party in honor of an intimate friend – a landscape painter. She was talented and more successful than most local artists. She held frequent one-man shows all over the state and in New York and often sold her pictures.

Tonight we were exhibiting a new landscape of hers to our other guests. We were considering purchasing it. It was sitting on the mantel piece. Already in previous years we had purchased two small pictures of hers.

For some time the conversation at the dinner table had been about her painting. Then one of the guests, a business man, turned to me and said he was delighted to have read the chapter on Freud and Jung in my book because he never had had time to study them. He was particularly interested in their explanations of why neurotic people were incapable of loving anyone.

The painter spoke at me angrily but *looked* at the speaker. "Freud did not know what he was talking about. And neither do people who praise him. He was neurotic himself when he stated that painters were neurotic because they messed around in pigment as a substitute for faeces. But he proved that all religions are infantile. And Jung was a doddering idiot! People who admire him should have their heads examined. The idea that the esthetic impulse comes from the unconscious is ridiculous. Why I am conscious every minute of exactly what I am doing when I am painting a landscape?"

Then she launched into a long tirade against art critics in general and some in particular – especially amateurs and laymen. She became so vehement that the apparent object of her attack looked bewildered and frightened. His wife attempted to deflect the flood but unfortunately employed my book as a dam. This made a bad matter worse.

I was amazed to hear myself involuntarily, quickly, begin a long recital of all the honors and prizes my painter friend's picture had won and I continued this accolade until the maid served the dessert.

When we went into the living room for coffee my husband climaxed the situation by passing around the liqueurs, proposing a toast to the poor upset painter, and announced that we were going to purchase her new landscape and hang it above the fireplace.

Then I took the guests upstairs to allow them to admire her other two pictures in her presence. When the painter said good night, she was glowing with happiness. So was I.

But afterward, as I lay awake, reason examined these three unprecedented episodes.

So Jesus was right!

All my life I had heard that Jesus exhorted us to "return good for evil." But how, how?

"Do good to them that hate you." But the Bible did not offer adequate techniques – that was what had always puzzled me. So frankly I never had believed it possible or at least natural. You never saw it put into practise around you.

But it *was* possible to attain a state of mind where you returned good for evil involuntarily and happily!

This was the first time in my life when insulted that I had felt no anger or pain but instead felt concern for my enemies' unhappiness rather than my own humiliation.

And it had been involuntary – not deliberate or conscious!

Did this mean I had progressed a step toward self-realization?

Chapter 5

SOLITUDE

Is solitude a way to renew contact with things and people, with the self, nature and the creative principle itself?

Today I sit alone in a quiet house – doing nothing – blessed nothing. Oh, the sweet relief of being alone for one brief once! This simple chair on which I sit is a blessed island of solitude in a heavenly sea of silence.

The solace of solitude and silence in a quiet house when the family – without which I could not live – is out; when the servants – without whom I could not write – are off. The burden of constant pressures is lifted, the prodding of endless distractions removed, the constriction of continuous tensions released. The bombardment by the electric vibrations of other personalities is noticeably absent. There is no necessity to constantly re-adjust myself to other people, to their wishes and ways, needs and ideas. There is no danger of being interrupted in the middle of a tenuous new thought or a fragile new feeling. I possess my soul in peace.

The whirling moving machinery of my life has come to a standstill at last. It is unutterably sweet to be still, to do nothing for a change, to sit motionless with idle hands and idle thoughts, no work clamoring to be done, no duties insisting on attention, no problems pressing for immediate solution. All household chores are postponed, all books closed, notebooks ignored, conscience curled up asleep in its proper corner.

How vibrant the silence is, bathing my over-stimulated nerves like warm healing waters. No voices to titillate my curiosity. No servants cleaning, washing, walking about. None of the rasping noises of our mechanistic civilization of the West. No dishwashers swishing, no vacuum cleaners grinding, no timers ringing. The telephone is disconnected. The doorbells are unanswered. Radio and television are turned off. The piano is standing restful and soundless.

I sigh and think, you cannot hear the music of silence unless you are alone, unless you are idle, unless you are still. Silence is filled with its own melodies, with faint far-off messages and subtle intimations.

I sit still as still and listen. Gradually my battered senses come alive again. I become intensely aware of my over-familiar surroundings. I actually hear the distant song of a bird usually half-heard through ears otherwise preoccupied. I really see the ineluctable grace of a Hepplewhite chair usually half-seen through eyes elsewhere engaged.

My heart leaps up at the vibrant color magically brought to life by a long finger of sunlight touching an ordinary red damask drapery. My eyes are mesmerized by the soft grey shadows of the leaves moving in the wind across a drawn window shade. It stirs my heart – why, I do not know – with all the melancholy of dreams unrealized, hopes unfulfilled.

Silence and solitude, idleness and stillness – how they free the mind to brood on the wonders of the commonplace, to find them full of unsuspected beauty. They reawaken my fondness for this beloved house which sometimes seems a burden.

They bring all the sweetness of marriage flooding back again. They reawaken awareness of the unbreakable bond with my husband more strongly in his absence than in his presence. I begin to feel warm and eager. My deepest self opens like a welcoming womb until I am impregnated with happiness, until I feel like a woman heavy with child. I feel reoriented, reorganized, ready for any eventuality.

Gradually I become oblivious to things, to people. I look with an inward eye, watch the slow surfacing of the self, usually submerged like a submarine. Now I am able to reassess my potentialities, redefine my goals in life, re-examine my progress and problems in the pursuit of the good life.

Now the body – undirected and unharassed – relaxes at last. Now the springs of action wound too tightly too long uncoil in delicious lassitude.

Then the mind, freed temporarily from the tyranny of conscious thought, flits happily about like an aimless butterfly from one brightly-colored idea to another, gathering nothing whatever, or culling the unexpected nourishment of perennial truths – that life is good, that man is good, that there is a supreme good beyond doubt, beyond reason – leaving a sweet certitude at the core of my being after I have been washed clean by solitude and silence.

Now like a spring that had run dry, I feel full again, filled from some mysterious underground source. I was empty – now the sweetness of life rises up when there is silence and stillness. "Be still and know that I am there." All the shattered fragments of my personality given to other people and things are now reassembled. I am whole once more. I feel rested, refreshed, strengthened and nourished.

Finally I rise and stand idly at the window. I gaze at the never-ending mystery of white clouds sailing across the endless blue sky. My lost identity with nature is gradually renewed.

I gaze and gaze into the clouds until I cease to see them, until I drift upon the tide of reverie, touching at the shores of enchanting islands of speculation, until all my doubts are washed away. My joy at being alive floats me along. Gratitude at re-establishment of lost contact with self, people, things, and nature swells my heart.

I look and look so long into the depths of the billowing white clouds that finally I am absorbed back into the enigmatic life force whence I originally issued, reassured that I rest securely in the vast arms of an ineffable and ultimate reality.

Chapter 6

DIALOGUE

We meet at the hotel in Florida by sheer chance. He is with his parents, I with my husband. All five of us exchange the amenities. The others drift away. He and I speak of books. It is the password. The sparks begin to fly immediately. That he is British creates no barriers whatever.

He is so young and handsome but so incredibly mature intellectually. Though still in college, he is responsive to the arts as only an experienced person is usually. We sit and talk hour after hour, striking sparks from each other's minds. I speak of poetry, new and old. He speaks of painting and baroque architecture, of Italian ceilings painted to swirl off into infinity, the limitations of the problems of design and the limitations of the human mind to know and create, and the close relationship between the esthetic experience and the religious.

We agree about the confusions of ready-made systems of philosophy and the necessity for personal experience. We speak about the conflicting ideologies of today, Communism and Democracy, and why Americans become Communists; about freedom and security and the meaning of human history; the unexpected psychological truths one stumbles on in the Bible. But we always return again to the universal language of the arts.

Words are exchanged in quick volleys, well-placed phrases adroitly returned. It is a conversational tennis game. Amazed and delighted at our own unexpected skill, we grow breathless with excitement. We laugh a great deal. Are we really so witty? Or is it merely well-being and rapport overflowing?

The tempo of the game increases. His fund of facts, I think to myself, is stupendous, his articulate expression astounding, his vocabulary prodigious. At twenty, I tell him, he seems to have arrived at the state of esthetic understanding and philosophic knowledge it has required a lifetime for me to achieve. Can it be he is a genius, I ask him? He laughs and demurs. He places 400 in a class of 1,000 students, he says. I am dumfounded.

So this is modern youth, I say to myself. How incredibly wonderful! If only I had such a son! How fortunate his mother is. I and my generation, I tell him, spent the first twenty years of our lives being children, and the next ten in making money and merely having a good time. He has a good time, he says, at week-ends and holidays but he is surfeited by parties and debutantes.

We talk on and on forgetting time and place. The conversational stream flows along, rippling and shining – swift, stead and exhilarating, carrying us away – away – into a timeless region.

Is that a danger signal appearing? Is that a warm tender glow in his eyes? Certainly I feel all the drooping flowers of femininity within me lift their sleepy heads again, ready and eager to blossom out again. But that's absurd, I reassure myself. It is only the stimulating conversation that intoxicates us like champagne.

Sternly I check myself. Carefully I remind myself, you are old enough to be his mother, God help you! He is very young, probably inexperienced, certainly defenseless as most men are (women being most men's Achilles' heel). He must not be hurt. He must be protected from you – by you!

But I did not seek it, I protest inwardly. He did not seek it. It merely happened. It was spontaneous combustion. Sparks ignited instantly on first contact. But you are the one to control this explosive situation, I admonish myself.

So painfully I clasp my hands together in my lap while listening to his scintillating discourse ranging rapidly from science to art to politics. Silently I rebuke myself: you must restrain your enthusiasm. You must remain dull and negative, merely a maternal sounding-board for the eager ideas of youth. You must resist flashing your eyes, laughing and tossing your head as every feminine impulse urges you to do.

I try.

Later we meet again, he and I, by accident or tacit design – in the public lounge at a quiet hour when others are outdoors playing tennis or golf or riding. We talk avidly for hours. He has read my last book and liked it. I have read the poems he lent to me – poems of genuine merit. He announces he is intellectually lonely. Lonely! That dangerous word! How it threatens my carefully erected barriers.

I hasten to ask him about his girls, about his roommate, his courses in college. He says he sits for hours listening to too much dull scholarship without fire, without imagination. I reply but find I must look alive, think fast to keep pace with his swift leaps from subject to subject.

Finally I rise and retreat to my room, exhilarated and deliciously refreshed by the unaccustomed exercise of the muscles of my mind. I happen to glance at the face of the woman in the mirror shocked to see it glowing like a Christmas tree. But how is one to ignore that magnetic undercurrent playing between the positive masculine pole and the negative feminine pole, charging the very atmosphere of the room with electricity, regardless of ages, regardless of good intentions, regardless of genuine intellectual interests?

I pace the floor thinking – thinking. I must send him away abruptly, permanently. That would be the kindest way, wouldn't it? Or the unkindest? But it's all too ridiculous, I say to myself. There's no danger to anyone. He certainly can see my graying hair. My maturity is apparent, obviously the discrepancies in our ages make everything absurd except conversational companionship. Must we be denied even that rare pleasure?

But what right, I demand of my invisible critics, what right has anyone to ask a woman to restrain her femininity? She couldn't – if she would. It is as natural to her as fragrance to a flower. It gives her a sense of fulfillment. It fills her with a sense of power, intoxicating and irresistible. If she controls it wisely and well, both may be benefited and no one hurt, I argue unwisely.

Through the years I had learned that to me my marriage was the supreme value, all else gladly sacrificed to it. So my marriage obviously was doubly safe. Did anyone's marriage ever embrace all interests? Husbands never pretended it did. All men fulfilled themselves through their business or profession or art. They did not expect their wives to speak their language nor offer professional companionship. That they sought in their colleagues.

But where could a professional woman or artist find it? Wasn't it a curse to be a woman with even the semblance of a brain, with any interest in abstract ideas or in the arts or professions?

It is a classical situation, I remark to the woman in the mirror. The young artist or intellectual attracted to an older woman. Perhaps I can help him with his poetry, I rationalize. Then an impish tempter recalls the famous French middle-aged writer, George Sand, and her wonderful friendship with the young composer, Chopin. Also there was Mme. de Staël at Geneva – fat and forty – and her salon of famous young writers and artists. The fabulous Ninon de Lanclose surrounded by a score of French philosophers and intellectuals at the age of sixty – even eighty.

Well, but you are not famous, and not French. This is not France. This is conventional America. Customs differ in different countries. Even the most innocent actions are easily misinterpreted by family and friends and strangers.

But – but – but my mind protests, isn't it high time that women be accepted as human beings, not forever and always on the basis of sex only? Hasn't the time come when modern talented women can train modern men to impersonal professional friendships – *after* the women have trained themselves? It is something I've longed for all my life.

We meet again one evening in the public lounge while others are laughing and drinking in the cocktail room downstairs. We talk enthusiastically as usual. I remind myself that I must turn my eyes away. I must keep my voice cool and impersonal. I must maintain it all on a plane of merest friendship. I must save him and his family and my husband from any possible misunderstanding at whatever cost to my feminine vanity and intellectual pleasure. I must act as I do not feel – like an interested aunt.

So I speak of his marriage someday, of the type of girls he probably likes, judging by his physique and temperament. I force myself to leave early, to say good-by impersonally, to a hurt young face and bewildered young eyes, hoping he will thank me – someday – perhaps.

Time elapses. It is all over, I think. How could I have been so cruel? Have I blighted in the bud a tender beautiful thing?

Then he returns – chastened perhaps? This morning plays the piano in the deserted ballroom of the hotel. Popular – classical – modern. His touch is warm and vibrant, the sounds expressing the inexpressible, forging a bond between us deeper than thought, beyond feeling, above understanding. Abruptly he stops. Apparently it is too poignant, too disturbing to him also.

Then he discusses Stravinsky and modern music, the intellectual approach and appreciation of technique, the pure beauty of mathematics. I say it is the Apollonian theory of esthetics. I admit it is all legitimate, that modern art has dominated the West for years. But isn't it the very emphasis on the technical in the arts, the intellectual and materialistic, the exclusive worship of reason and mathematics and science in all other areas of contemporary life that have brought the world to the present danger of total annihilation?

Is not something else needed desperately and quickly before it is too late? The ethical and moral principles derived from the undiscovered self, also altruistic love and even spirituality? I say that I feel the need to cling to the Dionysian approach, to the psychological purification which Aristotle says is the function of art. I know from glorious experience that it is proffered by the classical artists. A purification which, for me, at least, seems beyond the power of intellectual modern art.

Finally, I ask, isn't the ideal perhaps a union of intellect and feeling, of the conscious mind and the collective unconscious whence arise the ethical, the esthetic, the truly creative, the altruistic, and the spiritual? He agrees, and together we wonder if the greatest artists do not always combine reason and intuition because they are Whole Men?

Then I announce that I am amazed that so young a person as he seems already to be whole, already appears to have united reason and logic with feeling and instinct; whereas I, in maturity, was obliged to undergo a long and painful process of death and rebirth to attain this wholeness. Is this younger generation, I wonder silently, born with the qualities my generation struggled for so painfully? Yet acquired characteristics are not inheritable. How then to explain this phenomenon?

Bursting with enthusiasm, he suddenly throws his arms up in the air. Exultantly he explains that for months his thoughts and feelings accumulate like separate unrelated pools of water. Then in one conversation like this he feels them all merging, flowing together freely and joyously in a powerful stream, a blessed release giving unity and meaning to the fragmented and the puzzling. And I too am bursting with happiness for him. I too as a writer know full well the magic and mystery of verbalization – how it can clarify and unify. And I too feel radiant with joy, with no desire now to flash my eyes. No urge to flaunt my dubious charms. And gone is the look of personal tenderness from his eyes. Instead I see a look of exaltation – but impersonal. I feel the air of exhilaration – but it is sexless. I too feel alive, alert, strangely fulfilled – my body and mind and emotions expanding in a radiant glow.

A meeting of minds has lifted us at last above the personal plane. No longer are we man and woman, but two minds, two disembodied personalities, living, conversing and having our beings on another plane. A plane of mental and esthetic rapport. It no longer matters whether we are male or female, young or old, British or American. The true and the beautiful are ageless and sexless and universal. The danger – if there ever was one – is passed.

The next morning he and his family depart for New York on their way to Britain. I gaze at his empty chair in the dining room. Now the dream of my life has materialized. At last a man has accepted a woman as a person, as a mind, a writer, unencumbered by awareness of her womanhood. Heaven knows, sex in its right time and place is a thing of beauty and a joy forever. But a woman does not want to be a sexual object at all times and places to every man she meets. She longs for intellectual companionship once in a while.

This young man and I shall never meet again. We are content. We have given each other an enduring gift.

After their departure I seek the solitude of the beach deserted on this rainy morning. I walk along the water's edge mile after mile. I feel elated – exalted

– not quite ecstatic. I feel renewed – refreshed – released from the bondage of everydayness – of thoughtless routine, of the prison of womanhood, of sex.

Intense and prolonged intellectual discussion lifted us to the plane of the impersonal, clarified our thoughts, illumined truths we considered beyond us.

Can the verbal pursuit of truth create Platonic "love" even between persons of different sex and different age or perhaps the same sex? Is reason really a means to the good life, as Plato contends? Is dialogue an instrument for a discovery of the self, or the total psyche? Or is Platonic love something altogether different?

Chapter 7

LOVE AND RACE

Then one day I read a highly stimulating, nourishing, satisfying book. It was one of those books that becomes a milestone in one's intellectual life. It was a scholarly comprehensive study of mysticism. It particularly excited me because the author approached the mystical experience from several directions. From the rational scientific viewpoint of psychology, the philosophical, the spontaneous and poetic, and from that of various religions. He displayed warm insight into the mysticism of Hinduism, Buddhism, Islam, Judaism, and Christianity – though not of Taoism.

He maintained that the *only* religious experience was the mystical. Without mysticism there would be no religious systems. There would be nothing but ethics – if that. All the founders of great religious systems were great mystics – Buddha, Moses, Mohammed, Jesus and Paul and undoubtedly the early unrecorded Hindus – certainly Krishna and Ramakrishna. Psychologically the spiritual experience was the discovery of the personal self and the greater impersonal Self.

His book recommended a renewal of the individual spiritual experience as the best way to prevent the world from destroying itself senselessly. It also urgently recommended a synthesis of the various disciplines of science, art, religion, and philosophy and an end to dangerous specialization.

On the dust jacket appeared enthusiastic endorsements of his book by world-famous scientists, philosophers, psychologists, poets, and theologians of different organized systems.

This profoundly understanding book caused a great warmth to expand within me. Only half a dozen books in a lifetime so stimulate, so nourish, so move one as this book now demonstrated its power to do. It said the things I wanted to hear said, things I had vaguely thought or felt but for the utterance of which I lacked the courage or the knowledge.

I wrote him a letter. He invited me to tea. And so we met for the first time at his beautiful private house.

A maid admitted me. First I met his wife – a quiet, dignified middle-aged woman. She led me up to his study, introduced me and bade the maid bring tea then left us alone.

He was a very elderly man with beautiful white hair and a long white beard. He looked rather like Tagore, a sage or prophet. His face was delicate and sensitive. His skin olive, his eyes brilliantly black and penetrating.

We talked avidly for an hour, breathlessly for another hour. We forgot the teacups cooling on the table beside us, grew oblivious to all the shelves of books surrounding us.

We dispensed with the usual polite preliminaries, with discussion of families and work. We plunged immediately down to the hidden depths of the human mind, probed to the concealed foundations of each other's personalities.

I spoke again with ardent admiration of his scholarly book. He inquired further concerning my writings on psychology and religion. I suggested that he and I were travelling toward the same goal – he taking the high road of scholarship and I the low road of personal experience.

"And you may get there afore me," he murmured smiling.

"Oh, no, you so obviously already have arrived at full self-realization of your potentialities for the good, the true and the beautiful."

We talked on and on about philosophy and psychology, religion and art, about the obstacles to self-actualization. His erudition far surpassed my feeble efforts. It stunned me with admiration. His vocabulary dazzled me. I revered him as a possible intellectual *guru*, or my Socratic teacher. Frankly I did not understand half of his statements at that time.

I asked endless questions. He gave brilliant answers that often required me to think for myself more deeply. He asked me provocative questions. He did not lecture me as many a scholar might have been tempted to do. He listened, actually listened, understood, and responded warmly and clearly.

As we talked on and on I felt as if a cool wind were blowing through my mind – purifying it – purifying me. All pettiness fell away, everything personal sank out of sight. Age did not matter. Sex was unimportant.

We were no longer man and woman, merely two minds conversing, stepping like demi-gods from peak to peak of abstract ideas. Words, thoughts, flowed forth without effort. My sentences, my logic, my questions surpassed everything of which I had believed myself capable. He lifted me to new intellectual heights, raised me up to his erudite level. All the best buried deep in my mind and nature were liberated. This rare heady air of dialectic was intoxicating.

Finally, reluctantly, I tore myself away. I could easily have talked all night – so could he, I imagined. When we clasped hands to say good-by I was dizzy, exhilarated. When I emerged on the street I was deliciously disoriented as to place and time. I did not know which direction was which, whether I was walking North or South or West. I went the wrong way three times. Then I floated on down the street, my feet scarcely touching the pavement. I did not even know my destination. I did not care. I had found a person with whom I could be my utterly, utterly honest, deeper, better self without reservations, without caution.

Now I had a friend who could read my deepest thoughts, respond to my most poetic experiences. One who commented on my psychological insights with greater understanding than I myself possessed. The kind of friend I had longed for, hoped for, daydreamed of for years.

To carry on a prolonged, profound intellectual conversation with a scholar was a rarity for which I was starved. It was too good to be true but it was true! Younger scholars were too much under the pressure of their professional writing to have time for laymen. But now my light feet and laughing blood, my dancing mind and bursting heart proved I was admissible to the sanctum of the scholars.

I sailed on down the street mile after mile unaware of distance, oblivious to time, impervious to fatigue.

Days passed . . .

We met again. I was allowed to invite him to my club as my guest at lunch. We compared experiences in the difficult realm of human relationship and techniques of dealing with the inevitable problems. We discussed the role of religion in guiding daily behavior. Apparently he had traversed all the stages in actualization of the potentialities buried in his deeper unconscious. His conscious mind was brilliant, he was a whole man.

His international connections made it possible for him to contribute effectively toward the good society of tomorrow in a way I was unable to do.

Then we discussed abstract matters. He emphasized first principles. Again we asked each other searching questions. And again the dialogue was intoxicating.

He referred to Plato and Socrates as if I were as familiar with them as he was. As yet I possessed only a vague smattering. He commented on the wonder of recollecting universals, communicating with the Supreme Good, how it set one on the high road toward the good life.

Through Socratic dialogue, he commented, one was able to recapture some of the purity, goodness, and wisdom which Plato contended we all possessed before birth but lost on arrival on earth. I was too excited to comprehend fully. All I knew at the moment was that never had my mind and heart, spirit and body felt so cleansed, so purified. Never had I felt so wise, or so loving – toward the whole human race.

Socrates postulated in the *Symposium*, he said, that one may love first the beautiful face, then the beautiful soul, then beautiful ideas, and at last love beauty itself – absolute and everlasting – and it is love that lifts one to this high spiritual plane. This was what was meant by Platonic love, he said.

I did not understand such profundity intellectually at this time. I felt, however, that I experienced a joy, a perceptivity, a love of mankind that actually transformed my entire character – all stimulated by dialogue.

Finally we returned to his house. He invited me upstairs to see a certain book which had been dedicated to him by a famous international political figure. And to say good-by for a several months period.

The next day he was flying to the Middle East to deliver a series of lectures at various universities. He would discuss the influence that might be exerted on international crises by a possible universal religion composed of several disciplines. The best principles of all religions, also Plato's philosophy, the new trend in psychology toward individual self-development and science.

He gazed at me strangely and remarked that he was returning to his ancestral roots. Did this mean he was Turkish or Arabian or Jewish? Judging by his appearance, I thought he looked more Hindu. His name was no clew. I did not know his race. I did not care. I hoped I had risen above the prejudices of childhood even though such a malady penetrates one's very bones.

I had been raised to be a Southern "lady" in the traditions of an aristocratic class – a class all of whose ancestors had descended from the old plantation culture and mores. I was brought up by my antebellum-minded, maternal grandmother on stories of our Virginia forbears – Martha Washington, Governor Spotswood of Williamsburg and others.

When I was a child in the South, it was forbidden to allow a Catholic or Jew in one's home or to enter theirs. Negroes were accepted only as servants but frequently loved as individuals. We were imbued with prejudice against all other classes and races and religions, taught that white Protestant aristocratic Southerners were superior in blood and breeding to all other people on the face of the earth, too proud even to bend a knee to the Queen of England. Once I had been invited by an English friend to meet the Prince of Wales. I declined because I refused to curtsey to anyone on earth.

Today, however, I fondly believed that my initial awakening to the self had aroused me to the humanity of all peoples of all countries. I believed I judged others by their character and their mentality. Consequently I did not care from what race my newfound friend derived.

As I rose to leave he showed me the flyleaf of the book dedicated to him. The inscription read, "To my valued friend who began as a Jew and developed into a world citizen."

So he was Jewish. A few years ago I undoubtedly would have felt a sense of shock in spite of myself. Today I felt nothing – blessedly nothing. It was as if he had said it is Wednesday instead of Tuesday. For today had we not tapped the well-spring of the human mind, forged an indestructible bond beyond our own comprehension – a bond of kinship, of mental rapport, respect and affection? Not a bond between a man and a woman, not between two races but between two human beings.

Nothing could shake it, not on my side at least. And surely so great and wise a man could not entertain prejudice against any other race, or against me as a Gentile.

Previously I had imagined that I had shed all racial prejudices when the source of my love of mankind, the collective unconscious, had been aroused. Today I knew beyond the shadow of a doubt that any lingering shred had disappeared forever. I felt it was like a wonderful baptism, a moment of freedom from a lifelong burden of prejudice. He sensed my feeling. Rapport vibrated in the air between us like warm light. I felt his reservations about me as a Gentile melt away.

At the street door he grasped both my arms in his hands and looked deep into my eyes. It was a long poignant embrace, unlike anything I ever had experienced in my life. All the sorrows and suffering of the Jewish people for centuries seemed to flow through his arms and hands, his whole being, and shine in the unshed tears his eyes. All the compassion and love of which the Gentile race is capable seemed to rise in my heart, in the tears in my eyes.

And then I knew where there is a deep-felt love of mankind there is no difference of race.

But I did not yet understand that dialectic could arouse love of an individual, of universals, of mankind.

Chapter 8

CLIFFS

One perfect summer day I joined a group of warm, friendly Southern visitors who were taking a guided tour around Martha's Vineyard.

Finally at the end of the island we dutifully alighted from the car as directed by our bored and taciturn driver. Indifferently we walked up the slight incline he indicated. Nonchalantly we followed a sandy path toward the grassy green top of a promontory that promised nothing. Nothing more than another sand dune among those that are so commonplace, plentiful and unexciting around the shores of this island where Martha found her famous vineyard near the Cape of the Cod.

But the shock of that unexpected view from that unexpected headland of Gay Head Cliffs, to eyes unprepared and senses unattuned, stopped our speech, stopped our feet, stopped our breath. For there far below us, there a hundred feet below us, lay the open sea – incredibly, achingly blue. A dark, rich, indescribable blue – with scattered purple patches creating patterns beneath its transparency.

Motionless we stood on that high point projecting itself far out into the endless Atlantic like the prow of some mighty ship riding high above the ocean. Speechless we stood at land's end, at the edge of the world, staring incredulously at the intense blueness, at the vast stretches of unending water on three sides of us.

It stretched mile after mile beyond sight of land, beyond sight of man, clear to unseen Spain and other unknown countries.

We stood staring with all our senses at a summer sea, calm as a Cape Cod pond. Its mighty endless surface lay unbroken for once by so much as a small truant white wave. Can the Atlantic be so pacific I wondered? Is the Atlantic capable of so vivid, so brilliant a blue? Is any ocean capable of so profound, so provocative a color unaided by modern man's technicolor technology? It was a fabulous blue, suggestive of some fantastic world filled with buried treasures of feeling and thought and insight as yet unfathomed by us.

Finally my eyes were drawn away from the hypnotic water. And there along the shore – standing triumphantly against the sea, thrusting its white palisades proudly toward the blue sky for hundreds after hundreds of feet – rose a great indomitable white cliff. Its gay head was topped by green grasses, its base caressed gently by the ever moving, white sea foam. And across its beautiful face (so startlingly white in the strong summer sunlight) not marring its beauty but strangely enhancing it – was a wide vertical band of red clay, another band of yellow ochre, and another of white clay to make a pattern repeated over and over. Had some Gargantuan painter amused himself with a gigantic brush in some playful hour centuries ago?

And the air! That pure transparent blueness, that incredibly clear, cool nothingness filling the vast blue void above the ocean, before the face of the gaily striped cliff – what was happening to it? Was it actually vibrating? Was something invisible in it beginning to dance visibly as surely as the million silver "bees" I had seen daily dancing across the surface of the sunlit sea? Or was it merely the unaccustomed height making me deliciously dizzy? Or the unusual vastness and depth of space that agitated me so strangely?

Suddenly, behind all that blueness and whiteness, beyond all that space and those cliffs, within all that rare blue atmosphere, I sensed a mystery surging forward to speak to me. Would it impart some cosmic secret directly? Would it render ultimate reality visible? I waited breathless . . .

As I gazed at these incredible colored cliffs, they too seemed to move, to vibrate, every atom dancing furiously. It was incredible! Never before in my life had I beheld such a phenomenon. What did it mean? Cold chills ran over my spine. My hair threatened to rise on end. Was some vast secret of nature – a scientific truth even – on the verge of revealing itself to me?

But quickly jealous logic slammed the door on this encounter. That friendly-enemy, my conscious mind, must be vanquished anew each time the unconscious strove to speak to me. Why must reason, the male principle of the universe, strive always to dominate the female principle, intuition?

So the tantalizing illusion receded – if it was an illusion – which it wasn't. For did I not see the mystery and then see it vanish as surely as I had seen the silver "bees" of sunlight vanish from their shining path on the surface of the sea when a dark cloud passed across the face of the sun? The magic was gone now. Nothing remained except visible beauty – that half-open door to the unknown.

As we returned to the car I remained silent, for a change. I was thinking. Was Plato right when he said beauty was a window that reveals the true to us? But what truth?

I did not trust my own experience until much later I happened to read an article by a scientist. It said that the scientists today had discovered that all matter – even solid rock – is atomic energy and the atoms *move unceasingly* – though the naked eye cannot perceive it!

Was it possible that the beauty of Gay Head Cliffs and the summer sea had so stimulated my senses they had opened the door to knowledge of universals? Had I been on the verge of "recollecting" a great scientific truth as the Hindus have discovered they are able to do when their minds are operating on a certain high plane and they are sufficiently receptive?

Was it possible that this was what Plato meant by "recollection" of those Eternal Ideas we all have known before birth and have forgotten? This was a staggering experience, an exciting verification that I might be able to make contact with such Ideas.

But I must learn from my own failures. Why, why, had my conscious mind cheated me and slammed the doors of perception too soon? Was it because my reason was in the habit dominating me? Was this predestined by my type of physique? But no, I was not the extreme, intellectual, ectomorphic-cerebrotonic type of which William Sheldon writes? I was a 4-4-4 – that is, the type which is equally composed of ectomorphy, mesomorphy and endomorphy.

Then was I a victim of our Western culture that exalts reason, a tragedy for which Plato himself and most of the philosophers who followed him were to blame? To counteract the influence of my culture I must learn to relax more physically, to become oblivious to the presence of other people. I must learn to trust myself more. Did not Plato himself say that the senses could be an avenue to remembered Ideas? Were those forgotten ideas in the unconscious or the conscious mind? Did Plato elucidate this point? Did Jung explain it by comparing his archetypes to Plato's Ideas?

The whole point of the Socratic dialogues my Jewish friend had tried to explain to me, was that the use of reason and logic and the dialectical method could reveal universal truths. Did the conscious mind then perform two functions? And did this forgotten knowledge derive from the currents surging through the universe as Plato seemed to say or were they buried in our own psyche as Jung and Maslow maintained? Sometime, somehow, I must endeavor to clarify these matters.

Whatever the explanation, the experience today remained incredible, indescribable and thrilling – this unfinished encounter. I should remember it as long as I lived.

Perhaps next time this recipient might keep the doors of perception open longer as William Blake suggests. Then I might be more worthy of such a "recollection" of Eternal Ideas – I hoped!

Chapter 9

LOVE AND COLOR

One day not long ago I interviewed a new cook and something wonderful happened then and afterward.

A dozen times over the years I had struggled with my problem. If you are a woman who takes pride in running her house and yet wants to do creative work, you are faced with an almost insoluble dilemma.

While daydreaming of a domestic Utopia that never would materialize, I often exchanged my actual experiences with other women who also had had a procession of difficult women marching through their kitchens.

As employers we struggled to train our cooks to our ways, or adjust ourselves to theirs, or even to try to help them. Usually we retreated from the field of battle frustrated and defeated. Middle-aged woman cannot change – or will not.

We struggled with cooks so honest you could trust your life to them but whose penetrating voice and dominating personality left you battered and beaten, your self-respect trailing in the dust; with cooks who were shiningly, compulsively clean but could not cook; with cooks who cooked as expertly as a caterer but had one foot in a mental institution; with those who were neat as a nurse but cold and aloof; with those with heavenly sweet dispositions but during whose reign handkerchiefs and stockings and perfume disappeared.

And nowadays of course there were the saddest cases of all – the unemployables – the secret drug addicts, alcoholics who, I thought, merely had high blood pressure, and the extreme neurotics too mentally sick to hold a job in a factory for a week. Only a sympathetic or desperate housewife would tolerate them. Several times I endeavored to help such cases. I tried no amateur therapy but I hoped kindness and patience and understanding might ease their burdens. It was never sufficient.

So finally I had abandoned all hope of ever again finding a cook who was competent, possessed a pleasant disposition, clean habits, a normal personality and was honest. Then without warning the pearl without price appeared. That household gem, for which every woman hopes and waits, materialized at long last.

As I interviewed Anna that first day, our rapport was instantaneous. She was a middle-aged Negress, rather plump, with beautiful golden brown skin, a fine face and honest eyes. The difference in the color of our skins, of education and none, of religions (she was a Catholic) dissolved in a stream of instinctive harmony.

After a few days I felt intense respect for Anna's natural dignity, her pride in her work, her native intelligence and admirable skill as a cook *and* waitress. Most expert cooks refused to wait on table even for a family of two.

Every morning when I awakened my first thought was of her. No longer was there that seemingly inevitable conflict between employee and employer. No longer a household atmosphere filled with covert hostility. No longer those electric vibrations emanating from too dominant a personality, bombarding me all day every day in every part of my own house. They were conspicuous now by their blessed absence. Formerly they struck me physically like a rain of small stinging bullets – no less disturbing for being invisible.

No longer did I feel the employer's sense of continuous intrusion on her personal and family privacy by an alien personality. No longer must I censor all my conversations over the telephone, or conceal my check books and private letters.

This cook respected my privacy. She was wonderfully self-contained. She did not project her personality all over the house or attempt to dominate us like a surly sergeant.

What joy it was each day to relax in a warm friendly atmosphere, so real it was as tangible as a warm bath. This was what I had always striven for. Could it be that I too had formerly been unconsciously hostile? Could it be that my recent efforts to awaken the good in myself were now in operation?

Every day I said to myself, thank heaven for Anna. No longer are unavoidable minor problems inflated into major catastrophes as with other cooks. No longer are my suggestions interpreted as personal denigration as heretofore but now are discussed amicably and impersonally, the problems solved to the satisfaction of both of us. Now my wishes are carried out, even anticipated almost to the point of clairvoyance.

One morning after breakfast I went into the kitchen as usual to discuss the menu for the day. Later as I sat at the desk in the living room with my hand on the telephone to order the groceries, I paused and sighed in content. Oh, the pleasure, the satisfying harmony of two persons working together with emphasis on the job not on personal relations. Women workers too often, I discovered, consider every suggestion or criticism of their work as a personal affront. Men workers, yard men, painters and plumbers, understand your remarks as a discussion of the work – which it is. One of two must lead and direct in any work project. This cook was as aware of her employer's interests and rights as her own. I hoped I was equally aware of hers.

My husband now laid down his morning paper and stopped at the desk to say good-by and I told him what a blessed relief it was to have someone living in our house who slipped as easily into our household routine as if she had been living with us ten years. Instead of requiring a year to begin to commence to start to adjust herself. How restful to have a maid who remembered instructions given once instead of requiring their repetition twenty futile times as with the past impedimenta. He agreed.

He kissed me good-by and I sat there thinking: how incredibly soothing to be no longer assaulted hourly by unnecessary domestic noises. No more doors slamming, pans banging, heavy footsteps thudding on the back stairs all day long and loud voices talking to tradesmen. Experience had shown me that the most common type among cooks was the noisy, masculine, somatotonic mesomorph whose nature it was to dominate others, who loved to combat obstacles – and manufacture them.

No more shoes dropping like a cannonball on the floor above my bedroom. Heretofore the thick rugs placed strategically even on the closet floor of the cook's bedroom had been useless. For years I had been startled from my precious, hard-sought sleep night and morning.

Now I watched the cook clearing off the breakfast table. The movements of this Negro woman were quiet yet efficient with no loss of motion. She seemed in complete harmony with her job and with the things she handled. I felt intensely grateful to her for her comings and goings about the house with the noiseless feline assurance and self-containment of one of my beloved cats. It was a natural instinctive quietness.

I smiled to myself. What a relief to meet with no resentment about the unique habits of the master of the house and consequently no feeling by the husband that the cook's convenience took precedence over his comfort, as had been known to happen.

Every night when we sat down to dinner I carried on a pleasant little dialogue with myself (for I had learned that men do not care to hear too much about domestic affairs): when you yourself spend a hard day of work, mental or creative, or whatever, then any battle-scarred veteran of internecine household wars knows the joy of sitting down to a good hot dinner. One that is properly cooked and properly served by a maid who evinces pride in work, not resentment against the whole world in general and her employers in particular.

No longer, I say to myself, do your stomach muscles tighten in annoyance as they did at the stumbling and bumbling of her predecessors, or your digestion rebel at unappetizing food, or your nerves tense up in the hostile atmosphere. Now you eat with pleasure and gratitude. You double your enjoyment by watching your husband's enjoyment of the delicious food selected and prepared according to his preferences. You even laugh at his often repeated humorous sallies.

Nowadays if a dish is served that is not quite fit for a queen, you eat it with relish and forgiveness. The intent to please, the desire for perfection was there. And every successful dish receives the high praise it so well deserves the minute you rise from table. After such a meal by such a cook you leave the dining room feeling – for half an hour at least – that you love the whole world and everybody in it – especially your good cook.

Thus there evolved a new and wonderful human relationship. The kind that should be inherent in such situations. The kind I had hoped for, worked for, for many futile years. Not merely the usual lukewarm relationship of friendly enemies between mistress and maid; not merely the usual armed truce of employer and employee, not even the ambivalent neurotic relation of the mother-child I had so often observed where food and feeding was concerned but the mature relationship of two affectionate adult human beings.

Every blessed day I asked myself, is there anything so restful, so deeply satisfying as a harmonious household, freeing your thought for other activities, soothing your nerves, allowing your creativity for a book or whatever – to function freely, to flow unperturbed and undisturbed?

As the months passed I found myself gladly making sacrifices for this Negress of the kind I never thought I would make for anyone but my family. I found myself unconsciously thinking of her welfare before my own. And it filled me with a strange new pleasure. We understood each other, we laughed together often, and it was obvious that honor and honesty and integrity do not depend on color or race or education or social position.

It was a new attitude for me, a white woman who as a child was brought up in the race-conscious South, taught by my antebellum grandmother, whose father had owned slaves, to be kind to the Negroes who worked for us, to treat them as children never as adults, and to maintain an unbridgeable chasm between the races – all races except the white, aristocratic Protestant her Southerners of "good" family and breeding – ones who believed they followed the precepts of Jesus to love their neighbors as themselves.

Gradually there awakened in me a kind of blind devotion to this Negro woman of such fine character. I grew stronger because I knew she might need me someday. I knew I would protect – with my life it need be – a weaker person like this who might not be able to protect herself against the cruelty of those with unreasonable race prejudice.

I felt eternally grateful to her because she had enriched my life with an experience of profound affection – given and received.

I saw that when the best in one person flows forth, it calls forth the best in the other person – white or black. Love flowed forth from her to me and awakened love in me for her. Or was it the other way around?

And I saw that love knows no color barrier.

Then I put my face in my hands and wept unshed tears. If only to God the means could be found to arouse the love of all mankind dormant in all men – in varying degree! Nothing else could cure the prejudiced, hating citizens and the power-mad, war-making political rulers. Nothing had stopped hate or world wars or nuclear bombs or the ruinous armament race. Everything had failed.

In the name of obvious common sense and self-preservation, was not the most vital movement all thoughtful men of good will should dedicate selves to today before it was forever too late – too late – finding scientific infallible ways to arouse the love of mankind latent in all men? Teaching all men how to release the self through psychotherapy for the healthy unconscious, or Hindu, Buddhist, Zen or revitalized Christian practises, or by the rare means of Platonic philosophy or a synthesis of them all?

Chapter 10

AFTER A SWIM

We went to the Bahamas for a winter vacation. A former motion picture star sat on the far side of the dining room, at our seaside hotel. This morning she sat alone at breakfast as she did every day.

She had not appeared in a film for many years. When I was a girl I often went to see her. The stories were stereotyped, she could not act but she had been beautiful, had an exquisite figure, wore the loveliest clothes in Hollywood. Her voice had been warm, her personality appealing. She had truly merited the term glamorous.

Today I watched her as she left the dining room. She was short and fat and middle aged, dressed like a school girl, with dyed blonde hair. She was usually alone and her face was bitter. She possessed plenty of money it seemed. She roared about the island in a fabulously expensive, foreign racing car and played cards for high stakes all night, so the rumor went.

How sad it must be, I said to my husband, to have basked in the limelight for years and then to be completely neglected. Undoubtedly she looked so bitter for that reason. My heart went out to her. But she appeared unapproachable. Probably her arrogant manner was assumed for self protection because no one showered her with compliments anymore. Sometime, I promised myself, I would tell her how much I used to enjoy seeing her films. All artists liked recognition from their public, didn't they? And better now than never.

Later that morning I noticed her sitting alone on the beach near me. I strolled by and called her name. She did not answer. I called again. She rose quickly, gathered up her paraphernalia and said angrily with her back to me, "I'm late now and besides I am very busy."

I tried to laugh. "Oh, I just wanted to tell you how much I used to enjoy your pictures."

She strode off without a word. I stood there too stunned, hurt, and angry to move. Finally I turned, ran into the ocean and began to swim with all the vigor at my command. I swam on and on as if I never wanted to stop.

This tropical sea around the Bahamas was unlike any other I had ever known. It was a glorious jade green, a ravishing color. It was not warm yet not cold. It was rich and smooth like green cream. It felt delicious on your skin. It had a personality all its own. It rolled over you and around you, caressing you like some fabulous Circe of the sea.

Finally I rose from the ocean, cold, dripping, panting – and stumbled shoreward through the shallow water. Reluctant to leave its embrace, I lingered and stared down at my white feet in the transparent green water. I lingered and watched the white foam curling and purling enticingly around my ankles.

Then I dashed up the beach and sank gratefully onto the sun-hot sand. I lay there, cold and wet and weary. Suddenly a great rush of warmth flooded me, bathed me internally, my skin tingling with delight as if every inch of it had been kissed. My heart pounded mightily from my long play with the waves, my blood laughed in my veins.

After today's swim, more than ever before, a slow, sweet lassitude stole through my flesh as if I had been thoroughly loved for hour after passionate hour. I stared sleepily, stupidly at the moving water. The monotonous motion of the tireless waves actually hypnotized me. My restless brain sank happily to rest like a bird in its nest. Now my straining nerves lay luxuriously in a warm bed of peace. My muscles grew deliciously heavy. I never wanted to move again. I never wanted to think again as long as I lived.

As I lay on the hot sand, under the hot sun, with the green and white waves laughing at my feet, my body and mind melted and fused into one. Immersed in nature, my spirit flowed out into the sun and sand and sea and their essence seemed to flow back into me. We were one.

Now I was no longer I. I lost my personal identity. Like sunshine I was diffused in the universe as if partaking of the sun's purity, its power. I was united with some cosmic something – irrevocably – forever for one, long, delectable moment. This was the peak of perfection, all my doubts dispelled, all my hungers satisfied, all my searching ended – forever – for a brief while.

This was the moment of truth. I knew harmony was attained – harmony of body and mind, of myself and nature, my spirit and the creative principle of the universe. And through so simple a thing as swimming in the sea. I knew that our muscles, our bodies could transform us into our other, our better self. How could any religion renounce the blessed human body and its natural fulfillment and its spiritual function?

Finally, I rose from the beach cleansed internally and externally and walked slowly toward the hotel. At the top of the high steps I turned and took one last, loving look at the sea. And I laughed to myself at the follies of mankind in general – reported so urgently in the morning paper – and the foibles of the individual – like the unhappy motion picture star. Before my swim they had distressed me. Now such things diminished in size and impact. Were they not like minute grains of sand compared to the endlessness of the rich blue sky, the vast moving waters, the hot reassurance of the yellow earth under my bare, grateful feet, and the cool touch of the invisible wind as it ran its willful fingers through my hair?

Now my own pettiness and pride, irritation and egotism, like unwanted brown seaweed left on the sand, seemed to be washed away by the universal tide. I loved the whole world and everything and everybody in it. A gentle wave of compassion for the dethroned motion picture star washed through me, as I went up in the elevator to my room.

Without waiting to dress I sat down and wrote a note to her embodying all the honest compliments I could possibly muster.

Then I sat there motionless in a quiet kind of awe. At last I was beginning to understand Jesus and why he urged man to "do good to those that hate you." It was not impossible or unnatural as I had always assumed but natural after one had attained a certain difficult but glowing state of mind – not necessarily by therapy or religious exercises or dialogue but sometimes through so simple a means as the rhythmic motion of one's own muscles in swimming! It was simply incredible – until one experienced this beautiful truth.

Chapter 11

MUSIC

Night after night my husband and I sat in our living room listening to the classical music coming periodically over the radio by frequency modulation. We alternated it with the reading of our current books.

We listened to solo instruments, to concertos, symphonies, and opera. All brought delight. All did not serve as a means to purge and purify me, or prompt me to altruistic action.

We abandoned ourselves to the great concertos of Brahms, Beethoven and others. Serkin, Harrowitz or Rubenstein at the piano played with almost superhuman brilliance and skill.

The music of the piano seemed to me like a mountain brook, pure and sparkling, leaping and laughing, flowing serenely, then sadly, running along the whole network of my nervous system like healing waters, the treble reviving forgotten aspirations, the low resonance of the bass throbbing against the very core of my being stirring it from long sleep and apathy.

Only that music for the piano which was created by the best composers, and played by the most loving interpreters seems capable of satisfying your deepest hunger. Hunger for what I scarcely knew. The piano was my favorite instrument yet its music, however delightful, seldom prompted me to ethical, loving or creative action afterward. Why were concertos never so effective a catharsis as opera and symphonies?

On Saturday afternoons I listened alone to "live" opera coming direct from the Metropolitan Opera House in New York. My husband enjoyed playing bridge at his club on those afternoons. Then on Sunday nights we listened to opera records over the radio together.

Often as I sat there immersed in music, I thought, surely no musical instrument on earth can equal the emotional power of the human voice. All others are mere wood, wire and metal. The voice unlocks a dark mysterious realm of sorrow and joy and beauty, unlocks the deeper recesses of the listening heart.

Unashamedly we preferred all the old masterpieces. They possessed a magic the lesser or newer opera did not. The world's greatest opera poured from that small brown box between us – Verdi, Mozart, Puccini, Gounod, Massenet, Saint-Saens and others. The voices of the finest sopranos today – Tebaldi, Callas, de los Angeles, Sutherland, were so supernally pure they purified the listener.

When fine Italian tenors like Tagliavini or del Monaco sang the love arias, such beauty of sound melted my bones, seduced my will, ravished my senses, satisfied a deep instinctual need as completely as sex – almost. There was a finality about such perfection. It left me feeling that I too had participated in perfection, attained my goal – briefly.

Often the particular became universal and it was not a woman in a music drama who was suffering and rejoicing. It was I myself. This vicarious suffering and joy purified and fulfilled me strangely.

Some of these operas were positively overwhelming when passionately sung and played. *Aida* with Verdi's magnificent music and the incomparable Tebaldi singing the mysteriously beautiful aria, O patria mia. And the duet of the two lovers, Aida and Ramses, in *duct terra addio*, uniting them in love and death, freeing them from earth, bathed you in music that suggested the peace of eternity.

Somehow Othello singing of his jealousy, love and anguish personified the emotions of all young husbands and Pagliacci wrung your heart with the tragedy of the old husband with the young wife.

In *La Boheme, Manon, Tosca,* and *Butterfly,* the music, the voices, expressed almost unbearable human yearnings as it never before had been expressed. The exquisite sweetness of love was so poignant, so painful, it deepened all the love I had ever felt. It did more. It allowed me to participate in their love and anguish thereby enriching, enlarging, fulfilling me to my ultimate capacity.

These operas searched out the remotest corners of your heart. You felt that of all life's experiences surely nothing was so desirable, so evocative of our deepest feelings as romantic love – especially if it was hopeless.

As we listened to Lily Pons in *Lakme* and *Lucia de Lammamoor* the brilliant display of coloratura was uncanny. It was frighteningly beautiful as if she were a creature from another planet. It possessed such superhuman and unearthly purity it left me feeling un-worthy, humble, and all too human.

The dramatic music of the opera, the superb singing, like an ocean of sound, touched the barren shores of everyday life, bathed our desiccated days, filled all emptiness, flooded the thirsty world with colorful drama and high passion. Like waves of the sea it ebbed and flowed, racing, laughing, crying, touching dead griefs to new life, awakening old loves, deepening present ones, promising us the impossible. It flung up shining insights like sea foam revealing some of the profoundest depths of life.

After being immersed in opera for several hours, I rose up like a bather from the sea returning to the hard reality of the shore. I felt exhilarated, yet calmed, even ennobled. All weariness vanished, all worry washed away, all vague fears of unknown forces left behind me forever – for a few more hours.

But oh, the symphonies! We listened to the most beautiful symphonies by the world's greatest composers conducted by the finest conductors – Toscanini, Koussevitzky and others. I lay back in my reclining chair, closed my eyes, and – thoughtless – let the glorious sounds ravish me at their will. Beethoven's *Fifth in C Minor* with its unsurpassed exaltation in the fourth movement, and the joyousness of the *Ninth in D Minor*. All the power and passion of Beethoven in the Seventh and the noble *Eroica*. The grandeur of Brahms and his sublime *First Symphony in C Minor* and the sophistication of *No. 4 in E Minor*. Hayden, Cesar Franck and Saint-Säens were also enriching. And the lyric melancholy of Tchaikovsky filled me with mysterious happiness.

At times the majesty and beauty and power of the symphonic orchestra was almost unendurable.

The sweeping crescendo of the strings so piercingly sweet, so pure, aspiring to such impossible ideals, it carried you up to unbearable heights of hope. The cellos, warm and masculine and passionate like a voluptuous caress, touched the very womb impregnating it to give birth to you knew not what new wonders. The haunting melancholy of the English horn, especially in Cesär Franck, awakened the sweetness of old unrealized ambitions.

The occasional plaintive notes of the wood-winds, like the call of a lonely mourning dove, so poignant they pierced your heart with the sorrows of all the world. The low throb of the drums aroused unsuspected primitive power. And the triumphant blare of the brass stimulated you to new defiance, courage, and strength.

Separately the different instruments aroused different emotions. But when a hundred instruments soared together as one instrument under the baton of a great maestro, I too became unified and whole. My body and mind, feeling and spirit, and all my senses became a veritable living symphony in harmony with the music of the spheres.

But not Wagner's opera! We could not bear to hear Wagner sing – except *Isolde* with Kirsten Flagstad. The shouting voices seemed to be in discord with the glory of the instrumental music. My ears always tried vainly to strain out the voices and retain only the music but they drowned it out. Wagner in concert form we both loved passionately. It seemed sensuous and sublime simultaneously.

And the yearning in the *Prelude* to *Tristan and Isolde*, the ecstasy of love in the *Liebesnächt*, and the ecstasy of grief in the *Liebstod* – all seemed to me to be a mystical expression of the love of all men and women everywhere with its magic and sweetness, pain and sadness. It was human love raised to the highest degree possible. This music left me exalted, fulfilled, exhausted.

And the Valkyrie – their unearthly cry was positively electrifying. The music of the whole *Ring* cycle was unlike any other music I had ever heard. The effect was not that of man-made music but of some cosmic force. You felt as if the ancient gods walked the earth in Wagner's music quite apart from its story of them. It touched a region untouched by any other music, flooding the deeper unconscious. This was the region of the human psyche from which were born our racial myths and gods and heroes exactly as Jung's psychology claimed. Wagner's music penetrated to the origin of life, to the final depths. It was like those rare occasions when the phallus actually caresses the womb – than which there is no profounder experience possible to woman. Wagner's music touched the very roots of life as Beethoven revealed to us the ideal flower blossoming from it.

Night after night as we sat listening to all this unsurpassed classical music, the flood of beautiful sound was an inner baptism purifying and elevating. It invaded all my senses, melting the usual barriers right away. It broke the dam of consciousness, opened the sluice gates of the deeper, purer self.

Sometimes I felt myself to be a stagnant reservoir, the music flowing through me like a shining river, like a spring freshet, carrying away all the sediment of pettiness and selfishness, all the impure beliefs that the other person was always wrong and I was always right, cleared up muddy personal situations, leaving me purged, my own errors transparent as never before, my fresh course of action clear for the first time.

It also freed hidden currents too long damned up within me. It allowed them to flow out freely – my desire to create, love of mankind, stronger ethical values, intuitive insights into the meaning of life, deeper perception of beauty, spiritual yearning, urges to altruistic action. In short, it released those warm hidden currents in the collective unconscious common to the whole human race.

Occasionally it seemed to fill the reservoir to capacity with a mysterious flood of serenity, peace, and unearthly beauty. At times it did more. Music became a "path to Being." I felt ecstatic.

Invariably after a particularly fine piece of music my husband and I looked at each other in silence, our eyes shining with unshed tears, the magic mood too wonderful to destroy with words. Our enjoyment together of such profound music forged a new bond between us.

For hours afterward I longed to be of service to him. Sometimes I was immediately. I became more amenable to his suggestions which opposed mine, I gladly did things his way. It restored or increased the harmony between us. Our only quarrel was our effort to give precedence to the other's wishes. Our lives floated along on a high tide of tenderness that surely was the essence of the marriage relation. Such sublime music even made me eager to sacrifice myself for the human race, for friends and acquaintances. And if some small emergency arose in the next few hours I did so.

Often this musical flood unexpectedly uncovered ideas like submerged rocks. Even while the symphony was playing, it aroused my urge to write until it was irresistible. I took up the notebook always kept on my reading table and permitted any words that so desired to flow onto the paper. The profoundest thoughts frequently appeared then. Effortlessly they presented themselves in their final and most poetic form – for the language of the unconscious is poetry. The abstract, meaningless sounds of symphonic music released the creative stream more quickly and easily than any other art form – even more than my beloved literature – to my consternation.

So symphonic music was the means by which I experienced the meaning of life, gained insight into some of the eternal truths. It washed away the sediment of everydayness and pettiness, as Aristotle said art should, released the flow of my real self – for a few hours.

Chapter 12

AUTUMN

Can our senses and our intellect function simultaneously? According to the philosopher, F. S. C. Northrop, complete knowledge of anything must combine knowledge of the scientific, rational, theoretic principle and of the immediately sensed, intuitive, esthetic principle.

One fine day I step out the front door to pick up the newspaper. All unprepared, I am confronted by the most perfect Autumn day. That strange heady mixture – hot brilliant sunshine and cool, cool air – clear and clean and crisp.

But the world is filled with falling leaves. The year is dying, summer waning, growth and life ending. Death and sadness pervade the very atmosphere. Yet what is that unaccountable undercurrent of exhilaration?

Again and again I breath in the fresh coolness, drink in the flood of yellow sunshine. It is October's champagne, properly chilled, dry and slightly intoxicating. It quickens the blood, sharpens your awareness, awakens your senses, stimulates your mind, makes you function as a whole person.

Hurry, hurry! Autumn says. You must achieve all those wonderful things you have vaguely planned, of which you idly dream, before the dying year dies, before your own inglorious Autumn descends, before old age and death arrive and it is forever too late – too late!

I turn my head and there on our own lawn is an exquisite sight. It strikes the beholder motionless – a small young Maple standing all alone. Overnight its leaves have turned crimson and coral shading to orange and yellow flushed with faint pink like a blushing school girl. How delicate and tender, how young and defenseless! It's like a pretty little girl or an adorable kitten.

It evokes an indulgent smile, arouses longing to protect it from all harm, from death, even from growing up. Anything so perfect should be permanent. But already one scarlet leaf flutters to the ground.

One's pleasure at its unbelievable beauty is overlaid by regret at its transience.

To remain in the house on such a day would be a major crime. I toss the unimportant newspaper inside the door, leave word with the cook and catch up my companion, a walking stick. Irresistibly I am drawn to stroll through the bright golden weather.

I hasten across the car-ridden street and enter the wild natural park opposite our house. The woodlands surround those palisades known as East Rock. Everywhere I look – up the hill, down by the river, along the foot paths, and toward the bridge, the trees blossom forth in their myriad colored leaves. Every year the sight stuns one anew. Trees are supposed to be green. How can there be a whole forest of red trees, yellow trees, orange trees? Trees crimson and scarlet, yellow and green, coral, saffron and salmon, and every shade in between?

But ah, the Maples! They are certainly the royal family in the kingdom of trees. They light up the woods everywhere with their flaming beauty. The tall luxurious Sugar Maples, undisputed queen of color in this festival of Fall. They flaunt a glory of scarlet leaves tipped with yellow, yellow leaves touched with crimson, crimson leaves with green centers.

I pause at the edge of the park and glance back at the trees along our street. Is that the Black Oak which so carefully alternates yellow leaves with brown? White Oaks and the small Pin Oaks are an uncompromising brown – that "degenerate orange" as Whistler called it. Frankly they are ugly and depressing – brown all over and scarcely shedding a leaf yet – the bane of every tidy gardener all year long. But the Dogwoods are a rich burgundy. And one Maple is still entirely green. Has it not heard that Autumn has arrived?

I wander on along the high bank of the river. A large leaf floats down invitingly at my feet. Should I not be polite and pick it up? I turn it in my hand. How strange it is – the edges are brown yet the veins are vivid green. For the first time in my life I am not content merely to enjoy sensuously the beauty of the Autumn leaves. I feel an urgent need to understand them botanically, scientifically, intellectually, as well. Is it a Post Oak perhaps? But no, its lobes are too sharp. I shall take it home and identify it.

The grass is still green, thank goodness. The last of growing things to lose its greenness in the Fall and the first to assume it in the Spring strangely enough. Today the soft green carpet under the trees is fantastically patterned with variegated leaves red and yellow, gold and russet and brown. Avidly I begin to collect examples of each species and variety. I stare at them, study them in amazement. Apparently I have not really looked at a leaf before. The more closely you examine the familiar, the more unfamiliar and the more fascinating it becomes. I gather green leaves with red stems. Red leaves with yellow centers. Yellow leaves with orange edges. And what a variety of edges

– serrate, dentate, sinuate and – but I cannot remember my college botany very accurately. My ignorance annoys me. It is not enough to respond sensuously to the brilliance of the leaves.

I gather a large brown leaf with clumsy rounded lobes. Evidently it is an Oak but of what kind? I gather a simple, pale yellow Elm, and a compound leaf with six leaflets like the fingers of my hand, and a blood red Sumac spray with all thirteen leaflets arranged opposite each other on the stem. Then I find to my delight a green Willow with leaflets *alternating* on the stem. And the most beautiful leaf in the world, a Maple – yellow and red – exquisitely pointed lobes and a deep sharp sinus. It is a Maple of course but is it a Red or Sugar Maple or what? I shall carry my treasures home to gloat over like colorful jewels, and to classify scientifically.

On the stone bridge arched over the slow moving river, I pause and gaze up at the colorful hillside leading to the palisades of East Rock. Those great vertical thrusts of rock are no color on earth but pure henna! And there among all the usual colorful trees is one frosty grape-purple tree. Is it some unknown Oak or an Ash perhaps?

Occasionally I glimpse the delinquent Elm almost bare now, always the first to lose its leaves in the Fall, and the last to leaf out in the Spring, alas. I wonder why?

All along the river edge the lingering green of the reluctant Willows, the last trees to shed their greenness in the Autumn and the first to leaf out in the Spring. My heart goes out to the Weeping Willows, grateful that they are holding Autumn at bay. Oh please, please do not let the winter of our discontent come yet. Stay green a while longer. For green trees give us hope and joy and incentive.

I descend to the low path that follows the edge of the river. I break off the delicate, feathery spray that is still green. It is the Yellow Locust which in June paradoxically bears white flowers, not yellow, and fills the countryside with its aphrodisiac scent.

I collect the deeply veined leaves of the Beeches and the heart-shaped Birches and uninteresting Chestnuts, the polished Wild Cherries and the leaves of several other trees unknown and unsung. The shades and shapes are innumerable, the species and varieties infinite. But always in this orgy of color stand the somber Evergreen Conifers: the Pines and Spruces, the Hemlocks and Cedars – permanent, proud and reliable, bravely carrying on the tradition of greenness all winter long. They always cheer me immeasurably during those six long brown and white months that lie sodden under grey leaden skies. One month I could endure, but six! It is really too much!

Suddenly, a little gust of wind sends hundreds of small yellow leaves flying lazily across the path before me, filling the air like a flock of sleepy butterflies. Quietly they come to rest on the indifferent earth. Somehow the sight is so poignant – why, you hardly know; your heart turns over in your breast – why, you scarcely understand.

Finally, I sink gratefully to a fallen log, to rest my weary legs which care nothing for beautiful trees, to rest my chin on my walking stick, to rest my eyes and senses overwhelmed by the rich abundance of color and variety. But reason now leaps up quickly and demands attention. Why, it demands, does nature stage such an elaborate display to celebrate death? And why do leaves fall anyway?

I sit on the fallen tree trunk among the leaves drifting down all about me, observing them not only my senses but with my mind. I strive to remember my college text books. I recall how the band of cells at the base of each leaf dries out and prevents the sap from getting into the leaf, so that it breaks off falls.

And why all these glorious colors when they are to be destroyed in a couple of weeks? Is it the artist in nature? Then how can she bear to leave the skeleton of the trees so bare and ugly and black all winter long? Or is it the scientist in nature? Or is it the rare case where beauty is functional? A virtue beyond modern artists.

Suddenly, I feel that old familiar excitement. The inquisitive mind dashes hither and thither searching for explanation like an exuberant dog running after hidden quarry. I study the bouquet of brilliant leaves in my hand. Are these colors scientifically necessary? I reach back in my dusty memory. Didn't we learn – and promptly forget – that leaves do not "turn" in the Autumn? That the carotin and anthocyanin and tanin, which created the colors, are present at all times in the leaves? But these colors are masked by the predominant green of the chlorophyll until Fall. The chlorophyll, being an unstable chemical and requiring constant renewal, is destroyed by the sun when sap can no longer replenish it. Then we are able to see the red and yellow colors!

But why do the cells dry out in the first place? Well, the leaves draw up water through the branches and trunks and roots from the earth. And they spray it into the air continuously. In winter, when the earth is frozen, leaves can obtain no water. So as we turn off our outdoor faucets in winter, the leaves turn off their waterworks too. Thereby the tree retains the sap in it for its winter sleep. The beauty of the leaves apparently is functional. Also I learned long ago that frost has nothing to do with the Autumn colors though would-be scientists assure me it does. Their brilliance depends on the amount of sunlight and moisture in the air each Fall.

I still contend nature could have designed all trees to lose their green leaves quickly the way the Black Walnuts do. And nature would have done so perhaps, if she had not been a supreme artist. Or is it because she is a scientist? Has it something to do with returning nitrogen to the soil gradually? Oh dear, it is all very complicated. But the search   for the reasons for beauty is almost as exciting as seeing beauty! Yet intellect often frightens the shy senses away, but not today.

I rise and stroll on, pausing on the narrow suspended footbridge to watch the river flowing ceaselessly toward the sea. The homeward path describes a great circle through the densest part of the woodlands. Abruptly I stop. For suddenly a great shower of gold descends upon my head. Large, pure yellow leaves are being spilled like gold coins from some giant's generous hand. Startled I look up at the large Maple above me. Every leaf is yellow as yellow. The brilliant sunlight striking through those yellow leaves makes them luminous – unearthly – almost frightening. My heart leaps up. Incredulous, I stare into their golden luxuriousness. It simply cannot be, I protest, no tree on earth could be *that* beautiful! Overwhelmed, I withdraw my eyes. It is too much, too beautiful. I cannot bear any more.

Fear suddenly invades me. The trees threaten to open the door to the deeper unconscious. Reason knows it would be left behind. It tugs at my skirts. I should be drawn up onto that strange other plane of existence. I walk on hastily. Undiluted nature frightens man and his poor weak intellect. I realize I have missed a fine mystic moment. With a sense of guilty relief I soon emerge again onto the city street at the end of our block. To step over the threshold of the unknown is always disturbing.

But I am still drunk with a hundred colors of a thousand trees, dazzled by the whole dramatic spectacle of Autumn foliage. People are walking calmly along. I gaze at them incredulously. How can they go so indifferently about their daily business! How can they place their feet so carelessly on sidewalks carpeted with red and gold and green? How can they keep their eyes from the canopy of colors above them rich enough for kings?

Passersby are being showered with colored confetti of leaves. So why do they not sing and shout and dance in celebration of this festival of trees? How can they restrain themselves?

And look at the automobiles speeding blindly by! How can they bear to ignore this mighty pageant of beauty more spectacular than any parade of any circus ever devised by spectacle-making man? Why does New England not celebrate the Autumn harvest of beauty as European peasants celebrate their harvest of grapes each Fall?

If this tremendous, indescribable drama occurred suddenly overnight, we should all rush into the streets singing hosannas to the wonders of nature. If it happened only once in a lifetime, we should all fall to our knees in awe and reverence and gratitude.

As I walked on toward home, I said to myself, are we so rich in yearly natural beauty we do not appreciate it? Are Americans lacking sensitivity and perception? The Chinese place one single flower in a vase to contemplate, keep one single cricket in a cage to enjoy its chirping.

Is the poverty stricken East waiting patiently to teach the scientific, rational, materialistic West new values – to teach us that such simple things as the arrangement of a few flowers, the brewing and serving and drinking of tea can be more than an aesthetic ceremony, can merge us with the laws of the universe?

Will we in the West soon learn to congregate with friends, as the Chinese peasants did in the play, *The Tea House of the August Moon*, to celebrate natural beauty, intensify our own perceptions, enrich our lives by communion with our inner self, with our fellow men, with nature, and the great cosmic artist and super-scientist behind all the world's phenomena?

Already in the West we had experienced the excitement of pursuing scientific truths. Could we not offer this in exchange to the unscientific but intuitively wise, sensuous East?

And would we soon learn to attain *complete* knowledge by combining the scientific rational principle – which Plato called *logos* – with the intuitive, immediately apprehended emotional principle – which he termed *eros?*

Plato pronounced the former the male principle of the universe and the latter the female principle – and inferior, even evil.

The modern American philosopher, F. S. C. Northrop, however, pronounces the immediately apprehended as primary and ultimate and equally as valid as reason as a source of knowledge. He maintains that complete knowledge must combine the two sources and methods of knowledge.

Until today I had always felt that my reason interfered with my sensuous enjoyment of beauty and vice versa – though intellectual activity itself was also thrilling. But this afternoon for the first time in my life they happily wed and acted in unison. It was doubly rewarding.

All we need sometimes is a lovely Autumn day!

Was this a small step forward toward a more complete, higher life? Perhaps toward Enlightenment in the Western sense?

Chapter 13

AIR OF VENICE

One golden afternoon we sat on the broad piazza overlooking the Grand Canal, in delicious unpremeditated idleness – my husband and I. By tacit understanding we made no plans, suggesting no sight-seeing, speaking no words. We sat there in a warm satisfying immobility drinking in the very essence of Venice as it diffused itself into the early June air all about us. That extraordinary incredible air!

On the stone benches behind us old Italian women sat patiently staring off into nothingness; fat bambinos slept blissfully in the sunshine. Elegant tourists strolled by with unaccustomed leisure. The water at our feet lapped more musically than usual at the stone pier. Today the black and gold gondolas rose and fell more rhythmically while waiting for passengers.

But it was the warm balmy air, the palpably soft air. It had no fragrance yet it was redolent with a hundred subtle perfumes. It had no taste but was delicious on the lips. It had no movement yet it caressed my cheek. It fluttered the little red ribbons on the childish straw hats of the gondoliers loafing on the quay.

This air was unlike any other I had ever encountered. Not hot, not cool. Perfection beyond belief. More subtle, more mysterious than the breezes of a thousand provocative Springs. Did it not carry illusive secret messages? Surely this delectable mixture that bathed our faces and bodies and all our senses, surely it was composed of something more than mere physical gases. All the oxygen and nitrogen in the world could not be filled with meaning as the quiet pulsating air of Venice was on this strange unforgettable day. The epitome of all our glorious Italian days.

Surely for a few magical hours, all the beauty and color and history, all the pomp and tradition and romance of this unique city seemed to fuse together into an invisible but volatile stream. From it arose the essence of the most beautiful, most enchanting city in the whole world of men.

The atmosphere was permeated with the beauty of all those small architectural gems, those Venetian Byzantine palaces – pink and yellow, grey and gold – that had stood for centuries along the Grand Canal admiring their own reflections in the water. It was filled with the dignity and durability of the Doges' palace, with the skill and love of its amazing architects – dead for six hundred years. Filled with the indescribable charm and appeal of old mellowed stone, of the fantastic streets of water, of graceful bridges, rhythmically gliding gondolas, of the vastness of St. Mark's Square preparing the beholder for the shock of the celebrated cathedral, its Byzantine onion domes, its brightly colored mosaics decorating the spandrels of its Gothic arches.

Surely as we sat motionless under its spell there was borne on that mysterious air all the golden wealth of Venice when she was Queen of the Adriatic; all the genius of Titian and Tintoretto, of Tiepolo and Veronese, and the flesh of the voluptuous women they had painted into immortality. All the romance of the most romantic city on earth was distilled out into the air this day. *The spirit of Venice walked abroad.*

All the forgotten lovers and revels, the glow of its red glass full of melted gold, its exquisitely tooled leather, its people responding to the smiles of a stranger as eagerly as children. All the heart-warming Italian street songs and the unbearably moving lyric voices of its operatic tenors. All the glory that was ancient Venice and the grandeur that is its architecture today. That soft balmy Southern air was laden with the richness of the past. And it filled us with a strange quiet joy and utter contentment.

I sat there by the Grand Canal saturated by awareness of Venice, incredulous that the human imagination could even conceive of such a city, could create a city that was a great work of art as a whole. Who would have dreamed of building a city on hundreds of small islands, with nearly two hundred canals and four hundred bridges? Who would have dared such a fantastic impossibility, such a capricious impracticality? Only those early artists and visionaries – the Venetians.

This living work of art forced you to remember that despite man's wars and strife, he possesses greatness. Despite his follies and cruelties he loves beauty, he creates enduring beauty for the centuries. Despite each man's brief transitory life, mankind is eternal, mankind endures.

This incredible Arabian-night city expanded you with admiration and respect for the human race. You glowed with affection for that race of men which proved more enduring than the great cathedral itself. It all renewed your faith in man, who is more indestructible than the ancient stones of the Doges' palace – bombs notwithstanding.

Man, the city whispers to you, is a wonderful creature worthy of your love and respect and faith. You can never forget this – in Venice.

Chapter 14

CATHEDRAL

I stepped out of the hotel door the next morning and there it was. The unexpected sight struck me motionless. I stood there staring incredulously at the vast cathedral. How could anything so brown be so beautiful! How could anything so massive be so exquisite?

Its tremendous height – tall as a fifty-story skyscraper! Its great, strong twin towers supporting the delicate laciness of its pointed spires, their sides filled with open-work tracery, their edges outlined with hundreds of those amusing little curled crockets.

Again and again my eyes lifted up and ran along those great twin towers and slender spires. Story upon story of tall, slender Gothic windows with their pointed arches, the German richness of decoration, yet the incredible lightness of the whole cathedral, the mystery, the spirituality of it all.

That long unbelievable upsweep of the vertical lines of this Cologne Cathedral pulled the very heart out of you! Did the spires really pierce the blue sky? Now they began to sway. Or was I dizzy, slightly intoxicated from drinking in too much beauty too quickly?

Suddenly I felt something move inside my breast, something fluttering, struggling to escape from the prison of my body. Like a bird striving to free itself from the cage of my chest. What was it? Joy? Love? Sense of beauty? My heart? My spirit? I did not know except it surely was the essence of my very self.

Without my permission, this winged creature seemed by its own efforts to burst free from its physical restraint. I thought I saw it fly upward following the long length of the towers, then move up along the spire. It looked very white against the dark brown stone of the cathedral. It reached the uppermost pinnacle and soared on beyond. The invisible line, suggested by the pinnacle pointing toward the unknown, continued into space carrying the bird with it. And together they soared into the infinity of blueness and disappeared from my view.

For a moment I was left standing there on the sidewalk bereft, empty, as if the beauty of architecture had deliberately stolen the most vital element of my being. I felt like a lover who has "lost his heart" to a young girl merely because she is so beautiful!

Then slowly I walked on – feeling strangely, ineffably happy and fulfilled. I had given my most precious possession, the symbol of my inmost being, to beauty. A beauty so great that it led to heights greater than I ever could have attained alone, to a realm of unimaginable mystery. Would this imagined bird perhaps return to me – its wings touched with the golden radiance into which it had flown?

Wherever my unconscious mind went, however, the conscious mind was not far behind. To experience esthetic or spiritual flights was not enough. My reason must understand.

What was this "white bird" that seemed to burst from my breast? Twice in my life it had happened to me. Once before when I was watching a sublime winter snow storm in New York from a window high on the twentieth floor. Then it had solaced my grief. But today – ?

The only person I had ever heard of who had "seen" a white bird was Jesus when he was baptized by John the Baptist. Frankly I never believed a word of it, never understood its meaning. My strange unsought experience today, however, made me understand the Bible better than ever before, drew me closer to Jesus than all his teachings, than all his sermons, and exhortations. To *experience* a beautiful truth yourself – that convinced you beyond any possible shadow of a doubt. Convinced me of what exactly?

Could it be that the Biblical bird also was a projection from the unconscious – a symbol of something? But of what?

Not until we left Germany and returned home to Connecticut did I find a rational scientific explanation – in the writings of Jung. He seemed to be the Western psychologist who had conducted the deepest research into the psychology of religion and its symbolism.

In an article in *Spring,* Jung stated that the white bird was a universal experience of man's collective unconscious, a symbolic projection of man's spirit. Therefore, since time immemorial mankind has represented the immortal soul by a white bird because that is exactly how he experienced it, as an imagined image – imagery, not words, being the only language possible to the deeper unconscious.

Yet Jesus had seemed to see a white bird because of his deep religious emotion. Why should the beauty of a cathedral or of nature's white winter storm call forth the same kind of symbolic projection? Was it because religion and art and nature are fundamentally united in man's deepest unconscious? Because there is a unity in all things in the universe?

Anyway, Jung was correct, for the most beautiful truth is of no use until we experience it ourselves.

Was I gradually unearthing some of those ineffable treasures buried in us all?

Was my outward projection of a white bird a sign that my collective unconscious was being opened up deeper – down – down to universals?

Chapter 15

STAINED GLASS

It all began at Chartres. We approached the West facade of the cathedral famous for eight hundred years. How feminine and exquisite it was, as only Gothic architecture can be.

The two towers, unmatched and of unequal height, were rather disconcerting and detracted from its unity. The North tower however was elaborately decorated, lacy and beautiful, its slender spire the epitome of grace. The South spire was plain and octagonal and homely, I thought.

But all the uprushing vertical lines of the church, its slim buttresses, its slender spires, carried your eyes, your aspirations up toward – you scarcely knew what.

Its three superb doorways with their enticing pointed arches were invitingly recessed and intricately carved. They held my eyes so long I entirely missed the rose window high above them – until we entered the church, turned and looked back at it.

(Later I learned that those three tall lancet windows below the rose window and above the doors are the finest stained glass the world has ever seen. But it was not so for me this day.)

For there a great, round rose window glowed with a translucent blueness beyond belief. The morning sun was not shining through it but against it, making the light softly luminous. It was filled with the stylized stained-glass petals of a full-blown, open blue rose.

My husband whispered, "They claim melted sapphires were poured into the glass to make that extraordinary blue but probably it was only cobalt."

Whatever its magic composition seven hundred years ago, this lost art had produced a color that radiated some secret joy, some strange reassurance to mankind. It was a blue unlike any blueness I had ever seen or imagined existed or could exist. Could color mesmerize a person? It was truly uncanny. Its radiant glowing beauty melted your very bones.

To the statue of no person or god could I bend a knee. But the pure celestial blue of that stained glass window at Chartres Cathedral filled me involuntarily with the urge to kneel before it in homage to the mystery of great beauty – a symbol of a perfection somewhere beyond man's grasp or understanding.

So Chartres evoked the mood. But nothing could have prepared me for the indescribable sight that assaulted us the next day. We sought out a small church buried in the heart of Paris. We walked through a dreary, dirty old courtyard surrounded by commercial buildings and entered a small unimpressive Gothic doorway. I laughed with delight and surprise when we were greeted by a small chapel with a blue ceiling decorated with innumerable gold *fleur de lis*.

Free-standing columns of blue and gold supported the ribbed vaulting. The innumerable pointed arches were all painted gold.

It was all utterly different, startling, fanciful and delightful as if designed long ago to please some frivolous queen or some royal child. Not at all religious from my point of view.

Then we climbed an extremely narrow, circular staircase. Its stone treads were deeply worn by seven hundred years of footsteps. I expected nothing. I had read nothing about this little upper chapel of Sainte-Chapelle. During our trips through Europe I always preferred to allow the unexpected impact of historical places and famous works of art to strike my senses freshly with full force before my mind watered down my reactions with facts and figures, history and the critical opinions of others.

Today my husband and I were fortunate enough to be alone. No crowds of noisy tourists to detract from our pleasure by distracting our attention.

We stepped into the upper chapel and there – Well, truly I thought I should faint! The shock of such unexpected beauty, of such a glowing, dazzling sight was almost painful.

For there before us rose up a sublime work of art – a church like no other in the whole world. An *empty* chapel of noble height, of provocative space (unmarred by the usual, ugly brown wooden benches and their vertical lines). Its soaring vaults were supported by a series of slender piers all painted gold. The pointed arches were gold. They lifted your heart right out of your breast. The sweeping perpendicular lines of the golden wall ribs – all carried your eyes up – up to the blue ceiling strewn with gold stars.

Surely this is the most exquisite piece of Gothic architecture man has ever conceived, I thought. We stood in silent awe. To speak aloud in its presence was a sacrilege, we both felt instinctively, even the realist beside me who was not religious at all.

But the windows! It was a glass church. The walls on three sides were composed almost entirely of windows. Very high, very narrow stained glass windows of red and blue crowned at the head with traceries. But their light – it was so extraordinary it made the whole chapel glow like some exotic jewel. Their subtly colored light filled the air with a mystery beyond description, so powerful your logic automatically resisted it. (Only later did I learn that this church was designed by Pierre de Montereau for Louis IX in 1240 to enshrine the crown of thorns said to have been worn by Jesus.) Surely its architect had realized in this perfect little Sainte-Chapelle the ideal for which all Gothic architecture was striving.

For never was there such a light on land or sea. The red and blue glass was not transparent but translucent. I do not know whether it was morning or afternoon but the windows did not admit the sunlight. They diffused it, transformed it, informed it not so much with color as with poetry and music and fragrance and something else – something elusive, mysterious and deeply disturbing. This light was soft yet it penetrated your very flesh. It was motionless yet vibrant. It beat upon your senses like the sound waves of the noblest music. If Gothic architecture was finite man's effort to communicate with infinity, surely he had achieved it gloriously in Sainte-Chapelle.

So this was the reason churches preferred windows of stained glass rather than clear. Evidently their light was supposed to evoke the religious mood. I had wondered about this point all my life. Now at last I understood. Was beauty not one of the best means for releasing the self and discovering the cosmic Self?

In fact, had I not read once that Hindus believe God is light?

I continued to stand there as if hypnotized, speechless, staring, unable to move – how long I do not know, absorbing the magic of this incredibly beautiful composite of light and color, space and height, lines and perfect proportions – all bathed in a pervading luminosity. The longer I looked the more overwhelming it grew.

Suddenly, descending in that unearthly light pouring down through those magically colored windows on my right, I felt a radiant energy. I sensed a Presence descending – infused in the light, suffusing the entire interior space of the chapel – so real, so compelling it invaded the innermost recesses of my being.

Abruptly the church vanished right away. But the light remained. I was completely unaware of place. My body seemed to melt, to become light itself, to be drawn up magnetically to mix and mingle with that great radiance . . .

My personal identity was lost utterly, absorbed back into the greater ineffable identity . . . Was I dying or being reborn? . . . Was it a mystical moment of truth? The eternal verities seemed to live in that light, to flow into me.

I seemed to apprehend the harmony of all things, the unity of man, the world and the unknown universe. A flash of intuitive insight revealed that all was good. All was arranged in a sublime design beyond man's poor rational comprehension. I perceived that I, that man after death might become like this – a deathless wave of light, or a particle in a cosmic ray, an immortal but re-usable current of energy, and that science someday might be able to verify this insight.

Time had ceased to move . . . Nothing existed but that avalanche of resplendent light and my union with it.

Finally, I became conscious of my surroundings again; of my body, of my patient companion, of time and place and the church. I felt gloriously, almost painfully, enriched, enlarged, enlightened, illumined . . .

It was so wonderful, so frightening, I turned and fled down the stairs without a word.

Chapter 16

GREEN WOODS

Can the beautiful open the door to the good?

Today the summer weather is so brilliant I sit back in the car and relax in order to enjoy it to the full. I drive very slowly along the busy Parkway. I open my whole being wide – wide to absorb the beneficence of the sunlight, the intense blueness of the sky, the luxurious succulent greenness of the trees bursting with juice apparently. I feel marvelously brainless, blessedly thoughtless.

With obstinate leisure I drive along the edge of the rushing traffic of the Parkway. My eyes delight in the long curving lines of the road, in the lovely trees bordering it – dark evergreens there, light green deciduous here. They beckon to the city-starved eye with their waving arms to listen to their secrets.

Today even the incessant roaring swish-swish of hundreds of metallic machines flashing past us in mad futility fails to distract my eyes and ears and attention.

But how, I wonder, can these passing motorists see the wonderful summer world, when they race through life so fast? How can they enjoy anything? Speed is the enemy of beauty. Haste kills perception. Tension dulls the eye. Thought closes the senses.

The Parkway is lined with beautiful trees. Gradually I begin to see these trees at which I have been looking blindly for years. I begin to distinguish individual species from the vast amorphous mass of greenness I had taken for granted too long.

Look at the Maples. They are not merely green. They are yellow green or emerald green or silver green. Those yellow green ones – how symmetrical and round and beautifully shaped their whole architectural structure! Are they Red or Sugar Maples? My ignorance appalls me. The minute I arrive home I shall study, not glance at, my tree books.

The dark black pyramids of the evergreens, standing so motionless and dignified, appear at proper intervals like exclamation points in a long green sentence. Ah, that blue green – that must be the spruce pointing its finger heavenward like a saint in a mediaeval painting.

Those evergreens with such feathery and feminine sprays I recognize as Hemlocks. And those others we are approaching that lift their curved arms upward with all the grace of a ballet dancer – they are White Pines I believe. And look, even their long slender needles form a pattern too, great plumes of blue green foliage – or is it grey green? Anyway, the whole tree culminates in a tall, tapering green spire. A work of art when one looks at it long enough.

Trees! Trees! How amazingly different they are, presenting every gradation of greenness of which nature is capable, every shape of leaf imaginable, every angle of branch geometry permits.

Slowly we are approaching a beautifully arched overpass and there spreading its exquisite pattern against the grey stone is the delicate tracery of a green young vine with leaves so small, so beautifully designed, the whole so intricate and graceful it must have been painted there by some skillful Japanese artist.

But it is too tender, too unbelievable! Its beauty pierces my heart like a pain. It brings the real "moment of truth," the shining insight. I know there is a perfection at the heart of life. And for the briefest flash, I know all my conflicts are resolved, my fears, anxieties, and tension melted away. For that one illuminated moment, I know my whole being is harmonious arid orderly, unified and serene. For one fleeting second my life like the vine has achieved a small perfection.

In a mild delicious daze, I turn off the highway and ask my husband to drive. We roll leisurely along, following the lure of the country roads, uphill and down, swinging around a hundred sweeping curves. The car passes between great walls of beautiful green trees patiently awaiting man's responsive glance.

That little vine evidently has dilated all my senses. For over and over again the impact of another kind of Maple – species unknown – strikes joy into my breast.

Its large clusters of heart-shaped leaves hang before one's eyes like great clusters of flat green grapes, looking succulent and drippingly green. That must be a picture that is the delight and despair of a painter to reproduce.

It makes one smile to see the "frost" touching the tips of all the dark, blue green Silver Spruce. They seem to have no business here in this green world. And every school girl can recognize those mighty masculine Oaks towering over the lesser trees in the woods occasionally. How their polished leaves glisten like quick silver in the sunlight. I never had noticed it before. No wonder painters contend laymen are purblind. We are. The Oaks spread their strong brown arms fearlessly, indiscriminately in all directions. No neat disciplined pattern for these exuberant giant fellows!

Now we pass an aristocratic Beech bravely extending its incredibly long level branches in horizontal planes of brighter-than-bright green.

Naturally one expects all trees to thrust their branches upward or at least outward. But periodically comes the sweet shock of the exotic oriental Weeping Willows. They look as alien in American woodlands as some exquisite Chinese widow. All their long lines sweep downward. Like flowing green hair they toss and sway in the wind almost trailing on the ground. The grace, the delicacy and the luxuriousness of them pull the heart right out of one.

But what are those small delicate trees with the dainty fern-like leaves that flutter in the breeze when no other leaves are moving? I look and look, hardly recognizing them without their voluptuous white flowers. But they must be the Locust. How eternally young and feminine and appealing they look among all the larger, hardier trees. Little waves of poignant happiness seem to emanate from them and enter one's defenseless senses.

Finally, we approach the queen of them all, tall and majestic, presiding proudly over the Green of a New England village with its inevitable white, Wren-like church. They rise gracefully above the white Colonial mansions of proportions that satisfy more than the human eye – the tragically vanishing Elms. The soft grey shadows of their leaves dance across the white facade of the houses, moving in the wind, like an etching come to life. At this sight the sweetest sorrow of the world flows into one. It's absurd, it's inexplicable, it's full of meaning one cannot fathom though one has tried a hundred times. But how can shadows – the absence of sunlight – be so alluring?

What variety everywhere! What richness! Of trees and tints and tones of green, of hues and heights and forms. Are any woodlands in the world so enchanting as the Connecticut wildwoods? Not gigantic, not awe inspiring, not belittling man but friendly and designed for human companionship.

On and on we ride through the brilliant green and gold afternoon. Hour after hour we fill our eyes with the beauty of mass and motion, color and form. Pleasure intensified by companionship, concentration intensified by tacit silence, awareness intensified by leisure.

No destination today, thank goodness. No social engagement or lecture or business appointment. No invisible pressures on our backs to arrive any specified where at any specified when. For once I am free to look, to feel, to enjoy, to let go. Free from the necessity of reacting to a dozen other personalities. Free from adjusting to situations not of my own devising. Free from anxiety about a terrifying world I never made. No hurry, no cares, no thought, no conversation.

For words are like bright bait. They lure one to swim up from the dark pool of the deeper unconscious; whereas silence, leisure and relaxation allow all the wonder of nature's commonplaces and the sweetness of being alive to flow into one in full force like the surge of a great, green river.

Now we flash by another kind of woodland composed only of young trees, tall, straight and slender. Are they saplings or seedlings? They are dappled and splashed with sunlight and shadow. The sun strikes through the tender young leaves like unearthly green emerald fire. An enchanting spectacle. Perhaps an enchanted woods? I could believe anything today under the spell of these glorious trees.

Then we roll along the grey ribbon road winding around the side of a hill. I gaze down into the dazzling brilliant greenness of a sunlit woods below. Suddenly the light changes in a strange way darkening the trees to drabness. The woods are permeated with green gloom – uncanny – unlovable – unreal. Is this the spirit of evil showing its face? This light is weird. The sun has gone under a small cloud.

No wonder primitive man peopled the woods with spirits and demigods and the little people. Is this the other side of nature's Janus face, a reminder that not is beauty and harmony in this world, that there is evil and terror for man to deal with too?

Then quickly, the sun sails out from behind the one grey cloud in the sky. Once more the afternoon light, like a magic wand, touches every tree into startling green vividness again. And there ahead of us stands a beautiful tree whose name I do not know. But it is rich and luscious, flaunting all her charms like a voluptuous woman, ripe and ready. The arrogant wind comes along and runs its hands through her luxurious green hair, lifts her skirts shockingly, ravishes her carelessly, and passes on indifferently. But the sight pierces this beholder with sudden, sweet, erotic joy, to her utter astonishment. Could that be the reason the Greeks peopled the woods with Pans and satyrs seducing the half-helpless nymphs, with Daphnes being transformed into laurel trees to escape the pursuing Apollo? Myths and religions cannot be understood until the senses and the unconscious come alive – vibrantly.

Quietly the car glides along at the slow pace natural to man rather than the machine. Yet even this automobile moving over the ground seems to flow fluidly up the rises and down the dips like a well-trained hunter sailing over a stone fence, as if it enjoyed its own motion, as if it felt closely akin to the earth, no longer an alien thing of metal and motors. And my body and my nerves – never designed to race swiftly through life – now conform to the contour and slow rhythm of the machine. The car and I fuse in harmony with the earth and trees until my environment and I are one. And I know machines need not always be our enemies.

Finally, we turn homeward, all our senses fed to the fullest with the lush greenness of New England's festival of the summer woods. And now, like sap a Sugar Maple in the Autumn, my mind and body are flowing with the sweetness of life, functioning freely, eager to fulfill their destiny calmly whatever exigencies may arise – even nuclear warfare.

Satiated with too many sights and too much beauty, I say to myself, I shall look no more. I fasten my eyes on the soothing grey monotony of the road. But as if a climax of our drama of the trees had been prearranged, we approach a smooth grassy lawn, a greensward of vast extent. It rolls gently away from a white country house. Tall trees lay their fantastically long black shadows across it, enhancing its greenness in the late afternoon light. I catch my breath. Tears rise to my eyes – why, I do not know. Those elongated shadows lie there so motionless, so right somehow, presenting a picture that seems significant with meaning, promising to bring the peace all men seek – all self-actualizing men.

For behind that quiet, mysterious beauty, one can sense an elemental power, a natural and cosmic order, waiting to solve man's problems if he would but listen with the inner ear; waiting to release the joy, the good, inherent in all men – in varying degrees, of course. It promises to free the dormant creativity that beauty and nature stirs from its prolonged sleep. It urges modern man to create a new heaven and a new earth for himself and for others before it is too late – too late. Before man wrecks his own nervous system and his own sanity irreparably, by noise and speed and machines and power politics. Before he wrecks the world beyond repair by fear and hostility and hate; by nuclear weapons, bombs and crippling radiation.

For the green woods seem waiting to reassure perceptive and receptive modern man that good lies everywhere about him, in trees, in sun and wind and even machines – and in himself – if man will but fulfill his own potentialities.

So Plato was right – beauty can serve as a window that reveals the good.

SPECIAL NOTE

Here the notebooks of Clairene Myers ended. Past evidence indicated her experiences would have risen to a natural climax if death had not intervened unfortunately. This book primarily concerns the discovered self, only secondarily the inner life of any particular individual. Consequently I have taken the liberty of incorporating my own experiences in the last five chapters. By this time I have become so completely identified with her I scarcely am able to distinguish one from the other. I hope others will feel the same.

Chapter 17

WORK

Sometimes your thinking may soar aloft swift as an eagle, carry you to that pure height, that secret nesting place, where the harmonies are bred. And you discover that harmony of mind and muscle may transform distasteful menial work to a positive pleasure.

One September day a close friend of mine arrived from Florida to be our house guest. She was able to stay only three days. My husband and I had her entertainment all nicely planned. Fortunately she disrupted everything.

"May I read the manuscript of your new book?" my friend, M---, asked as we were having lunch at my club. "You said it was almost completed. I might be able to help you not with the content but with the technical details – syntax and such. *Discovery of the Self* you're calling it, aren't you?"

My first impulse was to leap at such an unprecedented opportunity. She was a distinguished newspaper woman, book reviewer, and author of several published books herself. I remembered my manners just in time.

"Oh but, M---, dear, that's work, that's no vacation for you! I think you work under too much pressure all year long anyway. Besides, you wouldn't care for this book anymore than you did for my last one. You know you are politically and scientifically oriented and my new book is psychological and religious. So your offer is doubly kind but – " I knew she was antireligious and skeptical of all psychological systems.

She won the argument, however – quite easily.

Immediately after we returned home, she unpacked, then we climbed to my writing room on the third floor. I unlocked the green metal file and lifted out the box of manuscript as tenderly as a mother lifts a new-born child.

"Why don't I sit there in the former cook's room next door while you work in your study?" M--- suggested.

"Fine. But remember this is still a roughish first draft, I'll write several more. It is completely uncorrected, unpolished by me as yet – so be prepared for shocks."

She laid the manuscript on the table beside an easy chair then seated herself in the sunny window of the former cook's room. I stood and watched her read Chapter I. She combed every sentence with a toothed critical comb. In the margins she made professional proofreader's marks with a pencil –] – ¶ – stet. – tr. (Oh, heavens, I thought, I could never remember the meaning of all those arbitrary symbols even though I had obediently employed them myself when correcting the galleys of my two published books.

Yet to observe anyone steadily applying herself to any task, concentrating and persevering in the manner of a true professional was a joy in itself. Most women would have stopped periodically to talk about their children or husbands, clothes or health – something personal and irrelevant.

As M--- finished each chapter I would take it into my work room, go over it carefully, pondering her penciled suggestions and make my own corrections in ink.

She changed half my *whichs* to *thats*; corrected my abominable spelling and my punctuation of which I was so proud; corrected my split infinitives and dangling participles; altered present tense to past and past to present; questioned the logic, or truth, or clarity of certain sentences; condemned all my clichés; questioned my syntax and lack of transitions from one chapter to another; in short, pointed out my many solecisms.

Yet to have some one care about my every comma and semicolon and adjective as passionately as I did made my head feel light with happiness. It was like having a male admirer observe intently the curve of your lips, the line of your eyebrows, the sheen on your hair.

For two years every morning of every day, I had labored to construct this house of words, this manuscript, never showing it to anyone, never discussing it with anyone, struggling alone in doubt and confidence, with pleasure and drudgery. Then to walk with another writer from room to room, as it were, through chapter after chapter, discussing the function of this paragraph, inspecting the strength of that sentence, examining the position of certain keystone words – oh, it sent the blood racing through my veins!

By the second day, however, I felt stunned by the number of corrections my friend was making in my manuscript. Was it merely my carelessness or my colossal ignorance? I was aware I could not spell – that seemed unimportant when a writer was striving to catch illusive ideas by the tail before they flew away.

I was not a purist or pedant but as a writer and omnivorous reader, I had entertained the illusion that my use of the English language was rather a bit above average. I realized I had forgotten more rules of syntax and grammar than I had ever learned in school. I assumed they were safely in my blood stream. They were not it appeared.

Now I carried my section of the manuscript into the other room and sat beside my friend. "Maybe I am stupid but would you mind explaining this? I wrote: 'Love of our fellow men does not originate in the conscious mind – unfortunately.' Why is it better to say 'does not unfortunately originate'? It splits the verb."

"Because the adverb, *unfortunately*, qualifies the verb, *originate*, not the noun, *conscious mind*. It should be as close to the word it qualifies as possible."

"Oh, dear, and I thought adding it at the end was a surprise and lent a note of irony."

"Irony," M--- replied, "comes as a shock in so serious a book as yours."

I placed a question mark in the margin to decide this matter later when alone.

"And in this sentence why did you change my word, *apparently*, to *evidently?*"

"Because," she explained patiently, "*apparently* means something that seems, but may not be, real. *Evidently* refers to something that seems, and is, real."

I stared at her in amazement and admiration. "How on earth did you ever become so wonderfully smart?"

"Fifteen years on a newspaper. They pound it into you every day of your life."

"Forgive me, but there is something I wish the editors would pound into those reporters on the New York papers. The first sentence in their opening paragraphs usually is so darned long I forget the subject they're talking about before I ever reach the end of it."

M--- laughed. "We reporters are so afraid the editor will cut some of our precious copy. We feel we must get the who and what and where and when and why and how crowded into it before that tragedy occurs."

"Well, they certainly set a poor example for the rest of us poor struggling writers. Now young lady, how do you feel about this controversial subject of split infinitives? Listen to this."

"I'm ag'in 'em!" she announced unequivocally.

"But listen to this. I wrote: 'to really learn a subject' and you changed it to 'really to learn a subject.' But don't you think that sounds awkward and pretentious. It seems more natural to say – "

"Ah, that's the point. Colloquially it's acceptable. But not correct when written."

I dashed into my writing room and returned with that most amusing and witty authority on modern English usage, Fowler. Foolishly I had assumed I no longer required his wise counsel. "Fowler says here that newspaper tradition is strongly against splitting infinitives but that usage among many good writers has made splitting preferable to ambiguity or artificiality."

She laughed, shrugged her shoulders and returned to her reading. I remained in the room with M--- now. We both read diligently page after page, hour after hour. We never disturbed the silence except to question specific details. We discussed my clichés and whether they were ever justifiable; why the present tense was correct when the facts stated were presently true; why it was correct to use the subjective, *were* instead of the indicative *was* after an *if* clause when the clause referred to present or future non-facts, and the reason the first definition given in the dictionary was the only correct one. Frankly I had never heard such a startling idea. I assumed all definitions were equally acceptable.

Now the process of learning itself was sweeping out the dust of my own bad habits and the debris of slovenly writing deposited in my brain after years of reading other careless contemporary authors. Never had the corridors of my mind felt so shiningly clean. Like the white brightly lighted corridors of a new hospital.

We were both working under the pressure of time. We wanted to complete the correction of the entire book before her visit terminated. We were tense, intense, and concentrated. It was as if we were dedicated surgeons performing some vital operation in a small operating room – quiet, bright, clean, a sacred little world in itself, everything extraneous banished, every distraction abolished, other people forgotten.

Nothing on earth mattered now but the successful operation on the body of this sick manuscript lying on the table between us. M--- was like the senior surgeon directing, instructing. I was assisting. All the joy of a professional exercising her skill welled up me. The pleasure of handling our shining verbal instruments to cut, remove, tie together, inject new life brought a satisfaction so keen it was almost painful to me. I had not known the mere *technique* of writing could produce such exultation. Was this perhaps the secret of modern art?

"Listen to this sentence," I said. "'To understand my own dilemma I must understand the society and the forces *which* caused it.' You changed it to '*that* caused it.'"

"Because," M--- explained, "*which* is a relative pronoun that explains the meaning of the antecedent or adds something to it. But *that* restricts the meaning of its antecedent and the relative clause it heads cannot be omitted from the sentence without wrecking it."

Stunned and delighted I shook my head. "Good Lord, I didn't know I knew so little or you so much. But what about all these other *whichs* and *thats?*" I flipped through back pages and read some examples. But the problem clarified itself each time as I heard the words read aloud. "But here's one: 'deeper study of Hinduism reveals that it is not a pessimistic religion but one that brings joy.' I think '*which* brings joy' sounds better than *that*. Isn't euphony important?"

M--- stood her ground. Again I consulted Fowler. He upheld her position explaining that *that* is the defining pronoun though he admitted euphony must be taken into consideration.

We worked on hour after hour. I loved every minute of it. I loved the mere sight of the black and white manuscript, the feel of the pen between my fingers. I loved my friend, her clear mind, her generosity, the problems of syntax, the entire English language full of words as resonant as notes of music.

Once I paused and savored my situation in silence. To be a creative writer is to live alone on a small exotic island in a vast sea of everydayness. It is to live in a beautiful dangerous country where everyone else seems a foreigner, a country where no one on the nearby mainland speaks your language though you flatter yourself when you speak theirs.

It is to be lonely but you cannot bear to live anywhere else. Every minute you are absent from your little, private literary island wandering about in the great outside world, you are homesick beyond belief. For that little creative island is your own, your native land. You scarcely realize how isolated it is until someone suddenly appears who speaks the same literary jargon as you do.

Year after year, day after day, you struggle with the fickle winds of creativity, with the storms of emotion, months of drought when not a sign of a creative idea shows its little green head above ground to nourish you. You dig determinedly in the stone quarry of your recalcitrant mind, often gathering nothing but useless dust, sometimes watching beautifully formed blocks of ideas emerge from formlessness, seemingly of their own accord. Gradually you assemble the accumulation of words from which you hope to build your fine house.

For a book is like a house. It is an architectural structure carefully planned in every detail, constructed according to an invisible blue print either in your conscious mind or perhaps your deeper unconscious.

It rests on a solid foundation of your own experiences and indestructible insights. It is erected around a skeletal framework of rational convictions and ideas sturdy as steel. A framework purposely indiscernible to the average eye but sensed easily by another architect in words. Each word, like a separate stone, may seem unimportant but is essential to the grand overall design. And all are cemented together by your blood and sweat and tears and joy – much joy.

I shook myself and returned to work. Today my friend and I were both keyed up to concert pitch, performing in marvelous unison like two pianists playing a duet. I forgot food, meals, comfort, fatigue, weather, and all my duties as a hostess. Time ceased to exist. I no longer knew whether it was morning or afternoon or last year.

So it went all day long. To know my friend was willing to work voluntarily all during her visit, especially on a book with the philosophy of which she was completely unsympathetic, proved the essential goodness of her character. It warmed me through and through. Never once did she attempt to dissuade me from any of my ideas so uncongenial to her.

It was obvious she simply did not believe some of these beautiful experiences. It was the usual reaction of those who have never had anything approaching an awakening to the self to those who have. She gazed at me frequently with burning intensity, incredulity, fear, aversion and awe as if witnessing an extraordinary sight never seen before, rejecting it with all her reason, yet fascinated against her will. It was as if she were watching the exhibition of some fabled sea monster with the tail of a fish, the body of a woman, two heads and the horns of the devil.

She respected my right, however, to record such experiences. Once only she murmured, "Of course, I have my own opinions about these matters."

This book was putting her friendship for me to the acid test. She was meeting it nobly.

I wrote something "breaks into pieces." She said breaks implies into pieces. So I suggested "into a thousand pieces." She laughed and admitted it, I mean, permitted, don't I? She corrected my *people* to *persons*, *allow* to *permit, whose* to *of which* and explained beautifully valid reasons to me. I enjoyed the reasons so much I forgot the pain of my ignorance.

"Honestly, my dear M---," I said, "it is a joy just to watch your mind work. It is like some delicate precision instrument cutting words and ideas and reasons into their proper shapes. You've even understood the meaning between my lines. It's like food to a starving orphan."

Never was my friend egotistical or dogmatic as she might well have been in the face of my abysmal ignorance of syntax. She was confident, clear, authoritative.

I had written "we cannot all be a Schweitzer or a Gandhi." She said it should be "we cannot all be Schweitzers or Gandhis." To me that destroyed the essence of it. Was it idiomatic or what? Secretly I left it as was.

We worked on and on. After a long silence I glanced up. "Here in this chapter about the Cologne Cathedral, I say: 'A beauty so great it led my spirit to a realm of unimaginable mystery perhaps to return to me touched with the golden radiance into which it had flown.' You changed it to 'perhaps it would return to me: But that is a flat factual statement. It takes all the 'flavor out of it. This is not a factual book. Many of these chapters were written first as poetry, at least as free verse. It has a certain rhythm. It may not be technically correct but I call it poetic license." I was being cruel to my friend but I must defend my brain child.

M--- smiled indulgently. "It's your baby. Do as you think best."

Never had the difference between creative writing and factual newspaper reporting of concrete events been so clear to me. I was attempting to arouse emotion in my readers, the same emotion Clairene had experienced when overwhelmed by the architectural beauty of that incredible Cathedral of Cologne.

Occasionally at the end of a chapter M--- would write, "Fine chapter." Once she looked up from the manuscript abruptly. "You've done a remarkably good job on the whole. It is expert professional writing. I like this *Discovery of the Self* about your Aunt far more than your *Awakening to the Good*. You have a rare gift for vivid description but honestly I don't see any point in this chapter."

I went into the next room, reread it, and the point I myself had missed before swam up into my consciousness so I incorporated it.

From then on I did not care whether I ever ate or slept again or not and it seemed I might never sleep again. My nerves felt like electric wires, crackling, humming, emitting sparks. I felt highly charged – physically, emotionally, mentally. Never had my poor old brain worked so smoothly, cleanly, with such shining sureness, all impurities burned away. An obscure point in another dubious chapter emerged of its own volition and I captured it in two sentences of which my mentor approved.

To work together on this high plane in a rarefied atmosphere of ideas and words and technique was as exhilarating as meeting on a mountain top after a strenuous climb. I felt it forged an unbreakable bond of love with my friend, not personal, not petty, but abstract, impersonal, enduring, platonic.

She marked several passages as too egotistical. "Claire, it must be extremely difficult for anyone to write an autobiography, even of a close relative, especially about her successes, without making it sound conceited, I suppose."

"Well," I replied, "I am grateful to you for this honest reaction. For it might sound egotistical to other readers too though to me it merely seems honest and universal. Mark it, dear. I shall find other ways of describing in more acceptable terms the steps in psychological and spiritual progress – for sometimes it's one and sometimes the other. Perhaps I should introduce this book with an Apologia."

On the third morning we sat out in the garden and worked on the last part of the manuscript. The September sun was deliciously warm but not too hot, the air cool but not too cold. The leaves were still clinging to the beautiful Connecticut trees though a bit dispirited and rusty and all the flowers in our garden had gone by. It was that magical period of Indian Summer.

By now exhilaration made my body feel light, weightless, like one of those balloons filled with helium gas that Macy's float down Broadway in their Thanksgiving parade.

Our work was proceeding at full tilt when without warning hunger struck me in the solar plexus like the kick of a Texas mule as it always does in an ectomorphic stomach. Why did the body always interfere with creative work, with mental activity? I was exceedingly reluctant to interrupt our marvelous rhythm of work.

"M--- dear, whenever you feel hungry, say the word and I'll drive us down to the club for lunch."

"Oh, but I want to finish it before I catch my train this afternoon. And it's all going so well and the sun feels so good on my back, couldn't we just have something simple on a tray out here by the birdbath? I'll help you."

I was delighted but doubtful on two scores. Did we have enough food in the house? And would I be able to prepare it without getting into a nervous tizzy that would dissipate my thinking ability?

"Thanks, I'll take care of the food while you continue correcting. I'm so eternally grateful to you. You are being a tremendous help to me."

"Well, you've done many generous things for me too."

This was the first time in my entire life I had ever entertained a house guest when I had no full-time, live-in cook. I was still a very nervous amateur at cooking.

For several months we had had no cook at all. This situation had revolutionized my life, my writing, and my social life. But it had not been able to revolutionize me – yet.

A few months ago I had formed a resolution of my own free will to attempt the cooking myself after twenty-five years of having a full-time cook. The main reason was that my husband, like most husbands, I had learned belatedly, derived a peculiar satisfaction from having his wife prepare his meals with her own lily white hands. Furthermore, good cooks were coming a vanishing race in our town.

Thus, consciously I was willing. I was unprepared, however, for the terrific unconscious resistance imbedded deep in the very marrow of my bones, in my whole nervous system. Intellectually I saw nothing demeaning about any woman cooking – it was an art and a science. Millions of women all over the world had cooked for thousands of years. I was no better than anyone else. Why shouldn't I cook?

Words – arguments – logic – chagrin – common sense – had no effect. All my so-called aristocratic Southern upbringing, all the traditions of the old South of our famous Virginia ancestors from Martha Washington to Governor Spotswood who built the Governors' palace at Williamsburg – rose up in fierce rebellion. As a child I had been told and had read a thousand times that "a lady never stoops to menial work. An aristocrat never works with her hands. Cooking, housecleaning, washing are work for servants."

As a child I had been surrounded by rich cotton fields, innumerable Negroes and ante-bellum values. The section of Texas in which I grew up had been settled almost exclusively by Virginia descendants. I never cooked a single meal, never sewed on a button, never washed out a stocking. In fact, I never even hung up my own clothes.

My mother considered that I should sit on a cushion and eat strawberries and cream and not even sew a fine seam. My father disapproved of this mode of upbringing. He said repeatedly, "I hope no daughter of mine ever has to do her own work but she should know how in order to instruct others properly." It was a cliché one heard all over the South.

Thus, against the wishes of my mother – who preferred for me to go to a finishing school in New Orleans and then make my debut – and against my own wishes (I preferred to go to a university and study literature and philosophy) my father sent me to a college where domestic science and home economics were taught. I scarcely ever had used my knowledge however in untold years. Certainly not in the last twenty-five.

Now for several months I had been struggling to learn to cook. Only my husband's enjoyment of my efforts and my own passionate pleasure in delicious food lent me the necessary incentives. But it was a silent internal battle. It was the war between the North and South being fought all over again and I was the battlefield. The emotional conflict made me physically ill.

I scoffed at my own folly. Nevertheless, it was impossible to bring myself to answer the front door with an apron on. That always had been the duty of one of the maids all these years. I snatched it off each time. I crept out after dark to the garbage pail buried in the ground by the back door. I pulled the shades down in the kitchen at night so the neighbors could not see to what abysmal depths the high and mighty had fallen.

No mortal could imagine what agony it all was unless she too had been subjected to the same kind of impractical upbringing as a child by an antebellum grandmother whose values had no relation to the modern world.

This conflict between Northern common sense and Southern gentility increased my nervousness and irritability to the nth degree. I coaxed the butcher and the green grocer for first quality food. Then I strained, tensed my nerves, hurried, concentrated, referred to six cook books to produce a five course dinner.

Knives displayed a diabolical will of their own and cut my fingers, pans deliberately fell to the floor with a bang, food willfully boiled over. I was determined to destroy my own inner resistance. I was determined to conquer my inexperience, to set a perfect meal on the table for my husband's delectation even if it killed me – and it looked as if it might. I slept very little on the nights I prepared dinner.

My effort to cook each dish by the clock so that every course would be finished at the same time left me so breathless, my nerves quivering so badly, I could scarcely eat my dinner. If I did not eat my husband would be distressed, if I did eat, it lay like a cold stone in my stomach. Fortunately my husband was very generous about taking me to the club for dinner frequently to relieve the nervous tension.

Today, however, I waltzed into the kitchen so elated over our three glorious days of work on the manuscript that no challenge, 110 catastrophe could faze me one iota. I felt ready to perform miracles. And it looked as if it might require a miracle to evolve a meal out of my meager stock of supplies and abundant ineptitude.

Our cupboard was bare purposely because we had been eating our lunches at the club while M--- was visiting us. Each night my husband drove us out into the country for dinner. Breakfast was not too great an ordeal. My guest slept late. My husband and I could have breakfast quietly together. I could devote my full attention to him – a doubly important matter whenever I had a house guest. Then later I would carry her tray upstairs and we would talk about the book while she ate.

Now I assembled the food, utensils, and tools on the long counter. Already I had evolved a system probably learned in college. For it had become increasingly obvious that gourmet-cooking, like genius, rests on a capacity for taking infinite pains.

Today the astounding thing was, my body was moving about the kitchen in a strange new rhythm. What was happening to me? Surely I could not be preparing a meal with pleasure?

I was supposed to feel resentful toward a society that made it impossible to find a good cook to free a woman for her professional work, to be irritated when household duties interfered with my writing.

But what to eat? Perhaps I could concoct a salad from left-overs. I tested the tomatoes which had been ripening on the shelf. I always nursed them carefully until that moment of perfect ripeness my husband liked so much. All our meals were planned around my husband's preferences. Three tomatoes were exactly right. Then I examined the avocado. Black as ink – had to be discarded. But what else could I put in a salad?

I dashed out into the garden and brought in some chives. I chopped them up fine and placed them in the bottom of the salad bowl. Now to peel the tomatoes. Like magic the skin come off sweetly and thinly indicating they were ripe. Thank goodness, they were still native and of the best variety – beefsteak. I cut them up and added salt. Standing with salt seemed to extract the essence of their flavor. None of these tasteless, sprayed, pale hard cold-storage objects. Carefully I covered the bowl and set it aside. Air, I knew, destroyed flavor and vitamins.

My body seemed to glide of its own accord to the pantry, to the stove, to the refrigerator. It was as if I was not working but was caught up in some old primitive dance. My muscles moved to an inner rhythm without consulting me.

Next I pulled the hearts out of the remaining salad greens, the chicory, escarole, and Boston lettuce. None of that hard, horrid, indigestible iceberg lettuce in our house! I washed them, allowed a little water to remain, tore them up with my fingers. Never a knife to bruise and leave a metallic taste. I placed the greens in a second salad bowl, covered it and slid it into the refrigerator. When ready to serve the greens would be crisp and cool while the salad itself would be room temperature as most foods should be if one cared anything about flavor. None of this icy American food to shock our stomachs and cheat our poor palates of their pleasure. We had learned that in Europe.

Now to make the salad dressing. I poured the olive oil into the bottom of the cup, then the apple cider vinegar – never grain vinegar – not enough minerals. It floated on top of the oil. I paused and smiled. In the same way my physical movements in preparing this lunch seemed to be allowing my thoughts to float on top. I was not losing contact with my manuscript and mental world by engaging in these humble manual chores. I seemed to be functioning on two planes simultaneously, mental and muscular – one as enjoyable as the other – almost. It was a delicious, unprecedented, indescribable sensation. Happiness ran through all my body like music.

But we should have one hot thing. Tea. I drew fresh water. Soon is was boiling vigorously. I scalded the pot, measured out our best oolong, poured the boiling water directly on it, and would allow it to steep four minutes. I must time everything so all would be ready to serve at the same moment.

Protein – we needed some kind of protein. Hot cheese crackers. I cut out the inside of the old Bel Paese cheese that was not too dry, placed it on crackers under the broiler flame. They behaved properly, cheese melted without the crackers burning black as too often happened.

In fact, everything in the kitchen was running with unprecedented smoothness. My hands appeared super-coordinated, no knives cut me, no pans fell on the floor, nothing burned, nothing spilled. Lids of jars twirled themselves into place as if delighted to do me the favor. Everything seemed part of me and I was part of it. A new unity prevailed. Why did I feel this new affinity with inanimate things, this actual kinship with the humblest pots and pans and paring knife? Was it possible that cooking might be as creative and joyous as writing – almost?

It was incredible but preparing a meal had suddenly become like a ballet – rhythmical – natural – joyous and effortless the way good ballet always appears to be effortless. I resisted nothing. I flowed along easily with this mysterious nature of things performing movements with my body that my mind had long forgotten but my nerves remembered well. My muscles seemed no longer under my control or direction but attuned to some mysterious rhythm beyond me.

But dessert! Mercy on us, there was nothing for dessert in the house. I examined the sad remains in the cookie jar. Too hard and dry. There were bananas and peaches. They were not very exciting to offer a guest.

Then suddenly there floated up to the surface of my memory that delicious dessert we had had all over Europe. They called it fruit salad but it was not. It was a dessert. A mixture of fresh fruits with a little sugar and that delectable Dutch *Kirshwasser* poured over it. The Europeans, however, used neither bananas or peaches in it. All fruits do not mix well and all do not respond to a touch of brandy. Would these taste horrid? I could but try it. The last peaches in the house also peeled thin and sweet indicating that moment of perfect ripeness. What unheard of cooperation from things! None of that usual innate cussedness of inanimate things.

I poured the brandy over it and tasted this odd concoction. The flavor was subtle, provocative, delicious beyond belief almost beyond bearing in my hypersensitive state. Somehow it set the magic seal on these three glorious days.

I leaned against the sink, grasped it with both hands, closed my eyes, and allowed this new-found felicity to roll through me and over me and around me in warm wonderful waves. This was a moment of truth. This was the high point.

Never had I felt like this before in my whole life. A subtle blending of thought and movement, relation to another person, to inanimate things and manual work. My senses felt in tune equally with knives and spoons, with the sun and trees and with creative writing. I felt in tune with my friend's mind and character, her kindness and generosity. Our mental rapport filled me with a glowing serenity.

Now everything in my life seemed in harmony – people, things, ideas, work, nature, food, my brain and my muscles. It was like being the conductor of a splendid symphony composed of many diverse instruments and yet playing in it too. I felt this grand unity was the nature of things – a unity derived from the same source of harmony with which I trembled on the verge of making contact.

Involuntarily the words spoke themselves in my mind, words I had not repeated since I was a girl in college, "God's in his heaven, all's right with the world."

And it was right in my immediate world, in the transcendent world and would be all right eventually, I knew, in man's world of global society – if man himself permitted it to be. This harmony of mine today was but a small sample of the possibilities of world-wide harmonies – among all men and nations.

I could feel my deeper unconscious straining like a prancing dancing horse to plunge ahead to greater heights – like a winged horse. I sank to the high kitchen stool and waited with closed eyes. Another minute and I would rise to union with ultimate reality, with infinity – perhaps!

But before the moment of climax, my conscious mind caused a lamentable embarrassment to overcome me, made an unwanted self-consciousness impede me from losing myself in – in what?

As I sat there I could distinctly feel the flood tide of joyousness draining out of my body and mind, spirit and senses as palpably as the sea water drains away from the sands of the beach. Oh what a pity! What a shame!

What exactly had happened anyway?

Was it not that excellent cook, St. Teresa, who had said she often found God among her pots and pans? Well, my stupid, domineering old conscious mind had not allowed my deeper unconscious to carry me quite to the heights. I had not found God – quite. And yet paradoxically enough was it not my reason; my intellectual activity with the manuscript that had lifted me to this plane of harmony of mind, body, and work? They were equally important, each was primary as Northrop maintained.

I had read frequent assertions in Hindu literature that once an aspirant of the higher life attained a certain psychological or spiritual level, menial work became easy and pleasant. Frankly I never had believed a word of it – until now.

The Hindus usually did not attempt to achieve this height by rational means but by religious means and yoga exercises of the body and through intuition. I had read also that in monasteries and nunneries, Catholics engaged happily in lowly chores – even cleaning chamber pots. They were told that it was all part of God's work. I always had wondered whether it remained a useful theory to get disagreeable menial work done or was it a felt actuality?

In any case, how astounding, how wonderful, that anything in life could transform distasteful manual work into a creative joy!

Was this an approach toward what the Mahayana Buddhists called the "fullness" of spiritual experience through people and things of the world?

I left our lunches on their trays hoping they would not be ruined, dashed into the living room, consulted my penciled notes in the back of Aldous Huxley's *Perennial Philosophy*, whipped through the pages and reread them with understanding for the first time.

Aristotle wrote of the Unmoved Mover, Huxley said, but only theoretically and from the outside. Perennial philosophers strove to know it directly, intuitively. That was why Aristotle's philosophy did not warm and stir me as Plato's did.

Now for the first time through actual experience I began to understand the profound psychology of Buddhism. Hinayana Buddhism, Huxley explained, was interested exclusively in attaining the *heights* of spiritual life through the inner self. Mahayana Buddhism advocated spiritual knowledge through *fullness*, through things and people of the world as well as through the heights attainable through the self, as the great Zen saint, Huang-Po said.

Zen Buddhists maintain that time and eternity are the same – *Samsara* and *Nirvana*. There is a way to Reality through the world and a way to Reality through the self. And the ideal way to union with Reality is to experience simultaneously the *fullness* of spiritual experience through the *world* and the *heights* through the *self* in order to obtain union with the source of all harmony, as I had been on the verge of doing.

Huxley warned that it is easier to discover ultimate reality exclusively through and within the inner self (as I had several times) than to discover it inclusively through and within the external world of people and ideas and things, as I had been so near doing now.

To experience both at once was a completely new experience to me and would remove forever – I hoped – the stigma and onus attached to cooking.

At least I had had a foot in the door of Enlightenment. And this took my breath away. I closed my eyes, clenched my fists against my breasts. It was too wonderful! This was what Jung had meant by saying the most beautiful truths are of no use until we experience them, what Assagioli meant by the different psychological states.

This was the unitive life that Maslow said was the ultimate aim of self-actualization.

This is what Plato meant too. My friend today had been rather like an amateur Socrates asking and answering questions. And I was the willing pupil. Plato had said that reason and dialectic, dialogue and verbalization not only could arouse the dormant good in one but arouse ideas and harmony with reality and, though he did not say so as far as I know, also harmony with the muscles; for was not that one object of the Greek games?

Slowly I returned to the kitchen in the most delicious state I had ever known. I lifted my guest's lunch tray and walked out to the garden glowing through and through with a new kind of truth and joy.

Chapter 18

JUNG AND GRACE

The house lights went out and there he was – larger than life! He filled the whole motion picture screen – this wise old man of Switzerland!

He walked in from the garden and seated himself in a chair. It looked like his living room. How strong he looked at 80. How vigorous and full of vitality, how healthy and happy and confident he appeared as he was approaching the time of inevitable death. A large well-built man, not shrunken with age at all.

We were witnessing a filmed interview with the world-famous psychologist, Dr. Carl G. Jung, in his home near Zurich. It had been made by the British Broadcasting Corporation. Now the Analytical Club of New York was showing it. I had come down to the city especially to see it.

The interviewer, thank heaven, was seldom visible. The audience heard only his discreet, courteous British voice asking the questions very respectfully. Then we heard and saw Jung as he replied. He sat there in his chair talking with great animation in English, never hesitating for a word, never forgetting a name, his mind working quickly and profoundly as if he were forty!

And how he laughed! His humor kept welling up irrepressibly. Yet all the while he was discussing the most profound subjects possible to man.

I remembered that unexpected laughter. It had disconcerted me the one and only time I had interviewed Jung in this same house in Küestnacht, in 1954, nearly ten years ago. The house with the vegetable garden in front and the famous study that overlooked the Lake of Zurich. At that time, however, I was still bewildered by my own involuntary awakening to the good. That had seemed a spontaneous progress through the same psychological steps which Jung's patients – normal ones at least – went. Then I was just beginning a study of his analytical psychology. His books were extremely difficult to understand. That was the reason I called on him in person. I was too ignorant then to understand the man or his system. Even today I was not certain if Jung himself believed in a God though I assumed he did personally if not scientifically.

For years I had been pouring over Jung's books alone in my study. They revealed his scientific, rational, scholarly mind. They revealed little of himself, almost nothing of his personal life.

Tonight what I wanted to know was – what kind of man was Jung? Was he neurotic as so many of the brilliant, most learned Freudian analysts were, alas? Or had he himself undergone all the psychological experiences he wrote about so profoundly? Had his own collective unconscious been released? Had it united with his conscious mind to make him a whole man? Had he himself achieved self-realization, individuation, the complete life, the good life?

In short, was he a good man, a noble man, superior to the usual man of achievement and fame and world influence and therefore worthy of being a leader of mankind? Genius does not guarantee goodness.

In reply to questions, Jung now began to ten the interviewer and us about his childhood. How poor his family was. How his father was a Protestant pastor who studied philosophy and oriental languages.

Jung revealed that he was afraid of his mother though he had gotten along well with his father. He was an only child until he was nine. Living in the country he was very lonely until he went to school. He related a fierce fight he had had with some bullies.

One day when he was eleven as he was walking home from school, he suddenly stopped still in the road. It was as if he were emerging from a great mist. He said to himself, "I am. I am me." For the first time he discovered his individuality, his identity. It marked a turning point in his life. It made him realize also that his father was not infallible. Evidently this moment of illumination lighted up the rest of his life.

This childhood incident warmed my heart. It was the open sesame to that magic world of the collective unconscious common to us all. At ten I had first lost my individuality, my identity, when I ran in the wild Texas Norther. I had merged with the wind only to return to the everyday world awed, frightened, elated – my identity strengthened with a new dimension, my communication with my inner being initiated, my introduction to the mystery of nature established for all time.

Jung now remarked with emphasis that he had always been quite intuitive. Ah, that word! It could be so full of meaning! It delighted me for it was often the password to self-realization. Some of my most beautiful truths had come to me through intuitive insight. I had feared Jung himself might be intellectual only. Rationality was fine and essential but alone it was not enough for the complete life. Intuition was necessary as a feminine consort to King Reason, as it were.

"Do you believe in God?" the interviewer now abruptly asked him.

It was not a matter of belief. He believed in nothing he did not know. He knew, Jung replied.

"Do you believe in life after death?" No matter what science or our reason told us, he said, our unconscious told us something in us would survive death. Death might be the greatest adventure in life.

He really thought so! It was obvious that at 80 Jung was unafraid. His manner, his tone, his personality far more than his words, convinced me that he had discovered Buddha's "secret of the golden flower."

As I sat there I felt I was sitting alone in the darkness conducting a conversation with that living man on the screen. He seemed larger than life in more senses than one. He was more alive to me now that he was dead, than he was when actually alive a few months ago. How could I mourn his death when he would live forever or at least his books would?

He continued to explain his analytical psychology in terms simpler than he ever employed in his writing. Most of the concepts he expressed tonight were familiar to me after years of battling with his books. But tonight he clarified my vague conceptions, rectified my misconceptions, reassured me on a score of points.

The interviewer questioned him concerning the origin and termination of his friendship with Freud. Jung said Freud believed sex was the major driving force in life. But as Jung himself had listened to thousands of his patients – normal and otherwise – talk intimately, he discovered there were other driving forces equally strong – love, hunger, religion. Freud refused to alter his original idea. So the friendship ended.

Also Jung had made further observations concerning the human psyche. In all his patients, normal or neurotic, there existed deeper layers to the unconscious than the upper personal layer containing the neurosis with which Freud dealt. Jung termed this the collective unconscious. It is common to all men. To release it, I knew from his books and from my own experience, is to seem to immerse yourself in the eternal cosmic processes.

He discussed the archetypes, those symbols that represent instinctual images. The wise old man, the great mother, the shadow, the *anima* and the *animus*. They were similar, I had learned, to what Plato called "ideas." I recalled that Jung had written that a religious element was part of the organic structure of the brain. So no one could escape the spiritual urge entirely.

It was not so much what he said tonight as what he was. I felt strongly that he was worthy of my admiration not only as a psychologist but as a man. All my lingering doubts were dispelled forever. He was a great man, a great moral, ethical, spiritual leader. This conviction elated me.

Best of all he offered modern man a practical system by which they could live a noble, happy, peaceful life – the first stage of it at least. The remainder of the journey up the mountain to that high plateau of Enlightenment depended on individual effort, as I was discovering to my consternation.

As he talked, my mind wandered but now it did not matter. Had not Jung appeared on the contemporary scene exactly at the crucial moment? For thousands of years all the higher religions had struggled to awaken the innate good in mankind. But modern Western scientific men had brushed all religions aside. They considered them intellectually and scientifically untenable – as I once had in my ignorance.

Then Jung the scientist had come along and offered frightened, confused modern man a practical method of therapy and self-realization that had scientific and rational bases. It could release the inner treasures our Western culture left buried in us – our inherent love of mankind, altruism, ethical principles, esthetic responses, creativity, spirituality, wholeness and communication with the creative principle of the universe – and oneness with nature.

It could unite the split personality characteristic of Western man, cure his dichotomy which Northrop says is almost becoming schizophrenic.

As I sat there tonight responding to the great personality of this great man on the screen, I said to myself, if the skeptics need proof of the validity of Jung's system of analytical psychology, Jung himself is the living, laughing proof!

He had defeated age. He evidently had carried his philosophy and psychology to the ultimate limit – as the Hindus and Buddhists carry their similar philosophy and psychology (with variations) to the natural limit. It had brought Jung a kind of perennial youth and joyousness and a sense of indestructible security. I felt all this emanating from him as powerfully as electric waves.

The very atmosphere he created by his personality, his laughter, his conversation, his biting honesty, and sometimes startling frankness, his laughing face, keen eyes, his gestures, his knowledge and wisdom and profundity but above all the assurance that radiated from him, the quiet authority – they all expanded my whole being like a warm inner light.

William James has said everydayness is always pulling us back, we must exert continual effort to keep channel open, the channel to our deeper, better self, to the super-conscious as Assagioli terms it.

This necessity for unremitting effort certainly was my individual experience and must be that of many other aspirants. So our own nature seemed against us. Also, our culture. Our Western society was not congenial to actualization of all our potentialities.

Many of our most brilliant contemporary intellectuals were materialists, atheists, scientists, and rationalists. They scoffed at the good and the spiritual. They made it difficult for aspirants like me to swim against the strong intellectual currents of the day. We needed frequent reassurance, continuous recharging of our energy and resolve during our struggles until we finally should have arrived at an unassailable plane such as Jung obviously had attained.

Tonight I felt I might be approaching that plane of certitude.

Periodically ripples of laughter swept across the audience. How good it felt to sit among people of like mind, people striving for the same goal I was, for self-development of the best in us, for wholeness. Until tonight I had felt rather alone. For all the well-known Jungians were at one remove.

To feel myself in the midst of those who also admired Jung, studied him, understood him even better than I, those who spoke my language – how deeply satisfying. How comforting to sit among those who would comprehend if I referred to individuation or the collective unconscious, the union of the conscious and the unconscious, archetypes or mandalas.

Were not all these aspects of the natural man about which most men knew nothing? Tonight it was like coming home after years of wandering in a foreign country. Jung had warned repeatedly that the road toward individuation brings a terrible loneliness of which I already had had a taste. Most Western persons lived on an extraverted, material, conventional plane employing their conscious minds primarily – though seldom in the rewarding way Plato advocates. They neglected their deeper unconscious and all its buried treasures.

Yet I believed, as Maslow did, that most people wanted to be better, to live the good life. They were afraid, skeptical, unaware of methods, or too indolent. They seldom would listen without prejudice, or believe or experiment. Their minds seemed closed even to ways for their own greater happiness.

I knew exactly how they felt. I was terrified at first of this strange, dark, unknown country of the deeper unconscious that might lead me to who knew what abyss, to fanaticism, insanity? I did not know then that it led to the greatest sanity.

Tonight, however, some of those present were professional Jungian analysts, many were analysands. One was not permitted to become a member of their club otherwise. I never had undergone Jungian analysis because I felt my spontaneous awakening to the good in the self, in others, and in the universe obviated any necessity of it. My involuntary awakening had been similar in kind – though certainly not in degree – to the spontaneous poetic renascence of Whitman, Goethe, Dante, Bunyan, and Millay of Renascence.

Jung's books explained such forms of rebirth. And the scientific, intellectual understanding was almost as exciting as the emotional experience itself.

Tonight the personality of that vigorous, laughing, wise, white-haired man on the screen had recharged in me what William Sheldon calls the "Promethean Will" to rise to my full stature, to fulfill my true destiny, to achieve my goal of the good life, develop my self to the fullest, as Maslow would say.

All too soon the film came to an end. The lights flashed on again. I said good night to a new friend I had made. Our rapport had been instantaneous on meeting here tonight.

As I emerged from the building I felt a strange unexpected exuberance. Jung's vitality had recharged me with vitality, with both psychic and physical energy. I felt fully capable of walking the 75 miles back to New Haven then and there! I had a strong impulse to walk all night all over New York. If I had been a man I would have. But how can a woman walk the streets of New York all night merely because her joy is overflowing? Who would believe it, understand it? In India, perhaps, such a thing might not seem strange to anyone.

I returned instead to the hotel. I was too stimulated, too happy to sleep. But sleep seemed marvelously unimportant. Feeling wonderfully buoyant, fulfilled, satisfied, I stood gazing out the window from the twentieth floor. From the North window Madison Avenue was strung with a gargantuan necklace of red and green stretching away into the dim distance. To the East lay the East River with its slender graceful bridge outlined in sparkling yellow lights. From the West window I could see the Hudson River with the long line of lights winking along the shore. I stood on the top of the world!

Obviously man's material accomplishments were admirable. Best of all, however, I could see the clouds sailing across the sky. So you *could* be near nature in the city if you were high enough. I felt very close to those clouds.

As I gazed at them, for one luminous moment I felt almost on speaking terms with the presence behind the phenomena.

The following day I did walk all over New York – mile after mile. I walked to all the distant places to which ordinarily I took a taxi. Never had my step been so light, my body so light, it was weightless as an astronaut's. Fatigue did not exist. Traffic jams did not phase me. The crowds streaming up and down Fifth Avenue seemed the great stream of life that carried me along effortlessly.

Everywhere I went people were unusually pleasant – clerks, waiters, cashiers. I purchased three dresses that fit perfectly without the customary, tiresome alterations. No wind snatched off my hat, no dust blew in my eyes as it too often did. My purse refused to fall and spill all over the sidewalk. I felt in complete harmony with things, and people, in tune with some vast universal rhythm perhaps?

At lunch my reserved New England friend never had been so warm, so expansive, interesting, or lovable. Later I had a very poor tea in a very good restaurant. Such troubles seemed marvelously unimportant.

On the train going home the porter was all smiles for no reason at all. My seat was directly over the wheels as I had particularly specified it was *not* to be when I had made the reservations. Usually that metallic clack-clack annoyed me. Today it sounded like distant music.

The afternoon paper lay on my lap ignored. I had better news. I sat there luxuriating in the atmosphere of well-being that enveloped me like a warm protective fragrance. Surely nothing could hurt, or frighten, or annoy me ever again! Why worry about old age, or death, or immortality? Why worry about personal problems? I felt sure I could solve them. Why allow the apparently insoluble problems of the chaotic, bomb-threatened world to keep me awake at night?

Perhaps mankind was now being put to the supreme test and would triumph in ways of which he had not dreamed himself capable. Perhaps today's tragic crises might lead to a world-wide psychological or even spiritual renascence. Remember Jung's law of opposites. The tension between things made the world go round and the reversal of opposites often created a new good, a new unity. Maybe Yin and Yang were right after all.

My husband met me at the train. As we drove home I recounted the Jungian lecture and the delightful aftermath.

"Well, if going to New York makes you that happy you should go more often."

My story lighted a spark in his eye that remained for days. I related the incident of the Jung film to half a dozen friends. Two of them cried with happiness.

Next morning my writing on the new book flowed smoothly. I felt in rapport with everything, in love with life.

My husband commented, "You have laughed more in the last week than at any time since we've been married."

"Than any time since I was sixteen," I corrected him.

The following week I returned to New York to see a second filmed interview with Jung, conducted, this time, by a Freudian analyst from the University of Houston, Texas.

After it ended the Jungian psychiatrist who was conducting the meeting asked if there were any questions from the audience. Dead silence.

"Surely," he protested, "some of you must have had some kind of reaction to these wonderful films of the great Jung."

My joy was bubbling over so I said, "I had a wonderful reaction but I don't quite understand it. Maybe you will explain it psychologically."

I related my reaction to the first BBC film last week and the wonderful aftermath, ending by saying, "That was a week ago and the glow still lingers. How do you explain it?"

He thought a long time and finally commented, "I think you had the gift of grace."

That was a month ago and the glow still lingers.

In the weeks that followed an incredible idea slowly dawned on me.

I had read of the great Hindu saint, Ramakrishna. His touch sometimes brought instantaneous Enlightenment to some of his disciples, or even his very presence would produce *Samadhi*, the highest state of bliss, in certain receptive devotees.

I had read how Jesus by his luminous personality had transformed the simple fisherman who were his disciples into holy men.

Never had it occurred to me that any modern *layman* might evoke anything even remotely approaching Enlightenment in anyone. Now I saw it was possible that Jung might be a great moral, ethical and spiritual leader similar to Plato and Socrates, Buddha and Ramakrishna, Jesus, Moses and Mohammed, Schweitzer and Gandhi, Whitman and Emerson.

How privileged I was to be present when his greatness and goodness illumined his whole personality – and mine. I had read that the radiant magnetic Walt Whitman affected men this way and so did the great Socrates. And one woman told me Schweitzer did, also.

So here was another means to the instantaneous revelation of the inner self – but all too rare, alas – the presence of a great enlightened personality.

Surely my receptivity this night marked a definite step in my progress toward Enlightenment – or was I now in that stage?

Chapter 19

ENERGY

Energy – both psychic and physical – appears almost miraculously, the story goes, when one really begins to achieve self-realization. Frankly, I doubted it even after the beautiful experience with the films of Jung.

Dr. Esther Harding, leader of the Jung school in America, has written a splendid scholarly book on psychic energy. She said Jung had demonstrated that the individual is able to hasten the evolution of his instinctive drives and transform this energy, once imprisoned in biological and instinctual mechanism, into a new form of psychic energy. For energy is indestructible. Psychological energy is subject to the same law as the physical energy described by physics in its principle of conservation. If energy disappears in one area it reappears in another.

The Hindus make fantastic claims concerning the energies of those who have attained *Samadhi*.

As usual I found it is difficult to believe certain abstract truths until I personally experienced them.

One day an invitation arrived from Texas Woman's University asking me to come to Denton and be an honor guest. What, I exclaimed in consternation, fly 2,000 miles just for a few days! And it will be hot as our August there in May.

I was always reluctant to travel anywhere. I did so only to keep my husband happy. I enjoyed it, my body did not. It did not seem to be designed to adapt itself to motion and change.

Certainly on all our European trips I found the ships too rough, the trains too dirty, the automobiles too small, the road too narrow and bumpy, the food too indigestible, the attendants too often indifferent or rude and my fatigue and indigestion too unbearable. Only the paintings, sculpture, the architecture and beautiful old cities of Europe were enjoyed by me – and those thoroughly.

My husband preferred to go to Europe every year. He never tired of the museums and cathedrals. But every time we returned home I was ill and it required a whole year for me to coax my poor insides into working condition again.

Now Texas Woman's University had invited the alumnae who were in *Who's Who of American Women* to be honored guests during Commencement week. The invitation had arrived only five days before it was time to catch my plane. I assumed that after reading of the White House invitation to the Nobel Prize winners, someone belatedly had the bright idea of doing something similar on a much smaller scale.

Ordinarily I would have hesitated, vacillated, worried, wondered, fretted, worked myself to a frazzle preparing for the trip. But it all appeared providential – though I did not believe in such things – as if arrangements had been completed for me by some power outside myself. I had just had the first permanent wave I had suffered in five years – for no particular reason. My summer clothes were all in order unusually early. I had sufficient traveler's checks left over from our last European jaunt. My health was never better. And my husband whom I never liked to leave alone, now that we had no live-in cook, actually urged me to go. I was well aware that he did not like dining alone at his club every night.

I wrote like mad on the manuscript of this very book every morning until the eleventh hour until I was dizzy with its abominable typing. Then I found myself embarking on the most strenuous journey of my entire life without the slightest hesitation – to my own utter astonishment. I gaily overlooked all the planes, taxis, limousines, buses, trains, and heat that would harass me.

True enough the limousine for the airport had been standing in the sun with windows closed until it was like some hellish oven. For once I scarcely seemed to feel the heat. The driver sped down the Turnpike at seventy miles an hour. Usually speed nauseates me. Today I actually laughed.

On all my previous airplane flights, fear had sat beside me. Today despite the ghastly airplane accidents one reads about in the newspapers, I was serenely unafraid. This was my first jet flight. I expected unbearable noise. I did condescend to put cotton in my ears – then ignored it.

Such an abundance of glowing vitality buoyed me up. It made me feel as if I could fly from New York to Texas and back, all the 2,000 miles, under my own power without any kind of airplane. It made me feel that I was not only above the earth, but above disaster, beyond trouble, free of all things and all people that might be unpleasant.

As I gazed out the window I beheld plain ordinary white clouds below us not the beautiful, fantastic, architectural cloud structures one usually sees. I felt I was a part, an extension, of the clouds, the sky and the wind, an integral part of nature, functioning in harmony with some great rhythmic rule that operates the universal order. I felt at one with the pilot, the plane itself. All the sweetness of life flowed past me and around me as palpable as a wind stream.

Thus I flew down to Dallas, took fourteen conveyances coming and going, passed nonchalantly from 95° heat in Texas to the cold drafts and noise of air conditioners in planes, limousines, private cars, buses, trains, hotels, dormitory bedroom, college dining and assembly halls. Everything in Texas was air conditioned except the hot, hot taxi cabs, terminal waiting rooms and the sunbaked streets.

I observed the comforts and discomforts of my body with an amused detachment entirely new to me, as if my body belonged to someone else and was not particularly important anyway.

I enjoyed every minute of that journey. The President, and the Regent with whom I had a fascinating talk at breakfast, could not have been nicer to me. My class was not in reunion. I did not know a human soul. But alumnae whom I had never laid eyes on before in my life offered to drive me in their private air-conditioned cars to various receptions and college affairs. It was too hot to walk a step outdoors. Besides, the college, I mean the university, had expanded so incredibly since I was a student there, the distances were too great in any case. And every building was perched on top of a hill.

They could not have treated me more royally if I had been Princess Grace of Monaco herself. The newspaper interviewed me, photographed me, people ordered my last book.

At the President's reception in his new, air-conditioned house, the Dean of Women asked me where I had found the fountain of youth. You cannot conceal your age from your college mates. They know the year you were graduated! Several others asked me why I looked so happy and youthful. I was happy but not youthful. But how could I stop long enough to explain that I had discovered a whole new philosophy of life, a whole new way of life when I myself did not quite understand it yet? I was more incredulous than they.

All the attention and kindness showered on me was not deserved. Maybe it was my New York clothes they admired. Or had I forgotten how exceedingly kind some Southerners could be at times? At the fabulous hotel in Dallas where I spent two nights, the bellboys, the chambermaids, the clerks took me under their wings and offered to attend to all my problems. The waitresses seemed to make my meals their sole concern. It was simply amazing!

The return flight from Dallas to New York seemed to symbolize the entire adventure – smooth – exhilarating – above the clouds. And looking up into that vast, endless blue brilliance and down on the foaming white clouds, I felt strangely close to the mysterious power that emanated from them. I felt eternally grateful to something, someone, for my initial awakening to the good and for all that had transpired in my life in the last few years.

It was not at all surprising to find a distinguished, interesting man sitting in the seat beside me. We talked animatedly all the way back to New York. Once the pretty young stewardess came and sat beside me wanting to know why I looked so happy. We struck a responsive chord in each other that went deep, far below the usual surface superficialities. The real, natural, simple me spoke to the real self in that young girl. It was a heart-warming encounter. The depths of humanity are warm and satisfying.

I longed to urge everyone I met to reread *Leaves of Grass* and Thoreau's *Walden*, the literature of Hinduism and Zen and Buddhism, the philosophy of Socrates and Plato, the psychology of Jung and Maslow and Assagioli.

Then they might be convinced that this happy, healthy, vibrant zest for life, this harmony with nature and the cosmic order, this love of all mankind, was the natural way to live. Wasn't Schweitzer "vibrant" at 88 and Jung vigorous at 80?

Yet such a natural self-actualizing way of living – even intermittently – was almost unknown in our wonderful, rich, technological America. But voices were being raised in our wilderness of materialism and extraversion.

When I arrived home my husband exclaimed, "Why you aren't ill or exhausted the way you usually are after a trip. You look as fresh as – as a Texas bluebonnet!"

"Guru"

No sooner had I returned home than I heard tragic news. A friend – brilliant, intellectual, highly educated, wealthy – had been struck down by misfortune. She had attempted suicide and was now in the psychiatric wing of a nearby hospital.

Recently when my *Awakening To The Good* had been published, she had generously sent copies to her friends but had not read it herself. When my husband was in the hospital for an operation she had been a great moral support to me. For some time, however, she had been avoiding me.

I telephoned the hospital to ask if she wished to see me. She did. I went and she talked at length. I listened. She neither looked nor acted like most of the other pathetic patients, sitting apathetically in the lounge. It appeared rather obvious to me that she was not neurotic in the usual Freudian sense.

As she talked I asked myself, was she emotionally disturbed because she had been rejected by her parents or siblings in early childhood? And now was some new rejection causing that old abscess to burst? Were her problems in the upper layers of her personal unconscious? Or perhaps in the deeper layers of the collective unconscious? Could this climax be due to her age?

I asked her how old she was. She was in her early fifties.

Was she, I wondered, quite unknown to herself, feeling an urge to release her deeper, better self, to reintegrate with her original source? I dared not utter one word of opinion in the midst of all these professional psychotherapists whose methods she found it difficult to clarify for me.

Had they gone back to her early childhood, I asked?

No. So it did not sound like the usual Freudian methods of depth analysis.

She talked mostly of the doctors, nurses, and other patients.

I urged her not to blame herself too much for what had happened. She had not brought disaster and sorrow on herself and her family entirely by her own free will. There was an inner force in the human mind stronger than the conscious will, stronger than logic or reason. Sometimes it took charge of people thousands of others like her. She must try to understand the operation of the human psyche then it would not frighten her.

"Remember," I said on my departure, "Jung says the psyche is a self-regulating mechanism. Give it a chance, give nature a chance to help you, your own inner nature."

She said she wanted to purchase a copy of *Awakening To The Good* to give to certain patients. She thought it would hold forth a happy goal of health toward which they might strive eventually.

I immediately sent her a copy as a gift of course. The inscription on the flyleaf reminded her of her own genuine virtues, her fearless intellect, unusual education, life-long courage and generous heart.

Soon after this she left the hospital. Then she telephoned me one night in great excitement.

"Something wonderful has happened! For some time I have been avoiding reading your book. I feared I was not ready for it. It might diminish me in my own estimation. I could not soar to your heights. But now – now I am reading it and am utterly overwhelmed. For I also have just had an inner awakening, a spiritual renascence – though not nearly so ecstatic as yours. I did not even recognize what had happened to me – until I started reading your book. I've been an atheist for years. And to think that a friend of mine had already written about such a glorious spiritual rebirth. I'm ashamed to say I been avoiding not only your book but you for some time."

"I know."

"Why didn't you get angry at me? Why didn't you strike me off your list forever? Why did you come to see me in the hospital and give me the book?"

"You know why if you've read my book."

"I haven't read the book – not all of it yet. This is a frighteningly new territory to me. I read only a few pages a day. I read every page several times – some six times. But already I see why all those university professors liked it so much. Your experiences have universality."

"That is its only value."

"But now you are the only person I know who can understand this mental, emotional, spiritual process I am going through. For I don't. And the Freudians certainly don't. I am alone, fearful that this joy, this religious feeling that supports me will disappear. I need your help desperately."

"Well, my dear, you know I will be happy to do anything in my power to help you – if I am able. I wish I knew a professional in this vicinity who is working with the psychic growth of the normal healthy unconscious in its efforts to realize itself. I am only a beginner myself and a mere layman. But whenever you feel you must talk it all out with someone who is deeply concerned, feel free to telephone me any night or day and – "

She actually laughed for the first time. What a wonderful sound "Like Alcoholics Anonymous, isn't it?"

"Not really. You are not defeated as they are. You are already on the way up – not through outside so much as through your own inner resources. Never forget that. And there's plenty more where that comes from. You have infinite capacity to grow into health and fulfillment of your potentialities – everyone has. Most people need help for they are unaware of own latent capacities. You are beginning to be."

"But I'm bewildered, confused, as well as on cloud nine."

"Don't let that worry you. It will pass – the confusion I mean. The happiness, too. Be prepared for that eventuality later. These things fluctuate.

The poor human nervous system is not quite up to this kind of evolution – if that is what it is and it seems to be in your case."

In the months thereafter she telephoned me often at all hours of the night. We frequently talked for two straight hours. Somehow the disembodied voices made it all easier. No self-consciousness, no face to face confrontation to distract our minds from her inner problems or small triumphs that were increasing in a heartening way.

After these first few long sessions I myself did not sleep. I trembled to touch so delicate a matter. Was I qualified? Could I really help her? What if I did her harm? Misled her? It was a dangerous responsibility for a layman like me to assume the burden of someone's mental health. But was that what it was? Jung himself said that an empathy, an entering into another person's personality had produced lasting therapeutic effect.

I was no scientifically trained psychiatrist but neither were all the thousands of Hindu gurus, Zen masters, and yogis. Yet they had been instrumental in liberating millions of aspirants of self-realization.

"But," she asked one night, "why did I have to be subjected to so many painful probings?"

"I honestly don't know, dear. They seemed to be experimenting with new methods. It sounds a little like the Zen methods. The master tries to induce utter frustration as Socrates did in the *Meno* – remember I told you about that yesterday. Then this brings a spontaneous flash of insight into the eternal verities, supposedly. So perhaps if you had not had that painful experience in the hospital, you might not now be feeling that the deeper layers of your collective unconscious are activated. I have observed several persons who after or during Freudian analysis have had a spiritual experience."

"I don't understand all this business about a neurosis in the personal unconscious caused by rejection by your parents and this other trouble in the collective unconscious."

I tried to explain it to her as best I could.

"At the Academy of Religion and Mental Health that I told you about a long time ago, I asked questions of men of different disciplines – ministers, priests, rabbis, and psychiatrists. Could religion cure a neurosis? One said it sometimes caused it. Another said they were not related."

"What's your opinion?" she asked.

"Well, I may be wrong, remember. But as I see it a deep spiritual *experience* can cure a neurosis because it opens the locked door into the collective unconscious – the source of so many of our virtues – love of others, desire to serve them, sense of security and so forth. I am not prepared to say it always does. Only scientific research can decide that."

She was hungry for intellectual understanding as well as emotional encouragement. She listened avidly to the theories of Jung, Maslow, Assagioli, Plato and Socrates, Hinduism, Zen, Buddhism, Yogi, and Jesus. She reveled in Huston Smith's little paperback I sent her – *The Religions of Man*. She commented that he approached each religion from the inside with warm sympathy and understanding, not coldly from the outside as most intellectuals did, who obviously never had had a spiritual experience themselves.

Her self-confidence and esteem had been dragged in the dust. I endeavored to rehabilitate her in her own eyes by explaining something of the laws that govern the human mind. I hoped this would prove that her disturbance was no private disgrace.

"In fact, as Jung says," I continued, "neurosis is a friendly warning. It is nature's way of warning you that something is wrong. Just as physical pain is nature's way of warning you that something is wrong with your body. Some psychotherapists today believe that an emotional disturbance erupts in us only because we resist being our deep, real, true self. I am not sure this is true of young persons. Age plays a large role apparently."

After some time had elapsed she began to employ unconsciously, to my surprise and delight, the very terms that were common in the various disciplines concerned with the growth of the normal, healthy inner self and its psychological and spiritual development. We were both amazed that she had stumbled on these terms herself. Finally, evidence indicated that the next step was warranted. I took my courage in my hands and suggested that Eric Neumann and the Hindus believed that age played a vital role in actualization of our potentialities. She accepted this with relief and reassurance. Perhaps biologically she was due for a spiritual awakening – about now. Another Jungian, Dr. Whitmont, claimed that in maturity symptoms which often appear to be neurotic and are so interpreted by the Freudians, instead are actually indications of a spiritual renascence.

The Freudians claim that one is merely longing like an infant to return to the mother's womb, to its warmth, security and peace when one has any sort of mystical experience. The spiritual experience, I said, is one where one seems to return to one's source, to become absorbed momentarily back into the warmth and security and peace of ultimate reality and to become part of the Supreme Good however briefly. Though some claim it is merely one's unconscious speaking.

"I warn you though," I continued, "I may be wrong about everything in your case. You must subject every word I say to critical scrutiny and doubt. You must follow your own 'inner oracle' as Socrates called it. You must fulfill your own natural latent abilities to attain the good and the true. Trust nature, trust your own nature – I mean your deeper, better nature. Relax and listen to its too faint voice. Don't imitate anyone, not me, not anyone. Develop into your own best individual self. Remember one's type of physique and temperament play a role in all this. Our two body builds and temperament are entirely different."

She confessed to days of depression but she progressed at a rate that surprised and pleased us both. "I'm still on cloud nine," she would say often. I was not, I was holding my breath.

She worried about her family. Did they love her?

"Don't worry about whether other people love you. Worry about whether you love them. Once you have fully released that love of mankind innate in all of us but locked away, usually, your human relationships should take care of themselves. Love of mankind can melt barriers, untie Gordian knots, solve insoluble difficulties. I know, I have tried it." I gave her a few examples from my own life. "This new fund of love has turned two entirely different kinds of temperaments like my husband's and mine into a tender, solicitous, humorous relationship I would not have thought possible. If one loves, it draws love out of others like a magnet."

"You are really my *guru*, aren't you?" she asked one night.

I laughed. "Not really. They are a hundred times purer, more selfless, more spiritual, more enlightened than I shall ever be."

"Why did you laugh?"

"Because a well-known Vedantist said some time ago, 'You may become a sort of Western guru.' But I won't. I want to avoid just that. Recently an acquaintance urged me to come out to Arizona and establish a school to teach my ideas. 'I wouldn't think of it,' I replied. 'I am not equipped for such an undertaking.' 'Well,' she said in farewell, 'if you ever do start a class to teach your principles, notify me. I'll come from wherever I am in the world. I need what you have to offer. I think most people do.'"

"I am beginning to agree with her," my friend on the other end of the telephone murmured.

"No, no," I protested. "You see, if I was able to help you it was only because you already had had some initial awakening of the self. I have no idea if any of my means or methods would do the same for those who required the initial discovery of the self. Only controlled scientific experiment would determine that."

"In other words you don't want anyone to get the idea that self-realization is some kind of emotional religious cult without scientific basis."

"Exactly. After all, even the spiritual experience is a psychological process. Science and religion will unite someday – you'll see. And don't forget Assagioli makes a distinction between the spiritual experience and the religious."

"Tell me again. There's so much to learn that – "

"Well he defines spiritual awakening as an awareness of the contents of the superconscious – like ethics, esthetics, altruism, creativity and so forth. This may not include an experience of God at all. The religious awakening does. I think 'spiritual' is a poor term but our language contains no terminology for this kind of thing – yet."

One night she said, "I hope someday I shall be able to do something for you."

"You have already. It is a great comfort to me to have someone to talk to about all these wonderful things. Except for a girl in New York, you are the only person I know intimately who is interested or understands. I can't go running over to the university and interrupt those over-worked professors every time I feel the need of discussion."

"Oh, you don't know how good that makes me feel! My relations want me to visit them for the Summer. But if you ever need me, if there's serious illness or death or whatever, send for me. I'll come no matter where I am or what I'm doing. Try me."

"Thank you. I feel you do mean it. And I shall never forget it. And another thing. You have caused me to clarify my own ideas, to organize my small body of knowledge derived from the different disciplines. The necessity to explain to you the processes of normal, healthy psychic growth of the deeper unconscious or superconscious has given me a new idea. I shall incorporate a similar explanation in front of my new book I'm writing now – *Discovery of the Self*. That is what you are doing – discovering the self. So you see I am doubly indebted to you."

That news seemed to be the best therapy I had given her yet.

She commented that she found a new compassion arising involuntarily in her toward persons whom she formerly condemned and a new tolerance toward other races and religions.

"Well, you probably would have gotten well without help of any kind. Psychotherapy is only one means, religious exercise is another, the practise of Socratic dialogues another, or it can be spontaneous, or even miracle drugs may perform this seeming miracle. Those who have taken LSD report that it seems to open this locked door of the deeper unconscious."

"Would you take it?"

"No. But that's another story. I want you to know that I am grateful to you for offering me an opportunity to repay a small fraction of my debt to life, the life force, God or whatever. My debt for my own spontaneous discovery of the self and the Self and for my progress toward Enlightenment."

As she grew better she began to help others. Not treating them but offering understanding, encouragement, and love. Thus a chain reaction was set up – I hoped.

Chapter 20

GREAT BOOKS

This was the night! The night I discovered the secret of greatness in great books and the strange power of dialectic. The night I made my irrevocable decision.

I had joined a local discussion group of the national Great Books organization. Every other week ten or fifteen members met for two hours of animated give and take about a particular classic. A scientist from the university, a doctor, a Catholic, several ardently patriotic Americans, some equally ardent Marxists, a librarian, writer, visiting nurses and other assorted men and women comprised our group.

Tonight we were to discuss Thoreau's *Walden*. I had sat at home reading it preparatory to our meeting. I had considered Thoreau's withdrawal for two years into the woods, his living there alone, as interesting, unique but rather eccentric behavior. I failed utterly to grasp its significant point and even less to anticipate its profound effect on my life.

A year ago I had joined the Great Books out of a sense of duty to myself. But who would have dreamed that the classics could be so exciting! Not I certainly.

Already our group during the year had read and fought heated verbal battles over Plato's *Apology* and *Crito*, Plutarch's *Lives of Lycurgus and Numa*, the *Gospel of St. Matthew*, the *Declaration of Independence*, the *Constitution*, the *Federalist Papers*, Tocqueville's *Democracy in America* and other books.

To my utter astonishment all these old books were as fresh and pertinent to today's problems as if written last week. They were not only exciting but illuminating and provocative. Some discussants pronounced Machiavelli's *The Prince* a true picture of real life and of human nature. It seemed to me and to others pure evil. It nauseated me to read it.

Like most of my friends I had been promising myself for years that someday I would read all the classics I had missed in college or been too young and ignorant to understand.

Like most of my friends I never found time to read the great classics on my own initiative. Yet I felt guilty because I feared in some vague way I was depriving myself of something important – just what I did not know.

Experience had proved that for busy, modern adult Americans actually to read the greatest books produced by the human race, a little pressure was needed, a little guidance, and organization. The real secret, however, was that another element was necessary which I understood very little – as yet.

Mortimer Adler, one of the founders of the Great Books idea, was correct, I discovered. He said the classics were far too advanced for college students. They were designed only for mature minds. Now I hoped I was ready and ripe for them at last.

For years, however, I had felt reluctant to approach Plato especially, assuming that his philosophy was too deep, too abstruse, too difficult and far beyond my comprehension. To my delight, however, the *Apology* and *Crito* were as lively and readable as a story in today's magazines. It literally took my breath away when I found that perhaps the wisest men who ever lived, Socrates and Plato, were struggling with exactly the same problems I was struggling with at this moment in my everyday life. The actualization of one's own potentialities for the good. The nature of the good life, of the good society and man's relation to the state and to the universe.

Until recently I had assumed that the only way to the good was the release of the collective unconscious. It was staggering therefore to realize fully that the means advocated by Plato and Socrates to achieve the good was reason and the method dialectic, that is, questions propounded by a wise teacher like Socrates and answers by his pupils or the populace or himself. In short, Socratic dialogues.

This method I found difficult to accept at first. In discussing the *Apology* the participants dwelt at length on the most famous dictum of Socrates, "Know thyself."

But what did he mean, the leader asked, by stating self-knowledge was paramount because from it came virtue?

Some of the discussants declared this simply was not true. As others argued back and forth, I sat silent for once, thinking intently.

Certainly my own experience of awakening to the good had brought me self-knowledge that amazed me and virtues greater than I ever dared imagine I or any other ordinary person possessed. But had not that process been a release of my unconscious according to the theories of the psychologists?

"Socrates," I commented aloud now, "believed that self-knowledge and the ensuing virtues were obtained through the use of man's reason and dialectics. How did that work exactly?"

No one else knew either. So we left this vital question unanswered for the time being though it puzzled me mightily.

We were never supposed to introduce any extraneous subject or cite any authority other than the author under discussion. Reference to previous books we had read in this group was permissible.

Before realizing that I was infringing on the rules, I burst forth, "The whole point of Carl Jung's and Maslow's and Carl Rogers' psychological therapy is to help the individual to know himself – his inner self. And from this collective unconscious flows certain virtues – his altruism, sense of ethics, love of mankind, creativity, esthetic receptivity, intuition, and even spirituality. But that is the release of his *unconscious* not his conscious mind. The Yale philosopher, Northrop, says in *Meeting of East and West*, however, that complete knowledge must be derived both from reason and intuition, that is, from the conscious and the unconscious."

My words of wisdom fell on barren ground.

"Did Socrates," asked the co-leader, "believe that man's chief occupation should be service to the state?"

"Every intelligent person knows that is true!" exclaimed one of the Marxists promptly.

"But," the Catholic protested quickly, "he says on page 24 that he was too honest a man to be a politician though he praised statesmanship."

"He says," I remarked, "that man's chief occupation should be the 'improvement of his soul' or psyche. By which I imagine he means his mind, don't you? Isn't it his implication that if man developed his virtues he would automatically become a better citizen of the state?"

The discussion continued at a fast pace. All too soon it was 9:30 and time to go home. We left Plato for the time being but I was deeply puzzled by his idea that reason and dialectics produced self-knowledge. I knew, however, that self-knowledge produced or rather released virtue.

Next we discussed Plutarch's lives of the Greek ruler, Lycurgus, and the Roman ruler, Numa. It was staggering to learn that there actually had existed in the world dictators who sought no power or glory or wealth for themselves or war or conquest of other nations but actually sought the good of their subjects and interstate peace and achieved both! Lycurgus achieved it through Spartan discipline of his subjects and Numa through gentle religious persuasion.

The vigorous anti-religious members of the group attacked Numa mercilessly for using myths and religion to create the ideal state. Others upheld his methods and turned the Marxists' favorite phrase on them, "the end justifies the means." What a light these two ancient benevolent rulers threw on our present day dictators and the theories of the ideal society. They proved that the masses of men could be led to peace as well as war, could be taught virtue by their rulers as well as hate and rivalry.

When we talked about St. Matthew there was unprecedented controversy between the ardent defenders of Christianity and the equally ardent Marxists who laughed at and ridiculed all the ideas of Jesus.

I attempted to be a peace-maker, "For me, Plato and Socrates throw much light on the teachings of Jesus. Jesus also was attempting to awaken the inherent good in all men just as the great Greek philosophers had but Jesus employed different means – not reason and Socratic dialogue but religious means."

This appeared unacceptable to both sides.

I had not read the *Declaration of Independence* since I was an ignorant girl in High School. Now I was amazed to find it such a noble document. It seemed to contain the whole philosophy of freedom and to reveal the deep wisdom of Thomas Jefferson. I wondered where on earth the framers of the American *Constitution* derived their wisdom. Had they read the great books of the ages and actually profited by them? The Marxists ridiculed the *Declaration* and the *Constitution* insisting that the famous signers of the *Declaration* signed it only to obtain power for themselves. This was vociferously denied. Obviously Jefferson had discovered the self and actualized potentialities.

Tocqueville in his *Democracy in America* suggested certain dangers inherent in democracy. He said a creeping dictatorship might easily arise under the guise of the benevolent state. He observed that Americans' love of equality was stronger than their love of freedom. Over-emphasis on equality might cause Americans to lose their freedom.

This stunned me. I always had assumed that each supported the other. These great books clarified my ideas, corrected my errors, invigorated my thinking, emboldened me to search for truth however dangerous or unpopular it might be according to the intellectual fashion of the moment. The greatest service they performed in my case was to disabuse me of all sorts of blithe assumptions, for which I had no corroborating evidence.

It was Plato's *Meno* that absolutely bowled me over. I was attending another group which had read it a special leaders' training course. Tonight as we gathered about the large library table, a teacher on my left asked me if I understood the geometrical problem posed by Socrates in the *Meno*.

"Not at all until this woman on my right explained it to me. Mathematics was always my weakest subject in school. She is a mathematician. I failed to 'recollect' any geometric truths."

Otherwise when I had read the *Meno* at home I found it so exciting that by the time the meeting started it was difficult to restrain myself from talking continuously. If I had not, the leader would have. The leader and co-leader were supposed to merely ask questions, never to answer them, never to express their own opinions on anything but to keep the meeting on an even keel. Otherwise we were inclined to rush off at tangents or relate personal anecdotes – a weakness we all had exhibited during the first few meetings.

On this particular night I was attending a leader's training course. Approximately 24 men and a few women were gathered about the wide library table in the directors' room engaged in an animated but friendly clash of ideas.

Some of the participants complained that they had not understood the *Meno*, others did not see the point of it. One businessman stated that he believed Socrates was merely attempting to humiliate Meno and expose his ignorance.

"Well," I said, "I agree with Mr. W--- that Socrates *appeared* to be putting poor Meno through a grilling. But isn't it possible that he was attempting to lead the man of average intelligence, typified by Meno, to release the eternal truths buried in Meno's own mind – as Plato says they are buried in all our minds? Socrates allowed him to advance step by seemingly-logical step only to demolish each step by Meno's own succeeding statements. Oh, I found the give and take in this dialogue so exciting I could hardly sit still!"

Everyone laughed. I did not laugh for it did not seem funny to me but a great joy.

"But," some woman objected, "he reduced poor Meno to utter speechless frustration."

"That's true," I agreed. "But isn't this the same method – " I stopped and raised my eyebrows quizzically by way of asking permission to overstep the rules. "Isn't this the same method used by the Zen Buddhists we hear so much about in America today? The masters in order to arouse the eternal truths buried in their pupils' unconscious, bring them deliberately to a state of utter frustration. This may induce a flash of insight. But I wish some of you would tell me this – was Socrates endeavoring to arouse the universal truths in or through Meno's deeper unconscious or his conscious mind?"

"His conscious mind!" several voices said simultaneously.

One man commented that Socrates had asked Meno what virtue was and could it be taught? Meno said it could be taught because it was knowledge. If virtue was knowledge then it could be acquired, could it not, Socrates asked? Then why had great and virtuous men never been able to teach their own virtue to their sons, Socrates demanded?

"Many men do teach virtue to their sons," several participants protested.

The same man across the table continued. Was virtue then merely opinion, Socrates asked? If so, it was not permanent for opinion changes. And if you sought the reasons behind the opinion then it became knowledge.

It looked to this discussant as if Socrates was merely going around in circles. Other participants agreed or disagreed.

"Plato," I suggested, "says true knowledge is not acquired but 'recollected.' Before birth each man possesses knowledge of eternal truths. At birth he forgets them."

Abruptly the discussion veered off in another direction. This idea of universals being recollected had excited me to a terrific pitch when I read the *Meno* at home. Now my excitement increased, my hands grew icy, my heart pounded, happiness surged through my whole body.

For suddenly I realized that now I had Plato and Socrates on my side as well as Jung and Maslow and Assagioli, Hinduism and Buddhism. All these believed that goodness and wisdom and knowledge of universals were inherent in man. Apparently some truths lay dormant in the unconscious and others in the conscious or were transcendent. They were all merely waiting to be awakened or remembered by one method or another.

One pretty woman now complained that she had read the *Meno* like a detective story – suspense on every page, at the end she expected to be told how to acquire virtue. But she felt sorely disappointed when Socrates terminated the dialogue abruptly by saying virtue is "a gift of God."

Others agreed heartily. Why on earth should anyone strive to attain virtue if it came only as a gift of God?

Suddenly as if mists were rolling away, my mind cleared. The urge to present my understanding of that phrase "gift of God" was almost irresistible.

But I did not want to monopolize the conversation. Fortunately, at that moment a handsome, large authoritative man who had offered answers to nearly all the other questions turned to me to my amazement:

"Well, how do *you* interpret the gift of God as Socrates uses that phrase?"

I laughed. I felt warm, eager, really confident for the first time. "Well, I don't mind telling you that ten years ago – even five – I would not have understood the *Meno* or believed a word of it! I would have dismissed as sheer nonsense all this business about 'recollecting eternal ideas.' I confess that all these ideas of Plato and Jung and Maslow and Northrop of Yale are fairly new to me but – oh, now – now they're just about the most exciting thing that ever happened to me!

They laughed but indulgently. I laughed too.

Now a sort of elated serenity surged over me. "To return to your question. I believe the gift of God comes usually as a reward after a long struggle to purify ourselves, as Socrates attempted to clarify and awaken Meno's memory of forgotten universal truths. Meno did not achieve this final gift of God or insight as Socrates apparently hoped he would. Yet I cannot help but feel Meno might have if the dialogue had continued longer. I agree with you – " nodding at the pretty woman – "it does end abruptly. Also Plato believed that in moments of great intellectual insight and memory of the eternal ideas he has forgotten, a man is communicating with the Supreme Good."

I emphasized the fact that Plato seldom used the word, God. I mentioned this because so many of our most vocal participants in Great Books were violently anti-religious. But did terminology matter so much as the pressing home of Plato's glorious conception that the good was accessible to man, that knowledge of universals could be recollected through beauty, reason, and dialectic, and that all this led to communication with the Supreme Good?

I also said Socrates seemed primarily interested in the problems of human conduct and identified knowledge with moral good. I said nothing, however, concerning another item I considered equally important – that Plato's primary interest was in the nature of ultimate reality.

This was not in the *Meno*. These books in our discussion group, however, had stimulated me to rush to a dozen other books of philosophy. We were not supposed to introduce outside authorities to prove our point. I restrained my tongue as long as possible. Then I asked permission of the regional leader to mention psychology as a parallel. He smiled and nodded.

"As I see it, the new growth psychologists use *psychotherapy* to stimulate the good and the true latent in man's deeper unconscious. Not the sick upper layers of the unconscious that interested Freud. Plato and Socrates employ reason and philosophical *dialectic* and the conscious mind to awaken the universals man knew originally but forgot at birth on earth. Numa and Jesus – according to St. Matthew which we studied recently, employed *emotional* and *religious* means to arouse the inborn good in man, as do Buddhism and Hinduism in yoga practise – though the *physical* plays a part too. The goals of self-discovery and development are similar but it's the methods and means that differ."

Everyone looked thoughtful and remained silent for the first time. The leader brought the meeting to a close.

Coffee and cake were served to us on this, the last meeting for the future leaders. Everyone continued to discuss *Meno* with great animation.

As we stood about I said to a man, "I would like to have continued discussing Greek philosophy for two more hours."

I drove a neighbor home and said to her, "Don't you feel it is ennobling to walk in the company of great men as they come alive in their books? They speak with amazing directness to the best in us and we respond more admirably than we ever had expected, with more understanding than we thought ourselves capable of doing."

She agreed but as I lay awake that night I thought of the points I would have liked to hear mentioned by the group. Aristotle, whose *Politics* we had read earlier in the year, said "the State comes into existence for the sake of the good life." Plato demonstrated that real knowledge was concerned with the world of Being, opinion with the world of change, of Becoming. I thought we should have emphasized Socrates' dictum that "the unexamined life is not worth living." And should we not have discussed the fact that Socrates believed in God, in immortality, in following the internal oracle, the inner voice, and maintained that death was not an evil? He himself was subject to visions and mystical transports. And he was willing to die for his beliefs and did in fact when he drank the hemlock. So far all the authors of the Great Books had believed in a God – except Marx.

As the year approached its termination, I looked forward eagerly to every new book, to each fortnightly discussion in our regular group though in the beginning it had seemed a chore. Sometimes in our smaller regular group we had difficulty in tearing ourselves away at 9:30. Who would have dreamed it could be so exhilarating to toss ideas back and forth like invisible balls across a table. Other people's interpretations often exposed my errors. I learned from them. It was incredible how many different opinions there could be about one book.

But I was still missing the most vital point not only in Plato but in these discussions until we came to the last meeting – the high point of the year for me.

Tonight our small regular group was scheduled to end our year by discussing Thoreau's *Walden*. First the leader asked several participants what they thought of it. One saw no point to it. Another considered Thoreau very peculiar to go off and live alone in the woods for two years.

The very resistance of some of the participants generated new energy within me. Their hostility to *Walden* threw a strong light across the words of Thoreau – dim to me heretofore.

"But how could Thoreau admire a bird of prey like the hawk?" the leader asked.

"It was on page 77," one woman replied. "And that showed his indifference and cruelty," she contended.

"Couldn't that be," I suggested, "Thoreau's acceptance of the unity of all created things, an example of that equilibrium of nature which science is only beginning to understand today? You know, if you kill off all of one kind of animal then the other animal it preys on will overrun the place. Maybe he accepted both good and what appears to man to be evil in nature as the Orientals do. Isn't it the *yang* and *yin* of Taoism? Thoreau mentions the *Vedas* constantly in *Walden*. Oriental books were very popular among the Transcendentalists like Emerson around the 1840's. We are scheduled to read the *Bhagavad Gita* in this course later. So couldn't Thoreau's philosophy have been influenced by these Oriental books?"

Well, another woman remarked, she thought it was very selfish of Thoreau to go off into the wilderness and live alone. He severed all connections with society. He was no longer dependent on his fellow men and that was bad.

I opened my mouth without the slightest notion of what I intended to say. Words emerged of their own accord. Little lighted doors in my mind began to pop open and ideas to pop out of them without my own volition. It was a strange but exciting experience – this phenomenon of verbalization.

"But," I heard myself saying aloud, "did Thoreau make the nails and hammer he used to build his house? I doubt if he cut the trees and planed all the planks he used in his house. Did he make the pots and pans he cooked in?"

"But," the other countered quickly, "he was antisocial. He produced nothing for society by living alone in the woods for two years."

I smiled. "He produced *Walden*. Was not that more valuable to mankind than nails and hammers and pencils? His book has been translated into nearly every language in the world. Millions of copies have been sold. And here after a hundred years we feel it is worthy of our serious study."

"Yes, but was it not very impractical," the scientist asked, "for him to advocate that all men should go off alone in the wilderness? All men could not do that. They had to earn a living for their families and themselves."

And if he, the scientist, sat alone in his living room and did nothing but think with the radio blaring and the children crying, he would be bored to death.

Several others agreed with him.

"Well," I suggested, "you might be bored if it were only your conscious mind that was working. Perhaps you would not feel bored if you released your deeper unconscious. For when it flows forth it frees the good in yourself, love of your fellow men, your creativity, and so forth."

He stared at me skeptically.

A pretty young girl stated she thought Karl Marx's ideas in the *Communist Manifesto* offered much better solutions to the problems of society than Thoreau.

The Catholic objected vigorously to this, saying that Marx wished to destroy all religions and then man would not be either moral or ethical – as witness Communism and Nazism. She did like Thoreau's relation to nature, however, but what exactly was his philosophy?

"Yes," the leader said, "what was the point of Thoreau's withdrawal from the world into the wilderness for two years?"

Someone read aloud the sentence from *Walden* – "On page 83: 'I learned this, at least, by my experiment: that if one advances confidently in the direction of his dreams, and endeavors to live the life which he has imagined, he will meet with success unexpected in common hours.'"

These words stabbed like a welcome dagger into my heart arousing me to their truth, they struck home when spoken aloud as they had not done when I read them alone in silence at home.

As others continued to talk I followed my own thoughts. Plato was right; discussion, dialogue, dialectic did arouse forgotten ideas. How many times at home I had sat quietly listening – interjecting a few questions and sometimes none – while my husband paced back and forth across the floor talking out his business problems aloud. The solution came to him as he talked, as he verbalized. It exemplified that strange law of the human psyche which Socrates understood over 2,000 years ago and today only the psychologists had learned to use in psychiatry, and people like my husband who followed their instincts.

It was the very act of verbalization in psychotherapy that awakened, revealed, and clarified the neurotic's forgotten feelings that were vague, confused, buried in his unconscious. It never occurred to me that the same law of the psyche might apply to normal people and their conscious minds.

I saw suddenly that I had been too stupid to grasp the obvious fact that it was the vocal *airing* of their views among the Greeks that formed one basis of the famous Socratic dialogues. And it constituted the fascination of these Great Books Discussion Groups – and the unsuspected benefits verbalization could bring the participants.

I turned to the scientist. "I was wrong. I said if you sat alone in your living room you might be bored if you used your conscious mind but not if you used your deeper unconscious. But Plato showed us that through reason, the use of the conscious mind in discussing *abstract* ideas we can recollect the profoundest truths. But don't you think he means only *after* we have risen to a higher psychological plane? Not when we are consciously thinking about last month's grocery for instance?"

"But wasn't Thoreau using his reason as he sat in the woods," he asked?

"No, not primarily," I said. "But judging by Thoreau and Plato, eternal truths can arise through arousal of conscious mind and the deeper unconscious. Different kinds of truths perhaps. I am not sure on that point yet. Plato says dialectic can help our conscious mind recollect the eternal ideas we knew before we were born – even scientific ideas – as he proved when the uneducated slave boy solved the geometric problem in the *Meno*."

The scientist looked at me with greater skepticism.

Someone objected, at this point, that the interpretation of Thoreau's words was not easy. Another commented that he did not use words in the same sense we did. There was great discussion as to whether he ever graduated from Harvard or not.

Finally I said, "Well, perhaps people who have risen to so high a psychological and spiritual plane as Thoreau did while alone at Walden Pond – on this high plane words which we use everyday have different meaning for him. Just as in science – " and I glanced again at the scientist – "when modern physicists use the words particle and wave they do not mean what we mean yet all physicists understand the words as the scientist uses them, isn't that true?"

He smiled and nodded.

"You mean," the Catholic woman murmured, "they hear a different drummer as Thoreau says here on page 85?"

We were always required to verify our statements by referring to the specific page in the texts under our hands. Most of us created our own penciled index of salient points in the blank pages at the beginning and end of the book.

I smiled at her. "Exactly."

Suddenly, a new idea swung a great searchlight across *Walden*. It also penetrated deep into my mind. It revealed the whole point of *Walden*. It made my heart pound, my blood race, my whole body expand with delight.

I saw what should have been obvious all along but was not – to me at least – that Thoreau had withdrawn to the woods because he was employing nature as a means to awaken the dormant good and the God in himself. Had not the green woods of summer, autumn leaves released the inner good and some of the eternal truths buried in my mind either in my unconscious or conscious – I was not quite sure which – perhaps both? Or did not a certain kind of stimulation of the conscious mind sometimes arouse the unconscious?

Thoreau advocated immersing yourself in nature, simplifying your life, seeking solitude. These actions and principles of Thoreau applied to me. How stupid I was not to see it before! Had I not made efforts to simplify my daily life? I had not withdrawn to woods alone, but I sat in my living room or study or garden for many rewarding hours in solitude in an effort to advance my progress toward the good life, to release the better self in my deeper unconscious.

"Now," a woman asked, "what was this life which Thoreau had 'imagined'? What kind of 'more liberal laws' would begin to establish themselves?"

"Laws of a more liberal state," promptly replied the Marxist.

No, the Catholic participant objected, she did not think he meant that.

"Could he mean the universal laws within himself," I asked? "For further on he says, page 83," I read aloud: "'In proportion as he simplifies his life, the laws of the universe will appear less complex and solitude will not be solitude.' Solitude can be wonderfully enriching. You can learn to 'know thyself' as Socrates urges. In fact, Thoreau quotes Socrates on page – let's see – here it is, page 82. I think he means the cosmic laws become clearer to you. That seems to be a law governing the human psyche. Thoreau expresses the same idea in different words: 'I wanted to live deep and suck the marrow of life.'"

Now *Walden* seemed to me to throw a stronger beam of light back across the other great books we had been discussing throughout the year, Socrates, Plato, Matthew, Plutarch. It also illuminated my own reading of Jung and Oriental religions, of Maslow, Assagioli, Carl Rogers, Moustakas, Gordon Allport and others.

Thoreau had advocated not only simplifying your life, immersing yourself in nature, and seeking solitude but he praised the joys of the inner life, self-knowledge, the transmuting of every bodily function into purity, – even cooking perhaps, and recollecting the forgotten wisdom with which we were born, and he believed in the importance of the individual and in God.

Suddenly this realization of his meaning caused all my thoughts and feelings to melt and merge together. All the fragments of my life slowly, surely fell into their proper places, coalesced into an ordered pattern of wholeness. Now I knew beyond the shadow of a doubt that I was on the right road to realization of my potentialities. From this night on I was committed to the good life and the good society, the kind that might eventually emerge if all men pursued both.

I had come home at long last! My life had found its center of gravity. Everything in my whole life came into focus. The picture of the true nature of man's psyche, of man's pursuit of happiness, of my pursuit for the rest of my days – it all came clear and beautiful. This was the night of my great decision! This was not the end of my search for individuation – that would continue indefinitely – but this was the point of no return.

A deep, quiet serenity and certitude filled my body to overflowing. I was flooded with an ineffable peace.

I began to speak aloud to the Great Books group though I had no idea what I was going to say. The words seemed independent of me. Plato was right, I saw, verbalization flushed out hidden thoughts like birds concealed in the underbrush. "Now, I may be wrong, but as I see it, Thoreau was employing nature as a means to induce his own Enlightenment, as the Hindus call it, to develop his own potentialities of the good. Whereas Socrates and Plato employed reason and dialogue (something like the method we are using here in this very discussion," I said, smiling at the leader who looked pleased). "And Jesus and Numa used religious emotion as a means. But Jung, Maslow, Assagioli, Carl Rogers, and Moustakas use psychotherapy. Each discipline employs different means toward the same end. Isn't that terribly exciting!"

No one disputed me for a change so I continued.

"Their goal as I understand it, is to awaken the dormant good in man's inner self – through the conscious *and* unconscious mind, to arouse him to live the good life in relation to the self, to the state, to things, and nature. The inference being in most cases that out of this individual transformation of character will eventually arise the good society for all."

The people around the discussion table stared at me incredulously. They seemed to be struck silent, to my surprise.

"Can the greatest men of the world all be wrong," I asked? "They all seem to believe that men possess innate good and wisdom and that they can be awakened by different means and different methods. And they seem to believe that this self-development of potentialities should be the chief occupation of mankind. And this concern with the good, the true, and the beautiful, with justice, and freedom, with moral and ethical principles in the individual and in the state and with religion seems to me to be the secret of the greatness of the great books."

There was complete silence, looks of disbelief and bewilderment on all faces.

At this crucial moment the janitor appeared in the doorway. This meant it was 9:30, the lights were going out.

We gathered up our books and notebooks, pens and pencils in unprecedented silence.

"Oh," I said sighing happily, "if you have ever experienced any of these feelings that Thoreau did in the woods, you know it is the most glorious experience possible to mankind!"

They stared at me with incredulity, disapproval, fear – and hope.

Chapter 21

ENLIGHTENMENT ITSELF

The previous week was the prelude. Yet it did not prepare me for the ensuing week – the most extraordinary of my entire life.

For days I had felt an unusual harmony with everything and everybody. Family frictions dissolved into laughter or did not arise at all. All the sweetness of marriage rose like a warmth. Each of us contributed to it, each was enveloped by it, comforted, and made happy.

Abroad all people seemed friendly. At home the Negro cleaning man and the upstairs Irish maid worked with unprecedented quietness. Everyone moved in the same harmonious inner rhythm. Even my cooking came more easily, more pleasurably.

I drove the car with unsuspected ease, letting it find its own rhythm, letting it run itself as it purred like a great contented cat.

Like a newly discovered tranquilizer, joy flowed through all my veins.

Then my husband departed on his business trip out West as planned. He said the maid would look after me. But a message came that her sister in Baltimore was very ill, would she come at once? Of course I let her go.

Now for the first time in my entire life I remained alone in a house day and night for a whole week. Was it solitude that evoked the beautiful experiences or what? Happy solitude – unlike those three weeks alone when my husband was in the hospital.

I moved about the house as though I lived on two levels simultaneously. My body obligingly performed its necessary duties like a precision-made machine, self-operating, all parts functioning with unaccustomed ease and efficiency, every atom warm and throbbing gently, fulfilling its respective purpose, directed by some sweet silent instinct, operating below the level of conscious attention.

I ate and slept with sweet insouciance, executing my daily chores with unprecedented dexterity. All recalcitrant doors opened. No obstinate windows stuck. Nothing fell to the floor perversely. Lids screwed onto bottles as if delighted to do me the favor.

Day after day, hour after hour, I floated along on a stream of quiet exaltation, as if carried forward by some unseen force, buoyed up by an inexplicable joy, living in a new dimension.

Can this, I said to myself, be the long-sought plane of Enlightenment?

It was not, I was amazed to discover, a mountain peak of ecstasy, not a drowning in the blissful sea of oblivion. It was a glowing serenity. At times I felt a mysterious sense of levitation as if my body moved and-skimmed along only a few inches above the floor. It was literally like walking on air. A continuous fragrance, as if from invisible flowers, pervaded the air at all times.

Did other more spiritual aspirants than I literally levitate? St. Teresa was reported to be always rising to the ceiling much to her annoyance. I felt as if I was almost as weightless as an astronaut in space but I thought I was not. But it was the most delicious state imaginable.

On some days I experienced the ineffably sweet sensation of floating on a universal river – slow steady – and strong. Was this the state of Being Plato and Maslow mentioned? Was this the super-consciousness the Hindu religion referred to? Or the cosmic consciousness suggested by Richard Bucke? A result of evolution or of my own efforts at self-realization – the further discovery of the self? One did not really discover the true nature of the self until one began to develop its latent capacities.

Then suddenly without my volition or effort there arose from the dark springs of my deeper unconscious, the creative stream.

Mysteriously a new piece of writing began to take form under my surprised eyes, under my obedient hands, guided by some inner power uncontrolled by me. The words flowed onto paper effortlessly independent apparently of conscious thought.

Thus, a new book was born.

This ineffable state of Being continued unbroken, unchanged all day everyday for one whole glorious week. The creative stream seemed to flow into me from some outside source and then flowed out again onto paper in a black stream of ink.

I wrote on and on, anytime – anywhere. No longer must I be locked in privacy in my quiet writing-room far off on the quiet third floor undisturbed. I wrote at the lunch table, when I should have been concentrating on my food, in the bathroom when my mind should have been on other matters, while walking around the garden when I should have been watching where I was going, while I was in bed at night when I should have been sleeping.

I no longer read the newspapers – they seemed too irrelevant, too transient. I no longer telephoned my friends – they could wait. But when they called I felt full of warmth and laughter. Underneath our conversation, however, ran the undercurrent of creative ideas, allowing nothing to distract it from its predetermined course. This creative stream was like a river at the flood sweeping all before it – mighty, implacable and deceptively smooth.

A general state of joy permeated my days and nights and every activity, eliminating all my social life and desire for it, all consciousness of other people. I was aware only of this delectable state of Being and my obedience to the insistent inner urge to write.

I wrote on and on in every room in the house, faster than the human arm was designed to move. No fatigue, no nerves, no stress or strain. No dulling of the appetite. No destruction of sleep. Everything in my life was caught up in this natural rhythm of effortlessness. It was as if I moved to some inaudible music. I enjoyed everything. Food was doubly delicious. Bathing a pleasure. Sleeping a sinking into fathomless depths where I seemed to return to my source, to awaken refreshed and reborn, like a child born into the morning of the world.

I watched the words tumbling out onto the paper hour after excited hour. Finally, one day I paused and flung my arms to heaven. I cried out that life is good – good! Everything is good – good! I am happier than happy!

When I walked in the park, packs of dogs no longer barked at my heels. They turned away indifferently sensing that I was no longer afraid and therefore would bring them no harm. As I gazed at the trees and flowers they seemed to flow into me, all barriers melted away.

At last I was in harmony with all things simultaneously – if temporarily – with nature and animals, with people, my body, my appetite, my conscious mind, and my unconscious, and creativity, with manual work – with the universe – with everything.

At this moment I would gladly have performed the lowliest act for the lowliest creature, risked my life for the most insignificant of drowning butterflies. I longed to do so. For the first time in my life I understood why Jesus wished to wash the feet of his disciples. This is what is meant by discovering the self, by developing it. It is the source of endless buried treasures, I said to myself.

Perhaps some self-actualizing person, I said to myself, can fulfill their deeper, better nature through serving others and through action, others through love and religion, and yet others through knowledge. And certain types through creativity – in thought, in scientific research, or in the arts.

At last I am whole, complete, free of all men and all ideas, of society and its laws and pressures, I shall henceforth live by my own laws even when seeming to conform to theirs. I laugh, I dance, I sing. I live in another world, on another plane. But I do not forsake the plane of everyday reality however great the temptation. But I have discovered something of ultimate reality and now the light, the ease, the joy and wisdom from the higher plane descends invisibly to the lower earthy plane and directs all my behavior – forever – I passionately hope.

The creative process continued of its own momentum. It seemed a fundamental part of everyday living, as natural and necessary as breathing, as natural as singing when you're happy or dancing when you're a child.

At last I understood why the scientist, Edmund Sinnott, tells us the characteristic that distinguishes man from the animals is not language, not love, nor honor, nor religious worship, but the creative imagination. And only an artist in a creative moment, in that first careless rapture of creation, would say man is created in the image of God. For only then does he feel himself briefly god-like.

Every minute of everyday for a whole delicious week I remained buoyed up on this plane of harmony and joy, love and creativity. External obstructions to individuation: international tensions, the threat of nuclear bombs, the vastness of outer space and social ills did not disappear but my courage to face them was strengthened ten-fold. Internal obstacles to a higher, better life diminished away. Fear had faded away completely.

Time melted into fluid timelessness. I felt I was fulfilling my purpose in life, realizing my best potentialities, walking miraculously on the waves of life above disaster, beyond fear, incapable of anxiety, bathed in cleansing water of the good, floating on the universal stream that flows out of the nature of things.

But paradoxically enough, I also was being carried forward by that same stream, forward – toward Ultimate Reality.

This is the true discovery of the self, I said to my self.

This is Enlightenment itself!

But it was not the summit – merely the half-way house on the side of the mountain. I stood on this high plateau – amazed and grateful – and looked back over the ground I had covered in the last several years in my climb toward self-actualization.

I saw the original place of my despair at the evil behavior of mankind. Then like an astronaut I had been shot upward to peaks of ecstasy, without my own volition – permitted to view the psychological and spiritual heights which man is capable of attaining.

This was Stage I, Awakening of the Self. I had foolishly assumed I should remain on this dizzy height as my permanent residence.

Thus again, by a power greater than my own, I had descended, as if by parachute to earthiness, exhaustion, doubt and disillusionment. This was the beginning of Stage II, Self-Discipline.

I also saw where I had struggled to regain the heights once glimpsed. I had asked my unconscious to be my guide up the mountain. It was too weak and inexperienced, reason too insistent.

Delayed and distracted by world crises, national social ills, mechanized noises, too active a life, I struggled on. I employed one means after another to arouse my dormant unconscious.

I abandoned myself to the arts, immersed myself in nature, disciplined my body, borrowed techniques from psychology, religion and philosophy. I simplified my life, reduced distractions, decreased stimulations, sought solitude and silence. I tried and failed and tried again.

Finally I attained this glorious plateau of Enlightenment, Stage III of my ascent – a modified form suitable to my limited capacities. Here I could live in the world but not of it. Here I experienced a happiness greater than I knew existed for ordinary man. I hoped to remain here the rest of my life. But could I?

I glanced down apprehensively into the abyss called the Dark Night by those who had attained the final peak of the mountain. It was said to be a place of utter exhaustion, a fall into helplessness. But this Stage IV also was claimed to be, by those who knew, a place of rest and preparation for the final ascent.

I stared upward at the shining peak far above me. It was the highest mountain in the world – the psychological and spiritual Mt. Everest – the fifth and final stage in self-realization.

Many artists, poets, and mystics attained the third stage, Enlightenment, but only geniuses, great mystics, and saints achieved Stage V. To the psychologist, Maslow, it is self-realization or the Unitive Life; to Jung – individuation; to

Platonic philosophers it is the good life. It is known to Buddhists as *Nirvana*, to Hindus as *Samadhi*, to Zen Buddhists as *Satori*. Taoists call it *Tao* or the Way, Christians call it the Deified or Unitive Life. They are different yet similar.

It was inconceivable to me that any aspirant of my limited abilities should ever attain the highest peak or even the edges of its shining periphery. Consequently there surely was no danger of my falling into the abyss of the Dark Night, was there? Surely I would be permitted to remain permanently on this plane of Enlightenment where I now stood, would I not? If I were only able to maintain my position at this precarious height.

For here I felt I was controlled by the universal laws of psychic and spiritual growth, a part of the great cosmic scheme, living, moving, and having my being in the rhythm of the universe. I was fun of love and peace and joy.

I looked about me and saw other types of physique and temperament who followed professional guides – psychological, religious, or otherwise. They progressed up the mountainside slowly but surely, apparently without falling into dark chasms periodically, as I had.

The type of aspirant in the West, however, to whom the initial awakening to the personal self and the greater Self occurred spontaneously usually passed through five stages of growth alternating quick ascents with quick descents.

But whatever the type of temperament and physique, however the terminology differs in the different disciplines, whatever the means and methods – whether scientific psychotherapy, self-therapy, religion, philosophy, or poetic spontaneity – all are agreed in both the East and West concerning the result of complete actualization of human potentialities.

What is the result of *full* self-realization?

It is discovery of the self, development of man's deeper better nature, release of the collective unconscious – that part of the mind common to all men but neglected too long in too many men of the West.

It is awakening to the good in the self, in others and the universe; a psychological "death" when the ego drowns in the collective unconscious followed by a "rebirth" when the treasure house of the deeper unconscious is unlocked.

It is elevation to a higher plane of daily living – where the individual's character is transformed beyond his belief; when he returns good for evil – to astonishment; loves others as himself – to his surprise; does not control his anger but does not feel it.

It is a state of mind in which solitude becomes enriching; menial work an effortless rhythm; creativity as natural a process as breathing.

Realization of man's potentialities is a new plane above everydayness. On it the self-actualizing man achieves freedom from other people's opinions, from convention and conformity in clothes, politics and materialistic standards.

Fear, envy, prejudice against other races, colors, and creeds – or lack of them – drop away like unwanted burdens.

Virtues – unsuspected but dormant flow forth – selflessness, courage and compassion, certitude and peace, serenity and security, intuitive wisdom and spirituality.

In his ascent toward the heights he may fall periodically into exhaustion, doubt and disillusionment. He may work and struggle and slide backward into frustration.

His path, however, is always lighted up by past experiences and illuminated by the shining goal ahead.

Individuation – or the good life – is a new world where incredible wonders occur. Beauty of nature and art form a window that reveals the true and the good – as Plato suggests.

"Recollection" of Eternal Ideas, of Universals, may take place if the aspirant engages in more or less Socratic dialectic.

He becomes purified in an inexplicable way, innocent and playful as a child.

Finally the dichotomy that has blighted Western man ever since the Greeks is cured – the painful duality between mind and body, spirit and senses, matter and man, the conscious and unconscious, man and ultimate reality. He becomes whole as nature intended all men to be.

He lives in harmony with himself, with people, inanimate things, and the rhythmic laws of ebb and flow in the universe. He feels the unity of all things.

He attains the unitive life, unites with the cosmic Self, with Reality, the life force, God.

To discover the self and develop it is to discover the secret of happiness, the meaning of life, the ultimate goal of living. It is to experience joy – joy greater than that derived from wealth, power or fame – from youth, love or passion.

Actualization of the potentialities of the self – complete and full – is the greatest joy possible to mankind.

And those individuals who achieve the heights will create the good life for themselves today – and the good society for all tomorrow.

ALSO BY CLAIRE MYERS OWENS

Awakening to the Good, **by Claire Myers Owens, Foreword by John White.** This inspiring volume is an odyssey of the author's search for what has been called cosmic consciousness. She explores a variety of avenues for awakening to the good in all human beings: religion, art, movement, meditation, nature and more. Abraham Maslow, the legendary psychologist said, "Exciting, fascinating, I read it in one sitting." In these often troubled times, this book offers a much needed confirmation of the basic, positive nature of human beings and the instinctive reach for something Higher that we all share, the quest we are all completing. 184 pages, 6 x 9, ISBN 1585091324, $17.95

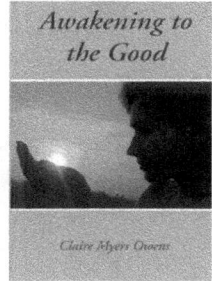

Zen and the Lady, **by Claire Myers Owens.** This is the personal story of a woman's journey into Zen, beginning in her 70th year and continuing into her eighties. When first published in 1979 it was praised by the most respected spiritual researchers and psychologists of the time including Kenneth Ring, Jean Houston, Ken Wilbur, Charles Tart, Jack Kornfield and Willis Harmon. In this book Claire brings the reader with her on the path to enlightenment and shares in her spiritual development. This book is already considered a classic of Western mystical literature. 192 pages, 6 x 9, ISBN 1585091294, $17.95

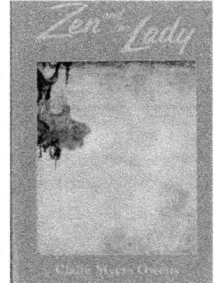

www.ingramcontent.com/pod-product-compliance
Lightning Source LLC
Chambersburg PA
CBHW050648270326
41927CB00012B/2932